Spiritual Resistance
Ita Wegman, 1933–1935

SPIRITUAL RESISTANCE

Ita Wegman, 1933–1935

PETER SELG

STEINERBOOKS | 2014

STEINERBOOKS
AN IMPRINT OF ANTHROPOSOPHIC PRESS, INC.
610 Main St., Great Barrington, MA 01230
www.steinerbooks.org

Translated by Matthew Barton
Book design by William Jens Jensen

LIBRARY OF CONGRESS CONTROL NUMBER: 2014933147

ISBN: 978-1-62148-065-5 (paperback)

ISBN: 978-1-62148-066-2 (ebook)

Contents

It seems very likely that freedom will no longer prevail in Germany, and that commissions may be established to rule on all kinds of matters, both in the political domain and in cultural and spiritual life—such as school administration and suchlike. The Jews may also be expelled. Naturally this is also our prime concern at present: the various members who can no longer remain in Germany either because they are of Jewish origin or because the particular work they were engaged in, of a more social nature, is no longer assured in Germany. And for me the uneasy question arises as to how we can organize ourselves as true anthroposophists in a way that serves truly human qualities; how can we continue to disseminate Spiritual Science in the right way despite and beyond nationalism, and how can we live in accordance with it? I can see a time approaching when the wave that now courses through Germany will not remain within its borders but will spread to various other countries, and when each country closes itself off until—since this is at odds with all true evolution—things ultimately degenerate into a widespread and major war. How should we relate to these convulsions—for this is also intrinsic to our tasks, otherwise Anthroposophy has no meaning at all if we merely acquire it for ourselves in quiet seclusion—and work in a way that enables us, perhaps, to prevent some of these developments through our right stance and right deeds?

—ITA WEGMAN, April 17, 1933

Foreword

*"These are strange times, and I am full of concern about the
future. It is certain that humanity will face extraordinary trials
as we move into the future, and even those who ought to have
some insight are blind to what is trying to happen."*

Ita Wegman, March 31, 1933[1]

This monograph describes the life and work of Ita Wegman
from 1933 to 1935, in particular her confrontation both
with Nazi fascism and with the internal dynamic in the General
Anthroposophical Society. My study of this theme began with
research into Wegman's trip to Palestine between September 29
and October 10, 1934—a journey inspired by an intention formed
by Rudolf Steiner during the last period of his illness,[2] finally realized by Ita Wegman in the fall of 1934 after her own grave illness
nearly ended in her death.

Newly discovered documents from her literary estate allowed
me to discover the places Ita Wegman visited in Palestine and to
gain a fuller picture of her experiences there. Closer scrutiny of
her correspondence during this period, arranged chronologically,
and her notes on the trip, also revealed the great biographical
importance to her of these travels and indeed the whole scope of

her spiritual experiences in 1934. The prime motive of my short study, as I intended it—in continuation of the work of Emanuel Zeylmans[3]—was to delineate this period in sharper focus. But as I worked on this it soon became apparent that the illness Wegman suffered and overcame in the spring of 1934, with her subsequent trip and further studies, are all aspects of a clearly configured biographical whole and can only be properly depicted in the overall context of this period and the inner developments involved in it. Thus it became necessary for me to review the documents that Zeylmans drew on in his survey of the conflicts in Dornach, along with other testimonies of this period, and to examine them again from biographical and existential perspectives, integrating them into the immediate biographical context I was studying. It was not my aim to enlarge on historical documentation of the General Anthroposophical Society and its catastrophic crises, but my focus, rather, was on the figure of Ita Wegman, her intentions and efforts during these three years, and the transformations she underwent.

Wegman had explicit, unambiguous perspectives and a uniquely clear view of both the political threat *and* the social-spiritual task with which she engaged in her own life from 1933 to 1935. There was however a radical change in her inner stance toward the opposition, aggression, and defamation she met within anthroposophic contexts at this time in reaction to her intense, purely motivated efforts. During this period, Ita Wegman tried to live and work in true accord with her inner impulses and ultimately with Rudolf Steiner's legacy, within a particular social reality in civilization in general and within the anthroposophic movement in particular. She sought this in her realization and inner acceptance of biographical and spiritual-esoteric experiences, particularly in 1934: "I feel my way slowly around these things, and as I do so they grow clearer."[4] There is no doubt that, in pursuing this process of spiritual "sensing," Ita Wegman increasingly found her way to her own very distinctive path, becoming ever more able to realize it in uncompromising fashion.

A closer study of what Ita Wegman said between 1933 and 1935, and the biographical realities of her life at that period, can give us deeper insight into her inner nature and development during a period of significant transition for her.[5] Such study also, however, reveals the general character of these three years and thus of a period whose distinctive spiritual and Christological task *and* dramatic dangers Rudolf Steiner had foreseen more than two decades previously.[6] Wegman's efforts in 1933 to confront the dark powers of National Socialism and the convulsions in Dornach, which she experienced firsthand, as well as her subsequent illness and the clarity of her "Christological conversion" in 1934 to '35, reveal a very specific, intrinsically comprehensible, and forward-looking quality whose spiritual signature is clearly prefigured in Rudolf Steiner's spiritual-scientific predictions.

If we try to gain greater insight into these processes, it seems advisable not only to direct our attention to the history of the Anthroposophical Society during these years but also to broaden our gaze to include the whole character of the time, Rudolf Steiner's comments on it, and, for example, to trace the development of a priest such as Emil Bock.[7]

During this period, in his studies of the Gospels, as well as Palestine and Rome, Bock achieved the "grace" of a breakthrough and was thus able spiritually to confront the powers surfacing in the Nazi regime with his authentic Christological orientation. The priest Eduard Lenz,[8] who had accompanied Emil Bock in 1932 in his first and decisive trip to Palestine, and later had to take the brunt of the conflict with the National Socialists, fell gravely ill during this same period, and may be considered part of this whole spiritual context.

I have not elaborated these—at least partly apparent—inter-relationships in detail, and thus refrain from engaging with deeper levels of the events of those times. Rather, quite intentionally, this book focuses exclusively on Ita Wegman, her development, and her words, trying simply to present the processes she went through and, implicitly, their extraordinary spiritual nature, without any further attempt at interpretation. This primary focus is by no means an impoverished narrowing of the gaze or even (in relation to internal Anthroposophy conflicts) a partisan approach, but arises from the governing premise that the mysteries of a great life such as that of Ita Wegman reveal themselves in the details. Tracing separate, subtle steps in her life as these become apparent, also at the level of spoken and written words, can lead us further and allow us deeper insight into Ita Wegman's being. She herself wrote: "In general meetings or gatherings people always understood me poorly because I lacked a smooth way of expressing myself. But people of goodwill always understood what I meant."[9]

This book closes in its epilogue with a moving letter to Maria Röschl on the future of the Anthroposophical movement and Society, which Ita Wegman wrote on February 22, 1935, on the occasion of her fifty-ninth birthday. This declaration brought Ita Wegman's inner position in 1935 to a point. However, it was not her final statement about the future of the General Anthroposophical Society and the Goetheanum—indeed, she hoped and worked for its possible resurrection until the end of her life.[9a]

I wish to give particular thanks to Gunhild Pörksen, who supported me in writing this book.

Peter Selg
Ita Wegman Institute
Arlesheim, January 2005/March 2014

I

"In Feverish Haste"

1933

"*It is as though everything has to be done feverishly before the great catastrophe occurs, for things do indeed look very grave in the world.*" (February 25, 1933)[10]

"*I feel like a hunted animal, unable to finish anything it has started, as though demonic efforts are being made to rob me of everything, so that chaos reigns.*" (September 1933)[11]

The year 1933 found Ita Wegman in a swirl of pressing activity, resolved to find something of real substance to counter the tide of political events in Germany, the powers associated with them and approaching dangers—for the whole of Europe and its future, and indeed for the whole world. Ita Wegman had been working and traveling more or less ceaselessly in her efforts to save the anthroposophically based medical, curative educational and social initiatives begun years before, which she had developed further with the help of active colleagues. At the same time, she continued to run her clinic, with its full complement of patients, and to direct medical training courses and seminars (and, as just one example, to help organize an anthroposophic conference at the Goetheanum for unemployed people[12]). Throughout the year, she repeatedly covered long distances to hold discussions on further steps during this time of such danger and foreboding—initiating new developments, encouraging individual colleagues, and helping to strengthen social and community spirit (*"It is so important in these times for us to stand shoulder to shoulder, at least knowing that, deep in our souls, the connections between one and the other are true and good and that wherever misunderstandings arise, this is not intrinsic to our inmost being"*[13]). At the same time she was also treating patients and special needs children and acting as Class reader. She was in Holland and Stuttgart at the beginning of January,[14] then from January 16—in temperatures of 30 below zero—in Berlin, and visiting the curative education homes in Gerswalde (Uckermark) and Pilgramshain (Silesia), before attending discussions in Dresden and medical studies in

Nuremberg on her way back to Switzerland. At the beginning of the second week in February she traveled to England for the rest of the month, and at the beginning of April once again returned to Berlin (via Stuttgart and the curative education institute at Hamborn); then in mid-May she went to Paris, traveling on from there to London and Birmingham via Holland and Germany. At the end of June came a further trip through Germany, and from the second half of August a six-week, extremely active period in England, repeated in November following further interim periods in France and Holland. Ita Wegman arrived back in Arlesheim from the travels of this year on December 11 (after intensive discussions in Hamborn, Berlin and Gerswalde on her way back from England). She undertook these trips in the clinic's car, accompanied only by one or two others, or took the train on her own, often traveling for many nights on end while plagued by grave concerns. Her chief cares concerned political events and the state of the world, the difficult situation in Dornach, but repeatedly also the medical situation in Arlesheim at the clinic she had founded and, with Rudolf Steiner's help, had developed between 1921 and 1924. Even when absent, she remained deeply connected with the clinic and its work. "*It also seems to me as though everything is at a standstill in Arlesheim. I hope I am wrong, but I am worried, and do not feel the clinic is emanating light.*"[15] Phrases such as this occurred sometimes unexpectedly in letters she sent while on her travels. Ita Wegman also continually requested full reports on the state and progress of all patients and felt concerned, too, about the Medical Section's fulfilment of its tasks for humanity. She was leader of the Section and wished to continue to realize and develop its esoteric, medical and social aims, even at a time of increasing darkness and violence.

Supported by Rudolf Steiner's unambiguous statements on the subject and a keen awareness of historical developments, Ita

Wegman had long foreseen the approach of this dangerous epoch of German National Socialism and fascism, even in its subtler nuances and prefiguring political maneuvers.[16] The political convulsions in the first part of 1933 found her inwardly prepared. As early as January 15, when the communist party held a mass rally to commemorate Rosa Luxembourg and Karl Liebknecht—murdered by right-wing extremists in 1919—and the local Nazi leader in Weimar had sworn unwavering allegiance to the party's leader Adolf Hitler, Ita Wegman wrote in a letter:

> I do want to try to intervene a little more in Germany. The times are strange: as if everything is stagnating; as if water that doesn't flow begins to stink. That's how things are in the world at present. Moreover, one has a feeling that something bad can come of it. Therefore, I'd like to see if we can perhaps achieve something in Berlin by intensifying our activities.[17]

Just two weeks later, in another letter (to Schloss Hamborn), referring to Adolf Hitler's inauguration as German Chancellor and the way this event was marked by torchlight processions of the SA and SS through the Brandenburg Gate, and by an upsurge of "grass-roots movements" in many German cities *("Those watching, who lined the streets, were gripped by this enthusiasm. They broke out in lengthy shouts offset by the relentless monotony of marching boots and the rhythm of songs"*[18]), she commented:

> It is bad that Hitler has come to power, but there's nothing more to be done about it now. We were too weak, and there will be bitter consequences. I've just seen an article in Berlin's *National-Zeitung* that refers to Countess Moltke as the "army sibyl." She's being accused of spiritualist sessions with the seer Lisbeth Seidler, who also played a part in the Sklarek trial. This is the start of the agitation that will come, since of course Dr. Steiner and his adherents will be labeled as national traitors. There is a good deal of significance in

the fact that the Nazis have already launched an attack on Dr. Steiner.[19]

In the first few weeks after Hitler seized power, Ita Wegman recognized the strategy of national deception and seduction that would unfold over coming months and years (*"The wave of nationalism seems to ensnare and discompose almost every single person on whom its gets a grip. People think this is the answer for everything, and that merely by participating in this national fervor—or 'elation' as it is called in Germany—the gravest problems have already been solved. One grows blind, and dull-witted, too, but currently there is nothing to be done to counter this momentum"*[20]). She paid close attention to the burning of the Reichstag building in Berlin on Rudolf Steiner's birthday (February 27) and the "emergency decree to protect people and state" passed directly after it, with its severe restrictions on personal freedoms. One day after the German parliament practically relinquished its own powers (with the aid of the "enabling act" to "remedy the distress of the people and the Reich"), and three days after the first concentration camps were established in Oranienburg and Dachau, she described these developments as follows in a letter to England:

> Circumstances in Germany are now quite bizarre and extremely difficult to judge, since evil intentions cleverly mask themselves as good and can even awaken an illusion that they are right and proper. Unparalleled ensnarement is being practiced here.[21]

Seven days later she continued:

> These are strange times, and I am full of concern about the future. It is certain that humanity will face extraordinary trials as we move into the future, and even those who ought to have some insight are blind to what is seeking to happen.[22]

Among those who really "ought to have some insight" but frequently enough were "blind" to the events that had been occurring and the carefully targeted preparations for them, Ita Wegman certainly included many who had formerly attended Rudolf Steiner's courses and read his books—in other words, many members of the General Anthroposophical Society. For Wegman, anthroposophic Spiritual Science was a methodical path of schooling to acquire a power of judgment not obscured by emotions: an essentially free capacity that could also be applied to historical developments. She expected her fellows in the anthroposophic movement— "students" of Rudolf Steiner and those who were fully conversant with his highly differentiated statements and their wide range of perspectives—to show a real capacity to understand the contemporary situation as the foundation for engaging in counterbalancing initiatives.

In the early months of 1933, however, Wegman found little such insight and next to no cosmopolitan outlook or ability to act in accordance with it. In many respects she was alone, as she had been in the preceding years. She saw what had already happened and what was coming, perceived what was afoot in now widely disseminated Nazi texts with their ethnic cleansing policies, followed intently the National Socialist electoral victory, the "cleansing" of radio broadcasts announced on March 25 by Joseph Goebbels, minister for "Public Enlightenment and Propaganda," the anti-Semitic campaign, "Fighting the Anti-German Spirit," launched on April 13 by the German students organization, and the anti-Jewish "Civil Service Restoration Act" that had already come into force (*"The grave conditions in Germany continue unstoppably. Books—by Thomas Mann, Stephan Zweig, and Wassermann—are now being burned. Those who subscribe to peace, humanity, equality and freedom are said to be propounding 'heresies'—the word used by the German student organization in Breslau. How will all this*

Book burning, Berlin, April 13, 1933

end?"[23]). On April 17 (thus a week before legislation was passed prohibiting "non-Aryan" physicians from practicing), she again wrote to England from Arlesheim, to Daniel Nicol Dunlop:*

> The situation in Germany is really one to be very alarmed about. A wave of blind nationalism is inevitably dragging into its maelstrom all who do not know something of the secret connections between the human being and the world, as we do from Dr. Steiner. This is what makes it so terribly difficult to talk with people at present and the anthroposophists are far too weak—again we see how weak they are— to form clear insights. It seems very likely that freedom will

---

* TRANSLATOR'S NOTE: The translation of this letter is from its original draft in German. According to archive records, Ita Wegman first composed her English letters in German then had them translated by a colleague; before sending them she made any further corrections she required. As one can see from the English facsimile of the letter, the result was often in a rather awkward style.

Arlesheim, den 17. April 1933.

My dear Mr. Dunlop,

I hope, you have had a good Easter and if the weather has been as beautiful as with us in Arlesheim-Dornach than you will have enjoyed it and it will have been very good for your health.

About a week ago, I came back from my journey to Stuttgart and the Institutions in Germany and came straight into the meeting. Dr. Vreede and at present we have the Easter-meeting. There was a great deal to do for me and having asked Dame Florence and Mrs. Wilson to give you a report of our meeting at Stuttgart, I knew you had already heard something about it; I wanted also to take a distance from all what had happened in Germany in order to give you a report in the right way. The situation in Germany is really such a one to be very much concerned about it. It is a wave of blind Nat&onalisme into which everybody is absolutely draged, who does not know more about the secret connections between man and world, as we do through Dr. Steiner. That makes it so terribly difficult also now to speak to the people and the Antroposophs are much too infirm in Germany. - It will come so far that freedom will not rule anymore. that commissions will be put up which have to decide in every thing, in political life as well as in spiritual life, in the administration of the schools and other things. May be that in spite of all, the jews will be put off. Our first care is now to see to the friends who cannot stay in Germany, be it that they are of jewish descent, be it that they are not quite safe any more through a certain work they used to do more on a social level.

Letter from Ita Wegman to Daniel Nicol Dunlop,
April 17, 1933, page 1

no longer prevail in Germany, and that commissions may be established that rule on all kinds of matters, both in the political domain and in cultural and spiritual life—such as school administration and suchlike. The Jews may also be expelled. Naturally, this is also our prime concern now: the various members who can no longer remain in Germany because they are of Jewish origin or because of the particular nature of their social work. Moreover, for me the uneasy question arises as to how we can organize ourselves as true anthroposophists in a way that serves truly human qualities; how can we continue to disseminate Spiritual Science in the right way despite and beyond nationalism, and how can we live in accordance with it? I can see a time approaching when the wave that now courses through Germany will not remain within its borders but will spread to various other countries, and when each country will close itself off until—since this is at odds with all true evolution—things ultimately degenerate into a widespread and major war. How should we relate to these convulsions—for this is also intrinsic to our tasks, otherwise Anthroposophy has no meaning at all if we merely acquire it for ourselves in quiet seclusion—and work in a way that enables us, perhaps, to prevent some of these developments through our right stance and right deeds?

Instead of preparing these "right deeds" through a "right stance" and clear insights, the general outlook of anthroposophists after Hitler seized power was primarily one of fear, horror and paralysis, but also on occasion of dubious diplomacy,[24] partial[25] (or complete[26]) misjudgment and an often self-referential opportunism (*"The sad thing is that many anthroposophists are allowing themselves to be seduced by nationalism and are joining in with it. The whole Schenk group in Nuremberg has left the Anthroposophical Society. I find this incomprehensible. It shows how many people have their heads in the clouds"*[27]). In another letter written to Dorothy Osmond:

Freedom is increasingly suppressed, and our anthroposophic friends seem not to notice the dangers of this, instead— whether out of blindness or opportunism—joining in with some of these developments. This makes everything more tragic than it already is. I pray that anthroposophists in other countries will be stronger, for otherwise Anthroposophy cannot fulfill its task.[28]

≈

For her part, Ita Wegman tried to organize an international gathering of anthroposophists in Berlin in March 1933 (*"I have chosen Berlin, specifically, because we need to do this right in the middle of Germany, so that we have something that can be effective in the whole atmosphere there."*[29] *"My choice fell on Berlin only because it seems important to me for a foreigner to gain an impression of the whole atmosphere there, since Berlin is the seat of all political activity"*[30]). This was a gathering of (primarily young) colleagues and members, connected with each other in their responsibility for Anthroposophy in general and for anthroposophic medicine and curative education in many countries (*"It would be good if we could try to make this gathering a truly earnest occasion, attending to the very grave situation in which the world currently finds itself and the dangers threatening our anthroposophic work, and discussing these issues"*[31]). Wegman aimed for a sequence of further meetings in England and Holland, but wished to make a start in Berlin among people with a cosmopolitan outlook, "who have the good will to work with each other and who also feel fully and completely connected with the impulses initiated by Dr. Steiner."[32]

It is important to discuss many things together. I'd like to call this gathering as early as possible.... I really would like to regard this meeting as a preparatory discussion about everything that needs to be undertaken in the forthcoming period.[33]

Wegman secretly prepared the location of the meeting in private premises (*"I don't want to attract attention"*[34]); and without revealing anything about the content of the meeting itself in her invitations—which included more than 43 personal letters in the period from March 5 to 29[35]—she repeatedly stressed to her addressees, to whom she already referred with abbreviated names, the importance of keeping spiritual connections alive across national boundaries and situations.[36] She emphasized the fact that fascist developments would by no means remain limited to Germany:

> I believe this meeting will be extraordinarily important, as I'm sure do all our friends, since times are growing ever graver and totalitarianism will raise its head everywhere. We will need to discuss ways of holding together and surviving. The anthroposophists will hold together very little, but we need to create a group of people who can do this.[37]

She tirelessly encouraged possible participants to attend the gathering, fearlessly combating all obstacles and anxieties (*"We all know of course that the situation is extremely precarious. But without finding courage the right thing can never happen in the world"*[38]), changed the time and location of the gathering frequently, and had enquiries made about any possible risk to people known to be active anthroposophists who traveled from England. Three days before the meeting, finally, she considered moving it to Switzerland after receiving warnings from Stuttgart. Finally, however, the meetings took place successfully in Stuttgart on April 1 and 2 (in the private premises of the anthroposophic physician Eberhard Schickler) and a few days later also in Berlin, to Wegman's great satisfaction.[39] The meetings were a success also

Boycott of Jewish shops, April 1, 1933

in view of the realities in Germany at that time, and imminent developments. On the first day of the meeting in Stuttgart there was a boycott of all Jewish shops throughout Germany, and thus a further palpable prefiguring of the extent of Nazi powers and proscriptions. Immediately before she departed for Stuttgart and Berlin, on March 31, Wegman had written from Arlesheim to her colleague and friend Mien Viehoff in London:

> Tomorrow I'm going to Germany, Stuttgart, and will meet our friends there. Maybe, too, there will be chaos in Germany tomorrow, since the Jewish boycott is taking place there on April 1. Nevertheless, it's good that I will be there, since one also has to do something for our German friends and must not be too timid and anxious. Very grave times are coming. We cannot yet be at all sure of what may happen.

The issues Ita Wegman wished to discuss in Stuttgart and Berlin with her friends and colleagues from various countries included not only acquiring a common awareness of the drama of the current situation,[40] but pragmatic concerns too: such as setting up an effective international organization for getting Jewish members of the anthroposophic medical movement out of the country and receiving them abroad, along with other persecuted people where needed ("*Those who have retained their healthy sense of judgment are not allowed to speak out unless they want the police suddenly knocking at their door one fine day to send them—also—to a concentration camp. There really is no other alternative therefore than for many people to leave Germany so as to regroup and reorganize abroad, and later perhaps to exert some influence again on Germany. The others, who remain, will have to continue work connected with Anthroposophy on the quiet, with great caution, so that the thread is not broken*"[41]). At the end of

April, and thus only four weeks after the meetings in Stuttgart and Berlin, Wegman elaborated these plans in more detail in various letters—in particular in letters to England (*"I regard England as the most suitable for granting freedom to those whom unfreedom has forced to leave their country"*[42]), Holland and France. She made specific practical proposals but at the same time continued to try to persuade her addressees of the need for full commitment and engagement. Thus in a letter to England dated April 28, she referred once more to the need for people under threat to emigrate, and gave exemplary reasons for this:

> These are people, after all, who are completely at odds with the current government, and because of this are at risk of all kinds of dangers; and also those of Jewish origin who are being expelled in consequence. I therefore urgently ask you to consider these questions. We need to create an international organization that will also work spiritually to combat the unspiritual nature of current nationalist regimes, which—it seems to me—are surfacing everywhere and taking similar routes.[43]

Wegman felt a sense of urgency not only regarding the current adversities but also the growing threat of nationalist tendencies in countries potentially willing to receive émigrés (*"I just have a feeling that we ought not wait too long. There is a great willingness to help from abroad at present, but this may decline if circumstances grow worse"*[44]). She tried to organize immigration visas, work, and guest accommodation for medical colleagues and friends who wished to leave Germany. She herself traveled to Paris to sound out possibilities there for Jewish students of her acquaintance to continue their medical training. Above all, though, Ita Wegman relied on Britain and her colleagues and friends at Clent [Sunfield] and in London, convinced that "from England, where the spirit of freedom is strongest, something like a fight back can arise. But

I believe this can only happen if we anthroposophists really put our energy into this."[45] Many people living in Germany in hard-pressed circumstances were already turning to Ita Wegman in their perplexity and uncertainty. Her key position as a physician, her location and status in Switzerland and all her powers of courage and initiative, as well as her inner connection with Germany, made her a focus of hope.[46] At the same time she was able to offer frequent training and work opportunities (for Jewish refugees among others).[47] At the end of April she wrote an explanatory letter to the anthroposophic physician Karl Nunhoefer in London:

> This is the most unbelievable thing that could ever have arisen in Germany—an unequalled ignominy—that is nevertheless regarded as humanly elevated. At present I am trying as far as possible to gather together Germans abroad and to form an alliance of them against this anti-spirit that is rampant in Germany now: to protest against it and to prepare for a time when one can achieve something in Germany again.[48]

Although the situation in Germany still seemed undramatic on the whole, Ita Wegman was more aware than most of her contemporaries of the real threat that was approaching. In mid-March, preparing for the meetings in Stuttgart and Berlin, she had urged a colleague practicing in Munich to make unstinting efforts to support the emigration of children from Germany to Switzerland, offering to accommodate them in centers directed by her:

> I am very concerned indeed about the whole world situation. The way things are going does not bode well for the future. I am often particularly concerned for the children who have to witness all this, whether the fervent delirium of joy, on the one hand, or the hate-filled persecution of people with different outlooks on the other—such as Jews and so on. I really feel like urging physicians to help get children out of

den 4. August 1933.

Fräulein

Hanna Lissau,

W i e n IX.
Fuchsthallergasse 10.

Sehr geehrtes Fräulein Lissau!

Auf Ihren Brief mit dem beigefügten Reifezeugnis
teile ich Ihnen mit, dass der Beginn des Ausbildungskurses auf
den 15. Oktober festgesetzt werden ist. Sie können in dem Kurs
Aufnahme finden und haben wir Sie zur Teilnahme vorgemerkt.
Es wird aber doch nötig sein, dass Sie etwas mehr Geld zur
Verfügung haben, um die nötigen Ausgaben für Wohnung, Steuern,
Aufenthaltsbewilligung etc. bestreiten zu können. Besonders
während der ersten drei Monate sollten Sie 40.-- bis 50.--
schw. Frs. haben.

Wir erwarten gern noch Ihre Nachricht, ob Sie dieses
ermöglichen können und senden Ihnen auf Ihren Wunsch Ihr
Zeugnis anbei wieder zurück.

Mit freundlichem Gruss

*Letter from Ita Wegman to the young, Jewish anthroposophist
Hanna Lissau in Vienna about her participation in a
training course in Arlesheim, August 4, 1933*

Germany. Please remember that we want to receive children here with love.[49]

≈

Ita Wegman's other continual concern since the Nazis had come to power in Germany was the future of "handicapped" children, adolescents and adults, and thus also the situation and outlook for various curative education homes and institutions with which she was either directly or indirectly connected. Rudolf Steiner's "Curative Education Course" of 1924 was formulated in absolute opposition to prevailing currents of thought about "eradicating lives not worth living."[50] The work that had begun since then was very much under Ita Wegman's auspices and the spiritual guidance[51] entrusted to her by Rudolf Steiner when she took over leadership of the Medical Section at the Goetheanum.[52]

In the eight years since Steiner's death, Ita Wegman had visited the different centers of this work on countless occasions, helping encourage and stimulate it and developing its medical aspect in close connection with those holding positions of responsibility for, and working in, these places. She knew all these people very well, as she did the children and young people under their care. In addition, she had founded the "Association for Social Support" and, with the help of its staff, established contact with welfare and youth services in numerous large German cities, developing modes of collaboration and initiating well-attended talks on themes of social conflict from an anthroposophic perspective.

However, as early as February and March 1933, powerful and targeted efforts were underway in Nazi Germany to resolve the "social question" by means of violent ethnic cleansing and social Darwinian approaches. "Degenerate individuals" were forcefully removed to Dachau concentration camp (as publicized on March 21 in the so-called *Munich News Bulletin*). Remedial schools were denounced; all forms of reduced "performance ability" and problematic social integration were declared the target of eradication measures; and finally, on July 14, 1933, a law to "prevent a new generation with inherited diseases" was passed, coming into force from January 1, 1934. This legislated for the compulsory sterilization of the "innately weak-minded" (which meant "any degree of mental infirmity diagnosed as being markedly abnormal"), of patients suffering from schizophrenia, manic-depressive disorders, or epilepsy (through to severe instances of clubfeet), and enforced a duty upon all medical practitioners to report such conditions.[53]

In the committees responsible at the time, plans for "euthanasia" of such individuals were already underway. In this situation Ita Wegman sought to save and preserve whatever she could. During her visits to curative institutes in January, April, May, and December, as well as at the meetings in Stuttgart and Berlin (to which she invited leading colleagues from all her curative homes), she discussed further steps, but at the same time restricted public

Dachau concentration camp, 1933

activity by the "Association for Social Support" due to the dangers of visible exposure (*"The work of the association has been put on hold to some extent because in B. [Berlin] things can no longer be done so freely. We'll have to see how things develop. Public lectures are no longer possible. I'm sure there's no need for me to explain this further to you"*[54]).

Wegman thought that the Nazi regime's—long-planned[55]—interventions in the pedagogical domain must be averted as a matter of priority, and that the medical orientation of the homes and institutes should be explicitly emphasized (*"Our curative education institutes are focused more on the medical domain. That's more of a specialism and may attract less attention, so that we may perhaps be able to continue our work there without interruption. We just have to be very careful"*[56]). Her advice was for each home to avoid any impression of an overarching anthroposophic organization; she suggested they limit correspondence[57] and maintain as much autonomy as possible (*"Increasingly I am proposing that each of us bear sole responsibility in all the steps that we wish to take during this period"*[58]). On April 11, she wrote to England:

> There is still no way of knowing how things will end, but we can have our suspicions about what is approaching. I have tried my utmost to ensure that each institute will do whatever it needs to, in entirely free initiative; and likewise to base everything only on curative education and medicine. All youth work or social work is suspended for the time being. And the "social support" work that started so wonderfully well in Berlin, and developed in a very fine way, now has to be limited so as to draw as little attention as possible. Letters, telegrams, telephone are under surveillance, and so we must be very cautious when sending news. The most important thing is not to place any emphasis on connections with other countries.[59]

All the larger curative education homes connected with Ita Wegman had an anthroposophic physician and therefore could handle diagnoses and medical reports autonomously and internally. Even after passing of the sterilization law there was no immediate danger since private institutions were initially excluded from the requirement to carry out compulsory sterilization. Without knowing the specific details of the legislation and its planned realization, however, Wegman wrote as follows to curative home director and physician Heinrich Hardt in Altefeld shortly after the bill was passed:

> It says in the newspaper that a sterilization law has been passed in Germany and will go into effect on January 1. This really puts our work in the spotlight. If these children who come to us are sterilized, naturally it will no longer be possible to work with them in a fruitful curative way. But as I have read, exceptions are possible, and here we must really make every effort to defend ourselves, by saying that we can still achieve quite a lot with these children. By this means, perhaps, we may manage to ensure that sterilization is only done at a later age, giving us the chance to work pedagogically. It is not clearly stated that children are already subject to this law. In your letter you said that you received some visits; it might be important to repeatedly emphasize what I've said here when you get such visits or questions. For us the age of sterilization is an important thing. If it is done later on, our duty must only be to work as energetically as we can to get these children, and to improve them as much as possible so that they may be able to avoid this law—and thus our curative education may still perhaps prove a blessing for many of them. If we could demonstrate that people with mental disability can improve, and later can be useful in agricultural work and so forth, we might create a safe means of continuing our work without interference. What we need to do is show the value of our curative education.[60]

Despite all difficulties—or rather specifically because of developments that had already arisen and others that were looming—Ita Wegman saw the curative homes and centers as essential cultural oases for the future, as places of true humanity and a therapeutic art of healing—indeed, as "places for the life of spirit to germinate."[61] During the first few months of 1933, alongside all pragmatic measures to safeguard the institutions, she was already also supporting her often insecure and unsettled colleagues, affirming the spiritual strength and importance of their task in Central Europe. In a sense, the demonic distortions of the image of the human being embodied by the Nazis was ultimately only the culmination of materialistic modes of nineteenth-century Darwinian thinking, and the powers of destruction associated with it. However small the anthroposophic curative homes were in Gerswalde, Pilgramshain, Altefeld and Paderborn (and likewise the efforts underway in Berlin, Stuttgart, Malsch, Bonnewitz, Arlesheim and England), they represented the first beginnings of a diametrically opposed culture of the future, specifically also in their esoteric and Christological foundations. Just one week after Adolf Hitler was named Chancellor of Germany, Ita Wegman wrote as follows to Erich Kirchner at Schloss Hamborn: "For Germany now there is really no more to be done than to develop and strengthen centers where the future can be cultivated, since these may perhaps be the only real centers of culture."[62]

Although Wegman traveled and worked in a very wide-ranging way throughout 1933, the outlook and orientation of her activities and intentions were without doubt focused primarily on England. The Goetheanum in Dornach was her base, along with Arlesheim and the Clinical-Therapeutic Institute, although she periodically spoke of this in a relativizing and open-ended manner: "I am here only to maintain continuity, because there is still much that I need to do here of course."[63] For years, however,

Heilerziehungs- und Erholungsheim
Schloß Hamborn
e. V.

Schloß Hamborn, den 20.6.1933
Paderborn-Land
Tel. Paderborn 2923

Frau

Dr. Ita W e g m a n

A r l e s h e i m
_____

Sehr verährte, liebe Frau Doktor!

Die Möglichkeit, durch Herrn Krüger
Ihnen ein Brief zu übermitteln möchte ich benutzen, um Ihnen ausführ-
lich über die Situation zu schreiben, die mich veranlasste, Sie um
eine Zusammenkunft mit sämtlichen Heimpädagogen zu bitten.
In Pilgramsheim bestehen die verschiedensten Machenschaf-
ten gegen Dr.König, die darauf hinzielen, ihn als Juden und Ausländer
auszuweisen. Tatsächlich hat man ihm bereits das Recht entzogen, den
Doktortitel zu führen, weil er das Doktor-Examen im Ausland gemacht
hat. Der Oberpräsident der Provinz hat einen Bericht eingefordert,
so dass man daraus ersieht, dass die Beschäftigung mit seiner Person
und Pilgramsheim schon an die obersten Stellen der Provinz geht. Bert
Keyserlingk erzählte mir, dass König sich dahin geäussert habe, dass
er dieses Kesseltreiben gegen ihn nur noch einige Wochen aushalten
könne und dann lieber fortgehen würde. Ein Vortrag in einer benach-
barten Stadt wurde von ihm abgesagt, weil ihm von nationalsozialisti-
scher Seite vorher mitgeteilt wurde, dass der Vortrag mitten drin
von Nat.Soz. gestört werden würde und er am Weitersprechen verhin-
dert werden sollte. Wenn auch unter den gegenwärtigen Umständen und
bei den Verbindungen, die zu den heutigen Regierungsstellen in Schle-
sien geschaffen werden können, ein Verbleib von König vielleicht
durchgesetzt werden kann, so bin ich doch der Ansicht, dass eine
Wirksamkeit von ihm kaum mehr vorhanden sein wird und ausserdem das
Institut aller Voraussicht nach sehr zu leiden hat.
In Gerswalde war zwei Tage vor unserem Aufenthalt der neue
nat.soz.Kommissar des Landes-Wohlfahrtsamtes in Berlin, der ein aus-
führliches Gespräch mit Löffler gehabt hat und ausserdem das ganze
Heim besichtigte. Das Gespräch hatte ungefähr folgenden Schluss:
Die Nat.Soz. beabsichtigen nicht, gegen die Privatschulen, Heime usw.
vorzugehen. Sie erkennen vollkommen ah, dass diese Heime viel gelei-
stet haben und dass sie auch bei dem alten System so organisiert
werden mussten, wie das geschehen ist. Man erwartet nur heute, dass
zu der individualistischen Erziehung, die nicht aufgegeben werden
soll, die bewusste Erziehung zur Volksgemeinschaft hinzukommt. Darin

*Letter from Erich Kirchner to Ita Wegman, informing her about
the difficult situation of doctor Karl König in Pilgramshain,
who was of Jewish origin, June 20, 1933, page 1*

23

in view of the political developments and atmosphere in Germany, and the generally nationalist tendencies in Central Europe, she had seen the need to create a foundation for anthroposophic work in the Anglo-American West alongside the center in Switzerland and the diverse, scattered institutions. This aim was one Rudolf Steiner had wished to pursue also, and which he had emphasized in his last days in relation to a possible trip to America by Eugen Kolisko.[64] Ita Wegman subsequently carried this further through intensive collaboration with leading and likewise cosmopolitan-minded anthroposophists such as Daniel Nicol Dunlop in England:

> After all, I have given a great deal of energy to ensuring that Mr. Dunlop became leader of the movement in England, in line with Rudolf Steiner's words that things would only start going well there, that the movement would only make progress, if Dunlop declared his willingness to unite with it. This was one of my first tasks in England: to help Dunlop to a leading position, and to encourage other friends to recognize this.[65]

Ita Wegman played a decisive part in big public events held in England, made it possible to establish a medical therapy center in London (at Kent Terrace, from September 1932), a curative home in Clent and a large, internationally oriented branch of Weleda under Dunlop's management:

> We must hold together strongly so that Rudolf Steiner's ideas are not suddenly overturned or even buried and forgotten. We must now scatter the seeds over the whole world and let anthroposophic life germinate and flourish all the more strongly.[66]

Wegman became increasingly aware of the rapid and drastic course things were taking, and the great urgency for necessary initiatives in 1933 ("*Soon it will be too late*"[67]). Germany was turning irrevocably toward the abyss, threatening not only to extinguish all humanistic tendencies and powers within its own borders but also to entangle neighboring countries in dire conflicts and war. The need for "feverish" activity *("It is as though everything has to be done feverishly before the great catastrophe occurs, for things do indeed look very grave in the world"),*

10, KENT TERRACE, LONDON, N.W.1

(A branch of the Clinical and Therapeutical Institute at Arlesheim, under the supervision of Dr. Wegman)

which Ita Wegman described in a letter to Madeleine van Deventer on February 25—two days before her major lecture in London[68] commemorating Rudolf Steiner—related primarily to circumstances and possibilities in England:

> My thoughts are very often of England, for the way things are now developing here [in Germany] seems to me to offer next to no opportunity to work properly here in the coming times; and so one must do all one can to create ways of working spiritually in England. To bring this about will of course require enormous efforts by individuals.[69]

In another letter of April 30, she wrote:

> You have no idea how restless I often feel, with a sense that things are happening so slowly and that time is marching onward mercilessly, that catastrophe is rearing its head and will suddenly break upon us. All I can do is say to everyone: Do whatever you can to bring everything under shelter as fast as possible so that things already have some form when dire circumstances overwhelm us.[70]

During her five longer stays in England in 1933, Ita Wegman tried energetically to help the progress of local anthroposophic endeavors. She was planning a larger clinic to be opened shortly in London, and a nursing home—for which she viewed premises and considered funding models—and made or consolidated human contacts and connections,[71] also with influential people in public life. She organized lectures with the aim of having some impact, and publications in well-regarded medical journals, as well as undertaking actual medical work with patients.

Examining Wegman's correspondence at this period, we can see that in her trips to England in February, April, June, August to September, and November to December—which she was always reluctant to end (*"I don't think I ought to stay away from England*

Arlesheim, den 9. Juli 1933.

Liebe Mien!

Ich beschäftige mich ganz ausserordentlich mit dem Problem
Nursinghome in England, und ich möchte hiermit fragen, ob das Haus
Hamilton Terrace schon wieder aus unseren Händen ist. Es ist doch
sehr schade, dieses Haus,was so nahe liegt, so ohne weiteres aufzu-
geben. Frau Leroi denkt nämlich sehr stark daran, nach England zu
kommen, und man müsste vielleicht einmal fragen, ob sie dieses
Haus nicht kaufen könnte. Oder ist denn gar keine Möglichkeit,dass
dieses Haus, nicht unter dem Namen "Nursing-Home", sondern mehr so
dass ein Arzt darin wohnt, geführt wird? Dieses Haus war doch so
billig und so sehr praktisch in jeder Beziehung. Bitte denke doch
einmal ein bischen darüber nach und sprich auch einmal mit Stein,
was er meint. Frau Leroi und Alex, auch Ellen, haben zugesagt,nach
England zu kommen. Ellen wird wohl mit uns Heileurythmie arbeiten
wollen.

Dieses einmal in aller Eile, weil mir diese Gedanken in den
Sinn kamen. Wenn die Arbeit in London nicht abgeschwächt würde,
würde ich ja auch schon ein Erholungsheim ausserhalb Londons wohl
begrüssen, aber damit wir nicht allzuviel Zentrums haben, wäre es
dann am besten, dass dieses dann auch mehr in die Nähe von Clent
Grove käme.

Schreibe bald!

Mit herzlichem Gruss

Deine J. W.

P.S. Wie geht es Frau Stein?
Viele Grüsse an sie und Stein.
Frl Clarissa Johanna schon in der Schule?

Letter from Ita Wegman to Mien Viehoff
about the plan for a nursing home, July 9, 1933

27

too long, since events are going so fast that one has no idea what might happen in a fortnight or three weeks"[72])—she repeatedly encountered very hopeful developments alternating with depressing reversals. Walter Johannes Stein (who would emigrate to England, finally, at the end of June[73]) held lectures in London that Wegman jointly initiated and attended; and on February 25, she writes about his work as follows:

> Stein has a very strong public presence, is giving lectures everywhere: at the German Club, the Goethe Association; ministers make his personal acquaintance and invite him to their houses, and he has any number of contacts. It is quite remarkable how things are progressing. We really ought to stay here another two weeks since it is almost a shame to break off.[74]

Yet delays, hesitancy and reluctance soon followed from those around her *("It is as if people have become more ponderous and anxious"*[75]). On May 29, Wegman finally found suitable premises for the "nursing home" and, in a hopeful mood, undertook laborious and initially positive negotiations—which however suddenly grew more complex and were sucked into the current of political circumstances. In a letter she wrote only two days later she said:

> It seems that everything here is paralysed by world events. The newly developing friendship with Germany has been swept aside. Instead, defensiveness and amazement prevail, but also a kind of very unhealthy mimicry. How will we make headway? It almost seems to me as if we are continually at the point of collapse.[76]

Immediately after this, the situation again grew temporarily more positive *("It's as if everything has suddenly awakened again; the rigidity has faded, and feverish work is being done"*[77]). Initially this did not apply to the nursing home (which failed to

*Ita Wegman in the curative education center of Clent,
Pentacost, 1933*

secure a permit) but to a large-scale conference to mark the opening of the curative institute in Clent, a health food store adjoin-
ing the therapy center in London, and an opportunity for Walter
Johannes Stein to work alongside Dunlop in organizing the so-
called World Power Conference.[78] Finally, in the second half of
June, Ita Wegman spoke of a "crucial stay" in England, fetching to
London an associate of hers, the chemist and pharmacist Rudolf
Hauschka, while she herself temporarily went back to Germany
and Switzerland, intending to return at the end of August for the
"Summer Conference" in Bangor, Wales (with a keynote lecture on
the "Fundamentals of Anthroposophic Therapy" and daily Class
Lessons[79]).

≈

When Wegman set off from Arlesheim to London on August 15,
she did not travel alone but was accompanied by two colleagues
(Werner Pache and Margarethe Bockholt), as well as numerous
medical students. For approximately the past four years, a continually growing group of students had been meeting twice a year
with Ita Wegman in Arlesheim for medical courses and study of
Rudolf Steiner's key medical works. Although it was harder for
many of them to attend this course in 1933 (for both political and
financial reasons), 22 students had, to Ita Wegman's great pleasure, nevertheless gathered in Switzerland during the first week of
March to study the laws and life forces of the etheric realm with
her and George Adams Kaufmann:

> Despite all outward difficulties, the spirit does break through,
> for—and this needs to be said—we have never yet had such a
> fine and intensive course with the young people as we did now.[80]

> Never before was such intensive, alert work undertaken as
> now in this course.[81]

Wegman was delighted by the spiritual clarity of the young students and their developing medical and social initiative. In her letters she repeatedly spoke of the great hopes she had in this new generation, seeing them as a new group

> that conducts itself absolutely as R. St. envisaged a new generation of physicians, for whom the primary thing is not having a practice but forming a community and thereby giving a powerful new impetus to medical work.[82]

In these spring months of 1933, Wegman had already begun to reflect on how these students could pursue their path—given the Nazi indoctrination and demand for "conformity" to Nazi principles at universities—in accordance with their innovative intentions. On April 30, she had written to London:

> Our dear physician friends have formed such a strong community that it really gives me pleasure. Some of them are here again to study; they help one another and are firmly resolved to put all their humanity at the service of Rudolf Steiner's ideas. In other words, our regular gatherings did have a sense and purpose. Naturally I include you among them, as one of those who now have an important karmic task to fulfill abroad.[83]

When Ita Wegman returned from London in the middle of June—her third trip to England in 1933—she found that some of the students wanted to hold the follow-up course on pastoral medicine in Great Britain in August.[84] Wegman responded positively to this idea (*"I saw great openness to the world in your proposal"*[85]) and led to further discussions both between the students themselves and with her. To travel to England in August 1933 was a difficult undertaking for many of them, in terms of both money and time, and in addition represented a break with the spiritual tradition of the student courses so far held in Arlesheim; and this gave rise to major internal discussions. In the end it was agreed to start the course in Arlesheim then continue it in England in a smaller group, and to give the gathering a different thematic emphasis (involving studies on Rudolf Steiner's second "Course for Young Doctors," studies on embryology with Karl König, as well as artistic therapy exercises in music, eurythmy therapy and painting). At the end of June Wegman wrote to one of the participating students in regard to the initial course in Arlesheim:

> We must regard the gathering here as another really very intensive nurturing of community, discussing in detail what plans we should form for the future. We really have to look the future in the face now and make plans.... I'd like to hold this course in a way that allows us to form a clear judgment, based on all that is available to us, about the impulses now living in the world.[86]

There were also many new students (from Germany, Holland, Austria, and Switzerland) who gathered in Arlesheim on August 2, met with Wegman and worked with her, Karl König, Edmund Pracht, and Margarethe Bockholt. Some of them, however, were filled with gloom: "The Germans brought a great sense of depression with them, and in the first few days we could hardly get down to work because of the cloud of affliction and worry surrounding them."[87]

From the second week in July, Ita Wegman had written numerous letters asking for financial support to enable the students to travel on to England, describing in detail the situation for young, anthroposophically oriented people at German universities:

> The poor people are really in a desperate state, suffering greatly from the situation they find themselves in, enslaved and subjugated from all sides and made to do things at the universities that run counter to the anthroposophic spirit.[88]

It is shocking to see how one has to divest oneself of all individuality there and merge with the will of the state, and how everything revolves around National Socialism.[89]

She also described the group's distinctive soul configuration and aims:

> Without being frivolous they want to form groups, wherever they are, that go beyond nationalism and can serve a new form of community that looks directly to Michael as its leader.[90]
> Among them are some really outstanding people who wish to bear Rudolf Steiner's Anthroposophy into the world without compromise.[91]

In several of these letters, each written individually and personally, that Wegman primarily sent to physicians in the anthroposophic movement with their own practice,[92] she asked for modest ongoing payments to support the students (*"I would be very happy with 5 marks per month. But you will understand me if I place more value on real action than on the amount of money, because such initiative itself will no doubt bring a blessing with it"*[93]). At the same time she indicated what she saw as her own task of mediation and preparation in accomplishing the planned trip to England (*"I will...personally bring this group there, and rather than working so much with them as course teacher, will introduce them to the circumstances there and give them opportunities to meet people"*[94]) and outlined further perspectives for the planned initiative:

> Naturally, I want to support this group of young doctors as much as possible. And so I think I will do everything I can to anchor this group—which may later draw others to it—in England in some way. This may only be a temporary arrangement to begin with, as a prologue to more permanent work later. We must give serious attention to helping the German

6. August 1933.

Sehr geehrter Herr Dr. Gutsch!

Ich möchte einmal mit einer Bitte an Sie herantreten. Unter unseren jungen Medizin-Studierenden sind verschiedene Schwierigkeiten aufgetreten, wodurch manche von ihnen keine Möglichkeit haben, weiter zu studieren. Nun habe ich wohl Möglichkeiten, diesem oder jenem zu helfen, ins Ausland zu kommen, um dort die Beziehungen zu benützen, die ich habe. Auch können eventuell einige hierbleiben. Die Freunde im Ausland sind sicherlich bereit, alles zu tun, um zu helfen, aber bis man erst dort im Lande selber ist, um die ersten Schritte zu unternehmen, dazu benötigt man doch ein bisschen Geld. Es ist jetzt gerade, wo wir einen medizinischen Kurs hier haben, so stark herausgekommen, wie viele Schwierigkeiten da doch sind. Und gerade nachdem der Kurs hier wieder von 55 jungen Leuten besucht worden ist, fühle ich es als meine Pflicht, dafür zu sorgen, dass die Sektion auch denjenigen hilft, die jetzt in ihren Studien behindert sind, hilft. Ich persönlich tue schon, was ich kann, aber es ist doch manches nötig, bis die Dinge laufen.

Wenn Sie mir etwas dafür zur Verfügung stellen können, so können Sie es auf das Postscheckkonto des Klinisch-Therapeutischen Instituts in Karlsruhe Nr. 70104 einzahlen. Ich bin Ihnen sehr dankbar, wenn Sie dadurch den jungen Leuten zu ihrem weiteren Fortkommen helfen können.

Mit freundlichen Grüssen

*Letter from Ita Wegman to the anthroposophical physician
Werner Gutsch, asking him for financial support for
the student journey to England, August 6, 1933*

spirit find a means to develop and express itself abroad, for otherwise much of value will go under.

These young people must be given the opportunity to meet others, to feel for themselves whether their karma lies in England, and whether the karma of the English wishes to connect with theirs. Karma must come to expression in relation to our task. We cannot just randomly advise people to go here or there, but instead they have to feel in their heart what is coming to utterance there.[95]

Wegman repeatedly spoke of an "orientation trip,"[96] one undertaken under fateful conditions[97]—whose outcome, however, was left quite open and unfixed. Ita Wegman worked tirelessly to bring this about, personally taking upon herself all the organizational logistics at a time when she was already fully and completely occupied.[98] Thus she not only organized meetings with young academics in Oxford but also arranged tents for camping at Clent (*"Might you have a tent stored away somewhere? Do you still know anyone who has some tents we might be able to borrow, or somewhere we could rent them?"*[99]) and, through Mien Viehoff, sofas and mattresses in London. She apologized to her correspondents frequently for making these requests: "I hope I'm not putting you to too much trouble."[100] During the second half of July and the first half of August these activities, alongside her clinical work at Arlesheim and everything connected with running the Medical Section, took up any remaining moments in her day, so that even her own efforts for additional funding for the innovative projects in London temporarily took a back seat:

I have not yet been able to do anything about additional funding since all my time has inevitably been taken up with ensuring the medical course will be a success. But we will find solutions I'm sure. So far things have always worked out, and they will again now.[101]

Right to the end, though, Wegman was fully convinced of the social and spiritual importance of her plans with and for the students, and four days before her departure from Arlesheim wrote as follows to London:

> I can't tell you how important it is for me to come to England with these 12 young people, to spend a little time there with them. One among them, Herr Marx, who has Jewish parents, cannot in fact return to Germany, and we must see what we can do to help him.[102]

Besides Lothar Marx (who was the only one of the group to end up staying in England and working there long-term) several

✓Walter Bühler, stud. med., Homburg, Saargebiet

✓Anneliese Feitig, stud. med. Siebeldingen, Rheinpfalz

✓Wiltrud Feitig, cand. med., Siebeldingen, Rheinpfalz

✓Marianne Hartmann, cand. med., Göppingen, Kelmenstr. 5.

✓Fritz Herbert, cand. med., Wiesbaden-Dotzheim, Idsteinerstr. 42.

✗Walter Holtzapfel, cand. med., Niebüll, Schleswig

✗Gisbert Husemann, Arzt, Holzhausen i/Westf. Kreis Lübbecke

✓Lothar Marx, cand. med. , Buchau a/Federsee, Württemberg

✓Maria Raszka, cand. med., Hamburg 25, Wallstr. 5.

✗ ✝Alexander Rust, Arzt, Celle, Emigrantenstr. 6.

✓Inge Ryssel, cand. med., Paderborn, Grunigerstr. 13.

✓✝Gerhard Schumacher, cand. med., Berlin W. 62. Schillstr. 11a.

Gertrud
Trudi Walther, cand. med., Mühldorf, Ob. Bayern.

✝Alexander Rust und Gerhard Schumacher sind schon unterwegs und jetzt zu erreichen unter der Adresse

Zonnehuis-Veldheim, Utrechtscheweg, Zeist, Holland.

List of names in the student travel group

other of the students making their way to England (such as Walter
Holtzapfel, Alexander Leroi, and Gisbert Husemann[103]) were considering continuing their studies and working there in the future,
and ended up leaving Germany on a cheap freight ship—but only
for a few weeks.[104]

≈

Ita Wegman stayed in England longer than the students did, remaining after the summer school in Bangor through to Michaelmas,
although she was urgently needed in Dornach and Arlesheim
and had herself organized a pastoral medicine gathering of physicians and Christian Community priests from October 4 under
the auspices of the Medical Section. Part of the reason for this
conference was to collaborate on revisions to the planned edition
of Rudolf Steiner's Pastoral Medicine Course.[105] Wegman's arrival
was urgently awaited for the necessary preparation of this important work; but at the same time she felt inwardly obliged to share
responsibility for developments in England, which she regarded
as so decisive for the future, by giving a helping hand there in the
last days of September. Finally, in the second half of September,
she wrote to Madeleine van Deventer and the Arlesheim college
of physicians in a tone of urgency, seeking their understanding for
her difficulties:

> I do not know what the situation is like in Dornach and
> Arlesheim, or in Germany, but here it appears to be growing
> very grave. One can feel a reflex response here to what is hap-
> pening over there; and if we do not stay alert, everything will
> fall apart here, too, and the good work will be lost.
> My situation here is a strange one: I feel and know that
> a great deal depends on me here, but also feel morally com-
> pelled to return to Arlesheim. The physicians' conference[106]
> is upon us, and we have to prepare for it. No doubt a great

deal depends on it. But how do we reconcile both these needs? There is only one way to do so, and it is as follows:

I will stay here until Michaelmas, celebrate the Michaelmas festival here and try to sort various things out here by then, do what is needed, and will then travel or fly to Basel the next day. I will be there for the conference, no doubt unprepared, but if the college of physicians is well prepared it will be able to carry the *conference and also me.*

We will work together in the early morning before the conference begins, and you can tell me everything you have decided on together. Please tell the college this. I am making this plea because I feel compelled to it by an inner need.

I feel like a hunted animal unable to finish anything it has started; as if demonic efforts are being made to rob me of everything, so that chaos reigns. But I have a strong feeling that other forms have to arise.[107]

Wegman made her final England trip of 1933 in mid-November. She worked energetically to develop the therapy center at Kent Terrace, organized the distribution of anthroposophic medicine and publicity work, and set up a vegetarian restaurant adjoining the therapy center and nursing home she had planned. She was again temporarily very optimistic and frequently brought Rudolf Hauschka to London (*"Hauschka arrived here with much vigor so that I hope we can achieve a great deal together. Study evenings with the physicians, visits to various scientists and academics, and setting up medicine production labs. Many things are progressing here, and I hope we can really make a good deal of headway this time. Much depends on whether, by the end of the year, I will have established the foundations for independent work to be done here, so that I can start working again as I'd like to"*[108]).

In December, however, Wegman had to realize that despite all her efforts over preceding months, real, transformative will could not be kindled there, even in association with her anthroposophic

Medizinische Tagung
4. bis 8. Oktober 1933.

	Mittwoch 4. Oktober	Donnerstag 5. Oktober	Freitag 6. Oktober	Samstag 7. Oktober	Sonntag 8. Oktober
½10 Uhr vorm.	Seminaristisches Durcharbeiten des pastoralmedizinischen Kurses				
½12 Uhr vorm.	Heil-Eurythmie				—
3 Uhr nachm.	Zusammenkunft der Arbeitsgruppe zur Bekämpfung des Krebses Thema: Besprechungen über die derzeitige Lage der Krebsbehandlung.	Referate und Aussprachen Bisher angemeldete Referate: *Dr. W. Gutsch* „Die Leber, eine innermenschliche Enclave der Aussenwelt"; *Dr. Oråil:* „Ueber Ulcus duodeni und die Kaelin'sche Blutuntersuchung"; *Dr. Rudersdorff:* „Betrachtung eines Arztes über Musik"; *Dr. N. Glas:* „Wie entsteht die paranoische Seelenverfassung?" *Dr. M. Cord:* „Einige Diabetesfälle".			—
8½ Uhr abends	Vortrag *Dr. Zeylmans van Emmichoven* „Grenzzustände des Seelenlebens"	Vortrag *Dr. K. König* „Ferdinand Raimund und sein Schicksal"	Vortrag *Dr. G. Suchantke* „Krankheit, Heilung, Bewusstseinsentwicklung"	Vortrag *Dr. E. Kolisko* „Das Verständnis des sacramentalen Lebens durch anthroposophische Menschenkunde"	—

Die Arbeit am pastoral-medizinischen Kurs wird für die Ärzte der medizinischen Sektion und die Priester der Christengemeinschaft stattfinden. Die Abendvorträge sind allgemein zugänglich.

Die Veranstaltungen finden im *Goetheanum* statt. Beitrag für den ganzen Kurs Frs. 10.—. Öffentliche Vorträge à Fr. 1.—, Anmeldungen erbeten an Klinisch-Therapeutisches Institut Arlesheim.

Für die Medizinische Sektion: Dr. Ita Wegman.

Program for the medical conference at the Goetheanum

friends and acquaintances. In the end, none of the developments Wegman had hoped and striven for in England during 1933 could make any real headway—neither the planned clinic or the nursing home, the new start to medical work by students or the intended progress in the public and academic domain. She returned for the last time that year from England—where at the very last moment she decided after all not to buy the house adjoining the Kent Terrace therapy center. Balancing up her efforts in England and describing her renewed experience of conditions in Germany (having returned to Switzerland via Hamborn, Berlin, and Gerswalde), Ita Wegman wrote in a letter of December 18, 1933, from Arlesheim:

> We have to be … fully aware that the fragmentation continues unabated in Germany primarily, and that no improvement whatever in outer circumstances will come about in the near future. That's something we'll have to accept with composure. And if we cannot accept the reality of what Goethe speaks of

as "dying and becoming," we won't be able to survive these times. This is the situation on the Continent. I also look back with great concern to England and London; for while on the Continent everything of real soul quality—in which the spirit connects with other, different spiritual natures—is collapsing, in England I was trying to set up a center where people might be able to live in freedom: the ideal which Rudolf Steiner showed to be the ideal for humanity. But these efforts seem not to have borne fruit. What I wanted, and regarded as salvation, was for a living circle of wakeful people to form around the prevailing death forces and give rise to new life: a circle consisting, as it were, of fortresses and Grail castles in the different countries—where people live but are at the same time so mobile that they can move from one place to another. To realize this truly seemed to me a new alliance of Michael, whereby one can bring something new into the world in order to make possible the new life seeking to emerge. Yet realizing it seems to meet with great difficulties. It is already difficult that people are not free to get over there; and then also that English souls do not have a lot of faith for things of such far-reaching scope. Of course, we can understand this as part of the solid English character, and have to reckon with it. But the depressing thing is that the world of spirit is asking for this new development and does so without regard to these national characteristics, which basically have arisen on the earth: what is needed stands there as requirement, and people must act to meet it. Whether such a thing will succeed or not depends of course on whether enough people can really become aware of the need. There are difficulties with expanding the Kent Terrace premises, and I think that we ought in fact to take the more cautious route and leave this for now. Without complete support, not just financial but also as regards good will—and invoked by necessity—such expansion will not find blessing. Perhaps we will therefore have to wait calmly until people see the need and so connect fully with realizing it. I want, after all, to avoid pushing something through that might be seen as taking its impetus from *my will—for it is not my will.*[109]

≈

Ita Wegman sent the above letter to Clent on December 18, seven days after she arrived in Arlesheim and Dornach—an arrival again overshadowed by grave fractures within the General Anthroposophical Society. After all the crises that had started soon after Rudolf Steiner's death—and indeed already before this insofar as they related to Ita Wegman[110]—and had caused grave divisions between members of the executive council at the Goetheanum for many years, by 1933 a certain, albeit superficial, tranquility prevailed. The Annual General Meeting at Easter had not led to accusations and denunciations as extensive as in previous years (*"The Annual General Meeting went pretty smoothly, without incident. I was still able to stand there and speak [I'm told I made a strong impression] and this is the important thing for me"*[111]). At the same time, given existing prejudices at the Goetheanum, she considered the demonstrative display of the English "summer school" program—with lectures by Walter Johannes Stein, Eugen Kolisko, Elisabeth Vreede and herself—as somewhat inept.[112]

Following a relatively peaceful period in the early summer (though naturally without executive council group meetings), the situation at the Goetheanum and in the executive group grew worse when Elisabeth Vreede and Ita Wegman disputed whether Roman Boos,[113] a highly problematic figure, should be in charge of planning the Michaelmas conference. They also decisively (but in vain[114]) rejected a thematic restriction of the conference to nothing but Swiss-related issues (*"Then I would also like to say that a Michaelmas conference ought really to have nothing to do with national issues. At Michaelmas something should be given that awakens interest in the whole globe"*[115]).

Likewise, Ita Wegman's well-attended Class Lesson during the October medical conference, and the wish arising from it to continue such work in the Goetheanum's terrace room, again accentuated the difficulties and conflicts that had existed for years ("*We are once again in the midst of a battle*"[116]). In October, Wegman had herself been surprised by the initiative of physicians Richard Schubert and Friedrich Husemann to found an "association of anthroposophic physicians in Germany" and place the management of this body in the hands of Dr. Hanns Rascher—who had exellent connections with the National Socialist leadership and worked for the SS news service.[117]

Although she was still the leader of the Medical Section, Ita Wegman did not hear of these plans until she read the circular sent out by Husemann and Schubert[118] and saw her fears confirmed not least by the fact that the leading Goetheanum faction (and the German physicians connected with it) did not take any clear, uncompromising stance against National Socialism, instead continuing to misperceive and cosy up to it.[119] Eventually, however, the situation in Dornach escalated during Ita Wegman's last trip to England due to Elisabeth Vreede's resolve to give a series of lectures of her own, on the theme of the old and new Mysteries, in the Goetheanum's terrace room at Christmas and—if necessary—parallel to the official Christmas conference. This led to fierce altercations in Dornach and among the general membership.[120]

Once again Wegman (whom Vreede had not informed of this) found herself confronted with a situation that she in no way endorsed but was compelled to share responsibility for, especially since some speakers at Vreede's event (such as Willem Zeylmans van Emmichoven and Karl König) were members of the Medical Section and close colleagues of Ita Wegman. Wegman wrote to Willem Zeylmans about this on December 13:

I had no idea that Dr. Vreede was planning to hold an event of a purely anthroposophic nature during the Christmas conference. If I had known of it, I would certainly have advised against it. I do not think she would have paid attention to me, but at least I would have had my say and pointed out to her that we invite all kinds of difficulty the moment that we do anything during the Christmas conference that does not directly relate to Section work; and in consequence cover over the divergences of view up in Dornach [between Marie Steiner, Guenther Wachsmuth, Albert Steffen and others in relation to Roman Boos] which have now started to become very apparent. This will again draw us into disputes that we basically really do not want. But now it's been done, and all of them up there have joined forces again to combat Dr. Vreede.

Of you the following is being said—and I'd like to know how much of it is true. Kaufmann told me in London that you knew exactly what was being done. And now I hear from Dr. Eckstein—though he told this to others and not to me—that you felt maneuvered into an uncomfortable position without being able to do anything about it. What is actually true? Did you know nothing about it? Or did you really want things to develop as they have? We must try now to get some clear insights since Dr. Vreede went ahead without discussing anything with us, more or less organizing the conference with colleagues who belong to the Medical Section; and I have to take a stance on this. It is embarrassing for me, after all, that I knew nothing about these things until Kaufmann received a letter from Dr. Vreede when everything had already been decided.[121]

She also wrote to Zeylmans as follows about the situation at the Goetheanum:

The battle drums are raging here and all kinds of demons are rearing their heads. It was a very good thing that we gradually succeeded in detaching ourselves somewhat from things and, through positive work that started outside the Goetheanum, had reached the point of slowly but very surely reintegrating ourselves into the Goetheanum, in a way that was justified through our Section work;[122] and gradually getting so many people interested again that they have come to appreciate and trust us. I have always seen this as the right approach. Through disputes and conflicts we bind ourselves to Ahriman, you see, and not to Christ. I regard the goings-on up there in the Goetheanum as a kind of maya, with old forces playing in. The less notice one takes of it, not even joining battle at all, but inwardly depriving it of oxygen, and the more we can shine out through the work we do, the better it will be. I have always thought this was the right stance as regards the histrionics up there. We nourish demons if we join in; and then they spread out and darken everyone's power of judgment.[123]

Five days later, in another letter to England, she wrote:

For the past week I have been at home again, though it seems to me as if I've been sitting here for months again already. There is so much going on here, things bubbling and fizzing, and we have no idea what will come of it. A lot of good things are happening too, things trying to come to the surface. One could even wish that a very great many good powers could come into play here now to help a breakthrough occur and repulse everything that breeds the demonic. Everything occurring at the periphery, which can also be regarded as demonic, is however child's play compared to what is going on here now.

It is really quite apparent that the Anthroposophical Society, in the form Rudolf Steiner gave it, cannot survive these trials and, with composure, we wait changes that may occur as a result. Every action one takes in this respect either to preserve or improve the Society, comes to naught. In fact, the good it contains is almost distorted into something bad as a result. In my view the best thing really is just to let the whole thing suffocate itself.[124]

≈

On the other hand, in these days before Christmas in 1933, Ita Wegman sensed many good trends surfacing in connection with her clinic in Arlesheim, and also at the Sonnenhof and associated training projects. After her return she witnessed the continuing activity that had first originated with her, and felt it to be strongly future-oriented (*"Courses are running here in Arlesheim. There are many young students here, a great many patients, and we want to try to experience the Christmas festival in as warm and inward a way as we can, despite all the conflicts occurring around us"*[125]). Writing to Mien Viehoff in London, she described the "very vigorous life" she found at Arlesheim:

> Despite the many problems in the Society—so extreme that it seems possible for everything to fragment completely— one has the sense nevertheless that the good realm of spirit is very strong. Let us keep faith with that and organize the Christmas festival here as it has always been—and maybe with even greater strength than before.[126]

As in all previous years, Ita Wegman invited to Arlesheim for this Christmas festival of 1933 many friends and colleagues from diverse institutions. The year was one of historical importance for the world, and on December 18 she wrote:[127] "It is certain that the Christ is now easier to reach than ever before." Gathering people together from the hard-pressed curative homes in Germany, she worked with them to develop the sustaining foundations of their anthroposophic efforts and to formulate perspectives for ongoing work in 1934 (*"We must after all be clear once more what needs to be done"*[128]). Politically experienced people with insight into international affairs, such as the prominent French journalist of *Matin* newspaper Jules Sauerwein, participated in the gatherings and discussions that took place at the clinic in the last days of 1933. Ita Wegman, though, in no way shut herself off from events at the Goetheanum but continued to take note of them with alert attention and without any illusions:

> Never before have things been so uncertain throughout the world, both from an inner and outer perspective.
>
> Our [Anthroposophical] Society is really broken, and we ought not to have any illusions about this. The only thing that now matters is honest appraisal of where the blame may lie. But that itself is the incredible thing: that this issue of blame is continually turned upside down and distorted. In the end something always happens so that the true picture is muddied and confused.[129]

The social situations that arose as a result were extremely complex and clearly no longer possible to resolve. Even Wegman, who was still trying to build bridges,[130] could not see any real way forward for the General Anthroposophical Society—no path of common anthroposophic endeavor to counter the anti-Christian powers whose workings had come to such dire expression during 1933. In a Christmas letter of elucidation to Joseph van Leer in Vienna she wrote:

> What we are doing here [in Arlesheim] is always concerned with forging an ever-stronger connection with Rudolf Steiner. Despite all the difficulties in the Society, we strive for this connection, and only by this means is it possible to survive and work.[131]

On December 23 Ita Wegman sent Violetta Plincke in London a photograph of Rudolf Steiner's sculpture of the Christ figure which Edith Maryon had taken many years earlier,[132] and had given as a present to her physician Ita Wegman:

> Among old pictures I still have one of the Christ statue given me by Miss Maryon. It was a small photograph that I once had enlarged; I have a few of them left. Since you can't buy them I have only occasionally given one to this friend or that, with a request that they accept it as something really very personal. As you can see it is the model, but it does convey a fine impression of the statue itself. I wish you a lovely Christmas festival and a good New Year.[133]

The Figure of Christ and the Adversarial Powers,, Dornach, 1916

2

"A Year of Reflection and Inner Work": Illness and Palestine

1934

"At a time of grave destiny within the Society, I was chained to my sickbed, and for a long time it was unclear whether my work would continue in the world of spirit or on the earth. However, one day I had a vivid experience that I still had things to do on earth, and from this moment on I felt better." (July 14, 1934)[134]

"I was not expected yet in the world of spirit—I learned this in an encounter I had with Rudolf Steiner, where the Christ being was present also—but there was still a need for me to do something on earth. From this moment on, I also found the strength again to take my own recovery strongly in hand." (February 22, 1935)[135]

The 1933 to '34 period of Christmas and the Holy Nights at Arlesheim was intense and light-filled. The numerous patients, many of whom had little connection with Anthroposophy, as well as the many invited guests, made for a rich, busy life with Wegman at its center. As every year, she was the spiritual and social focus of events, leading the gatherings each evening before the Christmas tree decorated with roses and candles: unobtrusive and completely unpretentious, but also conspicuously present through her inner certainty and vibrancy. In her first letters of the New Year, Wegman stressed the warm, inward character of the encounters and conversations she'd had during this time— along with a sense of shared anxiety about the coming year. It seemed to her that, after the extensive and expansive activity of the past twelve months, the coming period would be one of much more inwardness and spiritualization (*"We have been living under some pressure since we do not yet know what these times will bring. We have a strong sense that 1934 will be a year of reflection and inner work"*[136]). In addition, in a letter to England, picking up on comments Joseph van Leer had made before Christmas, she wrote: "We...had a lovely, warm Christmas in spite of many difficulties around us at present; and we feel very positive about continuing our work in true accord with Dr. Steiner."[137]

A little later than expected, Ita Wegman then set off for Holland after Epiphany for a previously agreed anthroposophic gathering, visited her mother and sister, and returned via Schloss Hamborn where she held further conversations about maintaining and safeguarding the curative institutes in Nazi Germany (*"It will*

not be easy to battle through to the end of this year. But as long as
we do not despair we may after all find the strength to prevail"[138]).
She also held conferences on the wellbeing of children and medical consultations. On January 12, she was back in Arlesheim, once again burdened by the circumstances in Germany she had experienced, and by the attitude of compromise she perceived in anthroposophic representatives, vis-à-vis the ruling powers:[139]

> Thus the anthroposophists are assigned to the class of unthreatening people, thereby assuring their survival.[140] It certainly isn't a courageous act that has been accomplished there. You get the sense that things are going the same way as happened when Christianity became an ecclesiastical organization, giving a very great many people access to it, but at the same time blurring and losing sight of the most essential aspect, knowledge of Christ, which became the preserve of only a small group of people. In the same way all that one can, really, call Rudolf Steiner's intimate teachings, is being blurred.[141]

At the end of January Wegman first indicated in a letter that at least some of her own correspondence to Germany was being opened and checked (*"Many of my letters are now being opened"*[142]), and she therefore greatly limited her written exchanges with anthroposophic institutes and colleagues.[143]

At the beginning of 1934, however, Ita Wegman was again extremely active and carrying much responsibility (in a New Year's letter she even spoke of the "huge amount of work I'm responsible for"). With great resolve she carried her social and spiritual tasks in Arlesheim (*"It is as if the workload continually increases and the clinic is almost at bursting point with the number of patients and others who come and go there"*) and other associated institutions and groups of people, though there were also moments when she felt weak and overstretched. During the first few weeks of

the year, Ita Wegman was again treating and counseling countless people experiencing health and biographical crises. She sent
overtaxed colleagues on holiday, elaborated means of dialog and
collaboration between those in positions of responsibility in the
various institutes, and created opportunities for recuperation and
convalescence for colleagues and friends who had worn themselves out through years of self-sacrificing work. As one instance,
in mid-January she wrote to Bernard Lievegoed in Holland, the
chief physician at an anthroposophic curative home, about the
need to continue faithfully supporting a nurse on protracted sick
leave, and remain responsible for her, also financially:

> We must do something for those who have worked for us;
> otherwise we will find ourselves in the greatest difficulties.
> This is something I learned from many years' experience: you
> can't just leave people who have fallen sick to manage on their
> own, even if they themselves bear responsibility for their con-
> dition. Human obligations are after all very great when one
> works with people. We have members of staff who have been
> ill for years, whom we must go on supporting because you
> can't just put them on the street. Something good in fact has
> always come of this if it is handled properly. Moreover, we
> have always been able to find the money to do this, as have
> the various institutes.[144]

Working very actively as a consultant in her clinic and out-
patients department, Ita Wegman continued the weekly lecture
series that she had initiated in the Medical Section at the end of
the previous year, on "Anthroposophic study of the human being
as foundation of healthcare appropriate in our time," inviting
other speakers to give talks on dietary issues and artistic therapies,
illnesses of the modern age and aspects of spiritual history and
social medicine. For instance, Eugen Kolisko gave a lecture titled
"The Riddle of Kaspar Hauser."

The Clinical-Therapeutic Institute in Arlesheim

Once again there were problems about room allocation at the Goetheanum, along with serious tensions, which for the first time made Wegman consider holding the talks at the Bernouillum in Basel (*"Naturally, it would be a different audience—fewer anthroposophists, but a great deal of interest, primarily for medical matters. In Basel recently there has been much interest in our medical work, and a very large number of out-patients come from there"*[145]). At the same time Wegman was still organizing big and extremely well-attended lecture series in the German capital, Berlin, and training courses in Arlesheim on anthroposophic nursing and curative education (*"My aim here is to develop a practical approach to the children, at the same time intensively reading and studying everything that Dr. Steiner gave us in this regard"*[146]).

Wegman managed all her extensive correspondence in person. She planned the next course for the group of medical students in March, further training courses in eurythmy therapy and painting

COURSES

AT THE

CLINICAL AND THERAPEUTIC INSTITUTE, ARLESHEIM.

NEAR BASLE
SWITZERLAND

IN

NURSING
CURATIVE EURHYTHMY

AND

CURATIVE-
EDUCATIONAL WORK.

BEGINNING IN MAY
EACH YEAR.

*Prospectus for courses in nursing, eurythmy therapy,
and curative education in Arlesheim, page 1*

therapy, medical lectures in London and, in more modest scope, a possible extension of the therapy center there. She even concerned herself with problems relating to the qualifying medical exams of physician Karl Nunhoefer who worked at Kent Terrace; and, through Hilma Walter, who still worked at Clent, she organized leaves of absence for him. Despite the reversals she had suffered in England, and her overview of the situation expressed in her letter of December 18, 1933, she still retained an open and undecided stance toward possibilities there. At the beginning of 1934 she considered another trip to England in the near future, even if with some reticence and amidst numerous tasks she was overseeing in Arlesheim:

> Here in Arlesheim there's a huge amount going on: the clinic is full with a very great number of patients, a great many physicians, many students; the courses are flourishing, and it is really very difficult for me to leave here for any length of time. But I can also see that this will not help the work in England to progress, since no one [there] is really interested in the Medical Section and can sustain the work in my absence in a useful way.[147]

Above and beyond this, at the beginning of 1934 there were also many requests for Wegman to give lectures, and enquiries about her visiting other institutions and anthroposophic initiatives in distant regions, such as Silesia (*"I would like to come to Pilgramshain again soon since I always so much enjoyed my visits there. But the strange thing is that my karma seems to be trying to bind me to the West, and matters there have to be concluded and completed. This means there isn't much time left over—if I am not to completely neglect Arlesheim—to visit other institutes that are not as it were en-route. Please understand that there is absolutely no lack of love and interest playing in here, but just a severe shortage of time"*[148]). Ita Wegman was also preoccupied by severe financial shortfalls at Schloss Hamborn and other places associated with it: shortages and existential crises to which, with the help of her administrator Erich Kirchner, she gave continual and seemingly endlessly optimistic attention:

> Of course things are difficult for us everywhere; but as long as I have lived and worked in the A[nthroposophical] S[ociety], this is how it has always been. Already in the Doctor's time it was always a battle to survive. We were always worried about how to carry on and where the funds would come from; and then people also always fought with each other. This latter aspect has come to the fore now, but it was always present.[149]

In the early weeks of 1934, Wegman was advising crisis-shaken Waldorf initiatives (such as the school of Dr. Blass in Essen), but in particular she was in contact with the wide circle of anthroposophic physicians, who asked for recommendations when practices were established and sought capable and willing colleagues for new positions, successor posts, or community projects (*"But it is very strange that among the young physicians who are now qualifying no one has the courage to start their own practice. They prefer to go to the schools or to an institute or work as medical assistant somewhere or other. At all events, we'll go on asking around"*[150]). People also came to her for all sorts of medical advice relating to illnesses and case histories that were often very grave or intractable.

≈

On February 2, at last, after all these initiating activities, Ita Wegman drove to Holland to give two Class Lessons and to hold crisis talks with Willem Zeylmans about the situation of the General Anthroposophical Society. Three days later she traveled from there to London on the night train, announcing her arrival and her need for accommodation in a forthright way to Mien Viehoff at short notice (*"I think it would be best if you get the mauve room ready for me. I hope the door is ready, but otherwise I can do without a door. Do leave Frau Leroi in the room above. I won't be staying long this time, but just briefly to discuss a few things with you all and to sort out a few things"*[151]).

Contrary to her original plan, though, Wegman stayed in London for over three weeks, also participating in the annual general meeting of the Anthroposophical Society in England, and not returning to Arlesheim until the end of February. Arriving there, she received news from Walter Johannes Stein that Karl Schubert was being forced to leave the Stuttgart Waldorf School due to his half-Jewish descent, and Stein's request that she try to help him (*"Schubert has been dismissed from the Waldorf School and will have to leave at Easter. Please see what you can do to prevent this invaluable man from going under. Holland won't take him—which would have been the obvious choice. Nor England, since they do not want too many foreigners in the school there. Maybe you could use him as a traveling curative advisor? He could be useful in many respects"*[152]). At this she immediately wrote to this highly gifted teacher of the remedial class in Stuttgart—whom she greatly esteemed and who was profoundly connected with Rudolf Steiner:

> I hear that there are some problems and that you may have to seek other employment.
>
> I just wanted to write to you briefly to say that I hope you realize we are ready and willing to do anything possible to stand by you and that your invaluable help will be appreciated everywhere. Therefore, I warmly ask you to let me know if there is anything in particular I can do so that I can make a proposal of some kind.[153]

Arlesheim, den 2. März 1934.

Lieber Dr. Schubert!

    Ich höre, dass einige Schwierigkeiten vorliegen
und dass Sie eventuell andere Möglichkeiten der Betätigung
suchen. Ich wollte Ihnen nur kurz schreiben, dass ich hoffe,
Sie sind davon überzeugt, dass wir in jeder Beziehung bereit
sind, Ihnen zur Seite zu stehen, und möchte Ihnen sagen, dass
Ihre wertvolle Hilfe überall geschätzt sein wird. Ich bitte
Sie also herzlich, wenn etwas Bestimmtes vorliegt, mir Mittei-
lung zu machen, damit ich Ihnen dann einen Vorschlag machen
kann.

    Wir sind alle hier kollosal tätig. Es gibt viel
Arbeit, aber es herrscht auch eine erdrückende Atmosphäre,
was die kommende Generalversammlung betrifft.

                        Mit herzlichem Gruss

                           Ihr
                       I. Wegman
                          I armed.

Letter from Ita Wegman to Karl Schubert, March 2, 1934

In the same letter to Karl Schubert, Ita Wegman outlined her own situation at the start of March in the following succinct words: "We are all incredibly busy here. There is a great deal of work to be done, but a stultifying atmosphere also reigns as regards the forthcoming annual general meeting."

On February 25, shortly before she returned from England, the annual general meeting due on March 27 and 28 had been announced in the Goetheanum newsletter, along with a brief summary of its agenda. While no clear mention of this was made—but only a hint given under Point 3 ("Motions Relating to a Petition")—it was known that seven staff at the Goetheanum had submitted a motion seeking changes to the statutes according to which membership of the General Anthroposophical Society in the future would be allowed *only* after the signing of the membership card by the executive council chair Albert Steffen, and that delegation of executive authority of any kind within the executive council would likewise require the chair's approval. After the events and conflicts of previous years, this procedure, if realized, would further weaken the position of Ita Wegman and Elisabeth Vreede, as well as the endeavors centered on Willem Zeylmans van Emmichoven, Eugen Kolisko, and George Adams Kaufmann or Daniel Nicol Dunlop in the independent national societies in Holland, Germany and England. Long discussions had been held on related issues during Wegman's visits to Holland and England. Ita Wegman herself composed a "counter-motion" immediately on her return to Arlesheim on February 27, in which she emphasized her view of the—esoterically or karmically based—importance of every single executive council member and the groups of people more closely associated with each one. Against this background she strongly sought preservation of the principle of plurality and freedom within the executive council of the General Anthroposophical Society. Her draft was worded as follows:

Gegenantrag

Die handelsgerichtlich eingetragenen Statuten können nicht derart verändert werden dass sie die Statuten der anthroposophische Gesellschaft, welche von Rudolf Steiner 1924 in der Weihnachtstagung neu gegründet wurde, widersprechen.

Der Gang der Ereignisse hat aber wohl gezeigt dass einige Veränderungen notwendig sind, ~~Die die~~ ... ...

Im Antrag der Herren ... ... wird dem Vorsitzenden ~~sollte~~ Machtbefugnisse zugeräumt, dass der ~~Vorsitzende~~ eigentlich die Macht eines dictators bekomt, ... was in einer spirituellen Bewegung nicht angebracht ist.

Ist der Vorsitzender von Güte und Weisheit durchdrungen, dann wird er ohne Paragraphen Machtbefugnisse haben die ~~er~~ dan vonselbst entstehen gemäss einer spirituellen Bewegung ...

~~Der~~ Vorstande ... ... der von R. Steiner ~~eingesetzt~~ wird, gewählt ~~soll~~ ~~waren~~, sollen gleichmässig die Möglichkeit haben im ... zu wirken mit denjenigen Mitgliedern, die sich ...

Ita Wegman: draft of a counter-motion, page 1

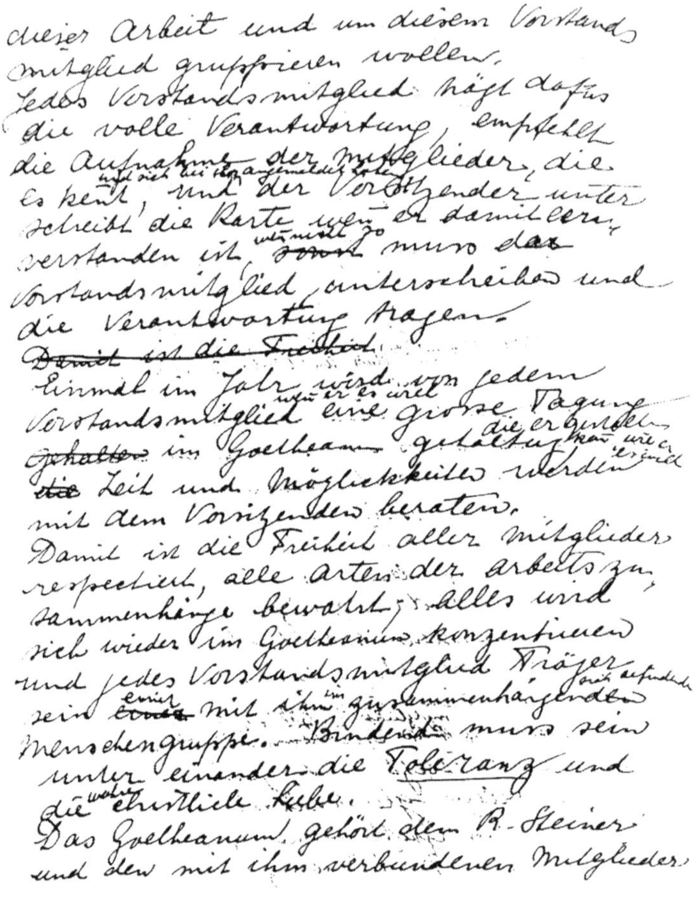
dieser Arbeit und um diesem Vorstands
mitglied gruppieren wollen.
Jedes Vorstandsmitglied trägt dafür
die volle Verantwortung, empfehlt
die Aufnahme der Mitglieder, die
es kent, und der Vorsitzender unter
schreibt die Karte wen er damit ein-
verstanden ist, ~~sonst~~ muss das
Vorstandsmitglied unterscheiden und
die Verantwortung tragen.
~~Damit ist die Freiheit~~
Einmal im Jahr wird von jedem
Vorstandsmitglied eine grosse Tagung
~~gehalten~~ im Goetheanum gehalten
~~die~~ Zeit und Möglichkeiten werden
mit dem Vorsitzenden beraten.
Damit ist die Freiheit aller Mitglieder
respectiert, alle arten der arbeits zu-
sammenhänge bewahrt, alles wird
sich wieder im Goetheanum konzentrieren
und jedes Vorstandsmitglied Träger
sein ~~eines~~ einer mit ihm im zusammenhängenden
Menschengruppe. Bindend muss sein
unter einander die Toleranz und
die wahre christliche Liebe.
Das Goetheanum gehört dem R. Steiner
und den mit ihm verbundenen Mitglieder.

Ita Wegman: draft of a counter-motion, page 2

Niemand hat das Recht und eine bestimmte Gruppe
Goetheanum für sich zu beanspruchen von Menschen.
Das Goetheanum gehört
dem ganzen ~~Mitgliedschaft~~ R. Steiners
Anthroposophie und dem ganzen
Vorstand.

Verweigerung der Mitgliedschaft darf
nur ~~auf Grund~~ aus dem Entschluss
des ganzen Vorstandes entstehen.

Vorstandsmitglieder, die Sektionen
führen haben Handlungsvollmacht und
führe für ihren Arbeitsbezirk Einzel
Unterschrift. Der Vorsitzende kann
verschiedene Arbeitsbereiche ~~neu einrichten~~
die oriell mit den Sektionen kollidieren
neu einrichten.

Ita Wegman: draft of a counter-motion, page 3

The lawfully registered statutes cannot be altered in such a way as to contradict the spirit of the statutes of the Anthroposophical Society that Rudolf Steiner reestablished in 1924 at the Christmas Foundation Meeting. Events have however shown that a few changes are needed. (These changes must not infringe the principle of freedom that holds sway in the anthrop. movement.) In the gentlemen's motion...the chairman is accorded powers and authority such that he really acquires the power of a dictator, which is not appropriate in a spiritual movement.

If the chairman is imbued with benevolence and wisdom then he will, without the need for statutes, have the authority to act that arises self-evidently in accordance with a spiritual movement. All executive council members of the Gen[eral] Anth[roposophical] Society that were appointed and chosen by R. Steiner, and enjoyed his trust, ought to have an equal opportunity to work within the Goetheanum with the members who wish to connect with this work and group themselves around this executive council member. Every executive council member bears full responsibility for this, recommends acceptance of new members that are known to him and who have made their application through him, and the chairman signs the membership card if he agrees to; but if not, then the executive council member must sign instead and bear responsibility for this.

Once a year each executive council member, if he wishes, holds a large conference at the Goetheanum and can organize this as he sees fit. Dates and scope are discussed with the chair. This respects the freedom of all members and guarantees all types of working affiliation. Everything is reflected and focused in the Goetheanum, and every executive council member will bear responsibility for sustaining a group of people that feels connected with him. Among us tolerance must be the presiding obligation, and true Christian love. The Goetheanum belongs to R. Steiner and the members connected with him. No one has the right to take advantage

of the Goetheanum for himself and a particular group.
The Goetheanum belongs to all who follow R. Steiner's
Anthroposophy and the whole executive council.
Refusal of membership can only follow from a decision
by the whole executive council.
Executive council members who are Section leaders have
the authority to act for their field of work, as sole signatory.
The chair can establish new fields of work that are not cov-
ered by the Sections.

Immediately after her arrival in Arlesheim, Wegman had
heard that Elisabeth Vreede was staying in Stuttgart with Eugen
Kolisko,[154] and now, in a letter of March 1, she requested a discussion with her. Kolisko replied that a detailed counter-motion had
already been composed or was in the process of being so (*"In the
last few days various discussions have taken place with friends,
and I will therefore be in a position to make you some very con-
crete proposals in relation to these pending Society questions"*[155]).
Four days later he came to Arlesheim where he read out to Ita
Wegman and the college of physicians the "Declaration of intent,"
a document that went on the offensive in regard to recent developments, and explained its political implications and aims within
the Society.

By now Wegman was feeling physically weak, had sent her
apologies for not attending an executive council meeting the day
before, was feverish and had difficulty in following what Kolisko
was saying. Nevertheless—after long hesitation and overcoming
inner reluctance[156]—she finally supported the text[157] composed by
Eugen Kolisko with the help of Elisabeth Vreede, which was later
signed by the Executive Council of the Anthroposophical Society
in Great Britain, working groups in Germany, and the executive
council and a majority of members in the Dutch Society (*"since
it really is important to assert ourselves now"*[158]). She therefore

withdrew her own effort, which focused more on a spiritually mediating approach, and on the evening of the same day wrote a letter to George Adams Kaufmann in London to express her agreement but at the same time also justifying her own striving in recent years:

> Events over recent years have shown, in fact, that a mediating approach is no longer appropriate, and all our physicians, and many who work in the Section, are fully of this view also....
>
> My way of proceeding—and I want to make this plain now—was always concerned to strengthen and consolidate work in the Sections. Through the doors of the Sections I hoped that a proper place would be found at the Goetheanum again, and that work that speaks for itself would slowly but surely make headway and then, eventually, would be recognized and accepted by the whole Society. I have always thought it necessary for the national Societies to stand upon the ground mapped out by Dr. Steiner, and that they ought never to accept something that did not proceed from the whole executive council, but were fully entitled to reject anything that was not right. And when I took a more conciliatory stance three years ago, I did so with this way of proceeding in mind. Within my Section I was still able to accomplish a fair amount, and thus collaborate with good people....
>
> Difficult times are coming, because it seems to me that the whole Society may almost be dissolved.[159]

In bed and "somewhat ill due to all these things that weigh heavily on my soul,"[160] in the following days Ita Wegman repeatedly pondered on the now established constellation of powers at the Goetheanum and in the General Anthroposophical Society which she had come to see as unalterable ("*Many people otherwise of sound judgment are still being misled by this saccharine sentimentality. And so we're facing indescribable situations. I don't*

believe anything can be salvaged except by putting an end to it "[161]).
At times, as Wegman wrote to tell Dorothy Osmond in London
on March 9, "I almost sense a desire rising in me no longer to
have anything to do with this false Society. No longer is there any
good will to be found in it, but instead an intentional distortion
of reality." Appalled by the agitation and perfidious slander that
had come to the fore since 1925, but not willing, either, to really
defend or justify herself, or join battle, Ita Wegman loyally shared
responsibility for the initiative of friends in Holland, England and
Germany but in certain respects she remained alone with her specific aims, task and intrinsic approach to things. Kolisko's intense
and tiring visit on March 8 did not end happily either.[162]

≈

The cause of Ita Wegman's feverish conditions was not clear. They
increased over the next few weeks and at the beginning of the second week in March prevented her from taking part in the ongoing course for medical students and newly qualified physicians,
who had arrived in Arlesheim shortly before. On the morning of
March 9, Ita Wegman was with them again to read lectures by
Rudolf Steiner. But she was too unwell to participate in the evening, despite her continual preoccupation with the students' inner
state of mind and outer circumstances, and her concern with the
complex processes of community building at an extremely trou-
bled period. Many students looked to Wegman for clarity and
guidance; to meet this need she wrote a long letter to them on the
afternoon of March 9 from her room in the timber house adjoining the Arlesheim clinic:

> My dear friends,
>   I very much regret that I shall not be able to be with
> you this evening. I had hoped very much to be there, for it

is so necessary for us to discuss certain things in detail. I have heard that, among yourselves, you haven't succeeded in collaborating with each other in the way you had hoped; and then it is tempting to lay the blame for this on the fact that our work has not been shaped in a way that nurtured a sense of community. You have in fact tried for the first time to introduce more differentiation into the common purpose; and that is healthy—as long as you do not forget, at the same time, to reincorporate this into a whole. This differentiation, which one can see as an out-breathing, and then coming together again as an inbreath, is precisely what can make a community stronger. Now, however, the question immediately arises: What really binds a community together? A community is, of course, always held together by a certain impulse of will. Moreover, in a community that seeks to dedicate itself to healing, the will to heal must naturally take the lead, but one that also includes and encompasses Rudolf Steiner. This will to heal must be conceived comprehensively so that at the same time you advance with it toward the real nature of the human being. To become a true human being, led by Rudolf Steiner, is after all what binds us together in our community. To reach this authentic humanity sometimes involves the most difficult trials, and certainly one does not accomplish it without suffering deep inner pain. One can be sure that a community that sets itself such a lofty goal will pass through tempests. It is not easy to stay upright through them, for nothing in the present world will endure. The world situation is uncertain and people's place in it equally so. The future is uncertain; there is nothing that can easily sustain us. We are really thrown back on ourselves entirely.

But just consider how rich we are since, in being thrown back on ourselves, we can make our own the whole knowledge of Rudolf Steiner—which is universal knowledge embodied in his works. We have to connect unwaveringly with Rudolf Steiner. And then the community of physicians will grow in the right way—a community you established 3 or 4 years ago by your own initiative in order to develop fruitful work with the Medical Section—or let us say within the institution founded by Dr. Steiner as the Clinical-Therapeutic Institute, which he appointed me to direct—and can achieve the great goals I have spoken of. Once it has grown in this way and achieved these goals, it will support and sustain the Medical Section that should have its rightful place at the Goetheanum. It seems important to me to nurture and care for this community since, as I said once in England, it could give rise to a true fraternity of Michael composed of true human beings who feel their home to be not just a single country but also the whole globe.

That is why I'd like to remind you of the many fine moments we have so often experienced together, which have given us a notion that our lofty goals might be realized.

The burning question at present is how our work will shape itself in the future. The only answer I can give is this: Take your lead from the physicians who have now qualified and are working at the Clinical-Therapeutic Institute. I don't mean that you should all work here; but that wherever you are you should realize the principles perpetuated in this clinic that Rudolf Steiner founded. No doubt, it is also part of our vital task to find young people who wish to develop their work in this way. It is clear that this will not be easy in the current circumstances in Germany. However, the work must be passed on from one person to another nevertheless. In a spiritual movement that sets itself high goals, the number of people involved is not the critical thing but instead the quality they bring to it.

That every community can engender strong powers is something you must see in a very real way. Rudolf Steiner said of the clinic, for instance, that if we can hold together and find the right relationship between physicians, nurses and all the staff, the work of our institute could be full of blessing. He said this to me in the grounds of the clinic itself, standing on the South Terrace during one of his visits here.

Subsequently, he often repeated similar words, in all kinds of variations. However, on one occasion, when someone asked whether the physicians might grow into a community such as that of the movement for religious renewal, he replied that this would not be possible in the same way because physicians are too attached to pursuing their own paths. He did however say it might be possible among the young physicians—and it was with this in mind that he gave the first course for young doctors.

May this community—this is my deep wish—not lose its strength because young students are now becoming physicians who can easily have many outside interests that make community life more difficult. I'd like to express my hope that, having perhaps overcome a few crises, the strength of this community increases in efforts to help and support one another.

I hope to come to the lecture reading tomorrow, and then we may be able to discuss together any questions that arise this evening.

Yours most sincerely,
Ita Wegman, MD

≈

Despite her wish, Ita Wegman was confined to her room for the next few days and often in bed. In letters she dictated to her secretary Else Koch, and in conversations with Madeleine van Deventer and a few other clinic physicians who visited her and tried to treat her, she kept herself informed of nearly everything happening in the Section and the clinic, also for instance taking note that the physician Jean Schoch had broken his leg and therefore could not give his intended lecture. Writing to him kindly, she referred to her own situation (*"Unfortunately, I am ill, too. I'm in bed with fever, whose cause is unknown"*) and went on in a somewhat laconic and knowing way:

I can well imagine that you are very thankful to fate for this—as you say—involuntary period of reflection. At such a time, after all, one can give tranquil attention to everything there is usually no peace or time to consider.[163]

Likewise she wrote on March 13 to Bernard Lievegoed, with pronounced clarity about her future path within the anthroposophic movement:

I am not planning anything other than to continue working as I have done thus far. Tasks were assigned by Dr. Steiner, and individuals each do what they can in their own way. It would make a mockery of Dr. Steiner to try to do things differently. If this is to be, it will happen by itself, determined by destiny.

In other letters during this period she encouraged a young student and former Waldorf pupil to embark on an educational initiative in Sweden (*"And if you say that every fiber of your being is connected with Germany, you might best help the Germans by taking German pedagogy abroad. There is no point thinking, if Germany makes problems for Rudolf Steiner's pedagogy, that it is the only country where it can take root. We must certainly try to realize this form of education in all countries. Naturally my own prime interest here is in making curative education better known"*[164]). Likewise she supported a physician colleague whose child's life was endangered by meningitis (or meningoencephalitis):

Arlesheim, March 17, 1934

Dear Dr. Liebert,

I was very shocked to hear about your little daughter. It is certainly grave and we must do all we can to save the child. I have already sent you a telegram and suggested giving her lemon compresses, Cochlearia applied to the calves, copper ointment on the soles of the feet, antimony on the forehead and neck, mild eucalyptus inhalations and Arnica 5x: 3 drops 5 times daily.

It might be a good idea to alternate the eucalyptus with equisetum inhalations, to give the child silica. You must do all you can to shift the illness back down into the metabolic tract. The condition involves an upward-inflamed metabolism that invokes a sympathetic reaction in the meninges. It might also be a good idea to administer an intensive silica enema.

I'm wondering what's actually happened here. Did she not get over the flu properly? Perhaps you'd like to tell me more again soon, on the phone possibly. Unfortunately I am not completely well myself, and am in bed, but one of the doctors here can pass me a message.

I hope for the very best outcome, dear Dr. Liebert, and my thoughts are very much with you.

Yours sincerely,

Dr. I. Wegman

It might also be good to massage the body with a silica ointment (crystal cream); perhaps the legs, too, one time, as well as the back one time. We will send you some more crystal cream.

～

As the annual general meeting approached, Ita Wegman was still ill with fever that grew worse in the evenings, experiencing great weakness and ongoing heart complaints, but no other symptoms. The possibility of her participating in the pending, problematic gathering increasingly receded. Nevertheless Wegman pondered every day on the issues connected with it, and repeatedly addressed various related aspects in her personal correspondence ("*Now I would like to mention a few things that have come to mind as I rested*"[165]). She continued to affirm the plans involved in the "Declaration of Intent" without however believing any longer at all that the General Anthroposophical Society could be saved, with the spiritual-social legacy of the Christmas Foundation Meeting (*"It is very good indeed that we are battling again on behalf of what Rudolf Steiner wished to give as stimulus and impulse through the Christmas Foundation Meeting. I do not believe that this can be achieved any longer as he wished it"*).

On March 22, she wrote to Dorothy Osmond:

> That's the situation, and I don't think that we should give very serious credence to what is currently issuing from the Goetheanum. Instead we should consider how to realize powerfully everywhere the spiritual wealth we receive from the doctor. Despite this, it is good that we're making one further effort to remedy things. If this fails, we should not make a fuss about it but just find renewed courage to let Rudolf Steiner come to vibrant life again somewhere else. Here it is already being said that young people no longer see anything new and innovative in the Goetheanum, but rather just the old ways—and this is very fitting given current developments.

At the same time, Ita Wegman was increasingly concerned with composing a personal statement for the general meeting that would, on the one hand, emphatically defend the "Declaration of Intent," and on the other also hint, in some ways at least, at her own distinctive views of her work.[166] Finally—two days after the letter to Dorothy Osmond quoted above, and at the same time as Hilma Walters and Mien Viehoff arrived to treat and nurse her— she sent this letter to Albert Steffen:

Arlesheim, March 24, 1934

Dear Herr Steffen,

Once again an annual general meeting is approaching, and once again the emotions of members are being whipped up to a frenzy. Yet again, decent people whom Dr. Steiner valued and loved are being attacked by means of these turbulent emotions: their standing is undermined and they are being systematically destroyed. Moreover, as chair of the Anthroposophical Society, you are allowing this to happen. You consider it good for people to correct each other; but you pay no attention to what is being left in ruins as a result.

Now a group of seven people is submitting a motion. In this way, Herr Steffen, they want to grant you further rights that go far above and beyond those of the chair. I see nothing good in this. This is distancing us further from Dr. Steiner's principles, and will promote a tendency to make the Goetheanum the enclave of one particular group of people, while others are excluded. For many years this has already been more or less the case and, as a member of the executive council, I cannot agree that this state of affairs, consistently enacted by three executive council members, should now be enshrined in the statutes.

I support the Declaration of Intent submitted by the working group members of the Dutch and English Societies because they are right to defend themselves against a one-sided governance of the Goetheanum. As far as my work at the Goetheanum is concerned, which relates specifically to medicine, I hereby inform the executive council and the membership that I refuse to approve changes that could be undertaken in the Sections. I will dedicate myself to the task that Rudolf Steiner allocated to the Sections, along with all those who wish to work with me and who feel the will to heal alive within them. Protected by the spirit of Rudolf Steiner we will still find opportunities to dedicate ourselves to this healing profession, far from the disputes and discords that now rage in the Society. Drawing on this will to heal we consciously raise ourselves above all disputes, and also intentionally remain at the Goetheanum, the place which Rudolf Steiner created for all, rather than for an advantaged minority. In addition, we wish to try, with those who have a sense of the importance of this way of working, to deepen, perpetuate, and disseminate the knowledge that Rudolf Steiner so richly endowed us with, and to do so in harmony and in Christian love, untroubled by the confusion within the Anthroposophical Society.

Dr. I. Wegman

P.S. I wanted to read this out myself at the general meeting, but since I have been in bed with fever for two weeks now, I have done it in this way.

≈

Three days later, the annual meeting that began in the Great Hall of the Goetheanum took a dramatic and highly emotional course. At the start of the meeting Eugen Kolisko read out (and substantiated) the "Declaration of Intent," Madeleine van Deventer read out Ita Wegman's letter to Albert Steffen and Werner Kaelin read a statement by the physicians in Arlesheim in support of Ita Wegman. Subsequently however, extensive discussion about the opportunities and risks of the proposed statute changes, and Elisabeth Vreede's stance toward executive council work and conference planning at the Goetheanum, were riven by fierce accusations about management of the Medical Section, its flawed methodologies, its "lack of scientific rigor" and its "dogmatic" and "sect-like" nature.

Speakers closely associated with Ita Wegman, such as Eugen Kolisko and Karl König, were accused of being "berserk" and "crazy" fantasists who distorted the work of Rudolf Steiner. Further accusations were (suggestively, in front of a lay audience) directed at the Sonnenhof and the Arlesheim clinic, where it was said that medical incompetency had led to the deaths of patients. Last but not least, some speakers asserted in rabble-rousing mode that Wegman, with "seductive tones of a supposedly occult or Christian nature" and her "mystical guruship" had sought to bring the Goetheanum under her dictatorial power after 1925,

Abschrift.   Arlesheim, den 25. März 1934.

                          An den

                          Vorstand der Allgemeinen Anthroposophische
                                                Gesellschaft

                          z. Hd. des 1. Vorsitzenden

                          Herrn Albert S t e f f e n ,

                                        D o r n a c h .

        Die unterzeichneten Mitarbeiter am Goetheanum nehmen die
bevorstehende Generalversammlung zur Veranlassung, Ihnen folgen-
des auszusprechen:

        Die Auseinandersetzung mit den vorgebrachten Vorschlägen
und Erklärungen hat uns zu der Einsicht geführt, dass wir auch
weiterhin innerhalb der Allgemeinen Anthroposophischen Gesellschaft an den von Rudolf Steiner gegebenen Prinzipien unbe-
dingt festhalten werden. Abstimmungen und Majoritätsbeschlüsse,
die in ihren Ergebnissen in das geistige Wirken von Persönlich-
keiten eingreifen wollen, werden wir nicht anerkennen, da sie
den Boden dieser Prinzipien verlassen.

        Wir sehen weiterhin unsere Aufgabe darinnen, Anthropo-
sophie so zu verwirklichen, wie es sich aus der inneren Haltung
des Heilerberufes ergibt. Wir erkennen aus den Erfahrungen der
täglichen Arbeit, dass die anthroposophische Medizin in der
gegenwärtigen Weltsituation immer dringender gebracht wird.
Wir fühlen die daraus sich ergebende Verpflichtung, in dieser
Arbeit kräftig fortzufahren. Wir sehen in der Zusammenarbeit
mit Frau Dr. Wegman, der Leiterin der Medizinischen Sektion
am Goetheanum, die Möglichkeit, die Medizin durch Anthroposophie so zu erweitern und zu vertiefen, dass darin die von
Dr. Steiner gegebenen Impulse wirken können.

        Damit schliessen wir uns den Aufgaben, wie Frau Dr.Wegman
sie in dem Brief an Sie, Herr Steffen, charakterisiert hat, voll
und ganz an.

                          gez. Dr. Kaelin
                               Dr. Boekholt
                               Dr. van Deventer
                               Dr. Stavenhagen
                               Dr. Suchantke
                               Dr. Knauer
                               Dr. Walter
                               Dr. Bort
                               Dr. Berthold
                               Dr. Leroi.

*Statement by physicians of the Clinical-Therapeutic Institute
at Arlesheim, March 25, 1934*

and to transform it into a "kind of military camp of Alexander the Great." Together with groups of people operating with unconscious motives and in dependency upon her, she was said—in contrast to the assertions of the "Statement of Intent"—to represent the real danger to the Anthroposophical Society and to be the "carcinoma" working to destroy it.[167]

As the last speaker at the meeting, and before it was aborted by the withdrawal of Albert Steffen, who left the hall, George Adams Kaufmann sought to establish sufficient calm and focus to emphasize the real intentions of Ita Wegman in her statement (previously the subject of cynical mockery). Among other things he said:

> In relation to what Frau Dr. Wegman wrote, which has been quoted again and stated yesterday, I have to say that you have profoundly misunderstood the anthroposophic method if you hear and reproduce words without engaging with the reality of what lives in the person who spoke them. I say this: Frau Dr. Wegman has the right, as healer, to speak of Christianity. She has the right to speak in this way of the Christ impulse. It lies in her very being to do so. And if you hear it as emanating from her being, then it is apt and justified. If you really practice anthroposophic methodology in your life, you are wrong to dismiss it so externally. And as to the attacks that were launched on the clinic yesterday...I have to say that I feel ashamed of our Society, for I myself know what lives as Christ impulse in many places, in curative institutes where Dr. Wegman comes and gives consultations late into the night.[168]

After the temporary withdrawal of Albert Steffen and Marie Steiner, and tumultuous scenes in the meeting, an overwhelming majority (774 to 94, with 23 abstaining) finally passed a motion that went even further than the original motion for alteration of the statutes, resolving that henceforth only Albert Steffen, Marie Steiner

*Ita Wegman's wooden house on the grounds at the
Clinical-Therapeutic Institute in Arlesheim*

and Guenther Wachsmuth would continue the work of the executive council "in accordance with the Christmas Foundation Meeting," and that their decisions would be considered binding for the Society.

≈

Following the general meeting Ita Wegman continued to be bedridden for many weeks, in her room on the ground floor of the "wooden house" that Rudolf Steiner had planned and commissioned for her at the Arlesheim clinic in the summer of 1924.

English friends such as Eleanor Merry suggested in letters to Wegman that she should move away from Dornach.[169] In mid-April, in a letter to her colleague Viktor Thylmann, Hilma Walter mentioned how complicated the medical situation actually was: "We consider the illness to be really very dangerous, though we refuse to relinquish hope that things will improve."[170] Ita Wegman herself certainly thought it possible that she would die. Fifty-eight years old, exhausted, and consumed by the tragic events since 1925, she hoped for death, seeing her task and work to realize Rudolf Steiner's legacy as being at an end. She increasingly regarded her illness and resulting distance from events in Dornach as a sign of her imminent farewell.

Madeleine van Deventer and others had given her an account of the annual general meeting, though spared her some details of wording and accusation. Others—such as the physician Ernst Marti—made written proposals to her for a future organized affiliation of those "no longer desired at the Goetheanum," and an extensive program of public conferences that ignored the "old" Society and the Goetheanum ("*I believe this need arises due to the fact that key impulses of Anthroposophy are not considered or realized in the world by the current Goetheanum leadership. A truncated and one-sided form of Anthroposophy is being offered*"[171]). In addition, Marti wrote:

We are as yet unable to perceive anything tangible, and all is in flux. But we are not impatient either, because we sense that something is being prepared that we must await. But I did very much want to tell you of these questions—not in the hope of receiving an answer to them, but in the feeling that for really fruitful work the plans must also be weighed within your heart, and in the wish to wait to see what you say about them and what you advise; and what impulses and goals you will suggest to us.

Only a few people apart from the Arlesheim physicians had access to Ita Wegman over these weeks (such as Maria Röschl who arrived for a conversation with her at the end of April). Ernst Marti and many others were deeply concerned to receive no further replies from her,[172] and experienced their own existential dismay.[173] In the second half of April, on the other hand, Hilma Walter and Madeleine van Deventer gave practical thought to moving Ita Wegman somewhere else, and, despite all anxieties about her condition, decided on the special qualities of the landscape around Lake Thun (near Bern, Switzerland).[174]

At the beginning of May, Ita Wegman received another letter of support from the priest Rudolf Meyer, whom she greatly esteemed and who also had good connections with Albert Steffen and Marie Steiner. This insightful letter praised her statement to Albert Steffen in the General Meeting, saying among other things:

> I found your letter to Herr Steffen, which was read out at the annual general meeting, to be the most apt of all the comments made there, and the one that best corresponded to the situation. I am convinced, too, that such words (and a course of action that follows from them) will be *effective,* even if majority decisions are at present drowning them out.[175]

At the time this letter arrived, Wegman's departure was being postponed daily because of continuing high fever. She eventually

left—lying down—on May 12, at the first signs of an improvement in her condition, but to the dismay of all physicians, nurses
and staff at the clinic, as well as many patients and friends in
Arlesheim. The evening before Wegman left, one of them, Georg
Moritz von Sachsen-Alternburg, composed a letter of farewell that
was taken to the wooden house:

> We all long to be reunited with you again. Not just for our
> own sake, to have you with us, but also so that we may
> accompany you if I can put it like this; if that is expressed
> correctly and you understand what I mean.
>
> We will all have to take up our posts again, and perhaps
> will have to occupy them in a very isolated fashion at diverse
> places. Nothing else is conceivable really as time goes on (and
> it will be necessary for us, after all, not to leave our posts,
> but to be where our destiny requires us to be, and to endure
> things and fulfil our role there). However, to do so we will
> need to achieve a deepening in ourselves and occupy a shared,
> tranquil place and awareness inwardly so that this gives us
> strength and stability. Thus far, I have no idea what this will
> look like or how it will appear; but I sense that something
> like this will be necessary, and that it will also be something
> different, of a different nature, from before. Maybe it's just
> that we adopt a different stance and that we "move" differ-
> ently from before. I feel that something like a circle ought to
> exist—but really I mean something new, more a condition
> than a possession: nothing static but in movement.
>
> This is hard to put into words. Thus far, I can't do so,
> and maybe it is not yet ripe enough to write down?[176]

≈

In Hondrich, near Spiez, by Lake Thun, where she continued to
be nursed and treated by Hilma Walter and a few helpers, Ita
Wegman at last overcame her grave illness and slowly but surely
regained her strength. This improvement,[177] which took everyone

Ita Wegman: Notebook entry (draft letter)
about her decisive spiritual experience, July 14, 1934

by surprise, was preceded by a profound spiritual experience
that had very probably occurred in the last days before she left
Arlesheim.[178] Ita Wegman subsequently wrote as follows of this
experience in mid-July:

> At a time of grave destiny within the Society I was confined
> to my sickbed, and for a long time it was uncertain whether

my work would continue in the world of spirit or on the earth. Nevertheless, I had a clear experience one day that I still had things to do on earth, and from this moment onward my condition improved.[179]

At the end of 1934, and especially on the occasion of her next birthday, February 22, 1935, Ita Wegman was to comment on this period in more detail, albeit still cautiously and with some reticence:

> My experience in the world of spirit showed me...something different from this [potential death]. I was not yet expected in the spiritual world. This was an encounter I had there with Rudolf Steiner, at which the Christ being was also present. I was still required instead to do something on earth. From this moment onward, also, I gained the strength to take my own recovery strongly in hand.[180]

Ita Wegman found herself directed back toward earthly activity, to take up again and continue, in a new way, the task of her incarnation in the twentieth century. In pain but full of yearning she had expected to cross the threshold into the world of spirit, and to end her earthly efforts to realize Anthroposophy in medical, social and humanitarian realms. Realization of the Medical Section at the Goetheanum in all its spiritual and esoteric implications was connected with "Christ-permeation of the world" (Rudolf Steiner), but this was something increasingly misunderstood in Dornach,[181] and eventually distorted into a grotesque caricature in histrionic outbursts there.

In a sense, Ita Wegman had been deprived at the end of March 1934 of further shared responsibility for the Goetheanum's development as a School of Spiritual Science, and thus as a place where Rudolf Steiner's impulse could continue. It appeared that something of incisive importance had come to an end. Rather than resigning herself to this, Wegman had sought to read the "signs of the times" and prepared herself for death. Now, unexpectedly, with great spiritual authority, she had been shown the path of return. "From this moment on... I gained the strength to take my own recovery strongly in hand."

≈

By the beginning of June, though still very weak and in need of ongoing nursing and care, Ita Wegman had reached the point of reflecting intently on the consequences of her "return" and of developing a new stance toward events in Dornach. Her first notebook entries of this period, still very much under the sway of her "spiritual experience," were jottings and letter drafts to the people who were no longer "desired" (Ernst Marti) at the Goetheanum, such as the anthroposophists now re-organizing themselves around Eugen Kolisko (*"I have been observing your efforts to consolidate the working group and national groups with interest"*). These notebook entries saw Wegman seeking to come to terms with the major inevitable spiritual changes that had arisen as a result of the general meeting's resolution, and now needed to be realized, pondered further, and established as the basis of all future steps:

> It is not so easy to gain the right overview of the whole situation. Something monstrous has occurred. We have not yet fully realized its nature. Yet everyone must be concerned with it. What does it mean when three of the executive council members say that they wish to continue to lead the Society in accordance with the Christmas Foundation Meeting? The Christmas Foundation Meeting is connected with Rudolf Steiner and then with five other executive council members, who were not arbitrarily appointed, but who, rather, were a spiritual necessity when the Society was reorganized and the

Ita Wegman in Hondrich, May–June 1934

Foundation Stone laid. Rudolf Steiner wished to give life to the new Mysteries; and, for this purpose, the old Society had to be newly founded and led by Dr. Steiner and the executive council? With each executive council member, a stream of human souls was to be led to the new Mystery center. Every executive council member has a karmic relationship with many other human beings. What Rudolf Steiner inaugurated there was living, practical esotericism in tune with the needs of the time. Sadly, people failed to understand this esotericism. They took it all as self-evident, and as if they were entitled to it. Apart from a few exceptions, they had little sense of what it signified, and its innovative nature.

Rudolf Steiner felt great anxiety. This could not end well. Therefore, he fell ill. When an initiate falls ill, that one is subject to laws other than those that apply to ordinary people. An initiate cannot fall ill through one's intrinsic nature, nor any longer through karma; initiates have gone beyond this.

In her notebook entries of draft letters, Wegman repeatedly emphasized the need to engage with the "karma of the Christmas Foundation Meeting": with its prehistory,[182] its active form, but also with its final earthly destruction through the dissolution of the karmic configuration of the executive council in Dornach (*"First and foremost we must be clear that the Christmas Foundation Meeting is broken, has been destroyed"*). At the same time, having been informed by Eugen Kolisko in a letter of initial steps designed to create a wider-ranging affiliation between members in England, Holland and Germany,[183] she warned against efforts to create a new Anthroposophical Society or similar organization in these circumstances. It would be better, she said, to continue working individually, also at a national or regional level (*"I have...the impression that the existing national societies such as England, Holland and France, which still bear within them the continuity of the Doctor's founding plan and programs of work,*

Ita Wegman: Notebook entry (draft letter) about
the destiny of the Christmas Conference, June 1934

should make themselves very strong through active, individual
work"). The aim of this would be to "intensify Anthroposophy"
and thus a deepened spiritual schooling of each individual, in particular with the help of the Foundation Stone Meditation ("We
need a prevailing insight that each individual's inner development is essential nowadays") but without creating new external
forms ("We're not forming a Society but spiritual connections
encompassing all countries: connections that have no earthly
form but are a spiritual power"). Anything spiritually new, she

said, requires the old and is concerned with preserving its existence while transforming it with patience in a long process:

> Let us regard ourselves within the old Society as the ferment in the dough, taking the freedom we are spiritually entitled to, but no more than that. It is self-evident, and therefore an inner law for each of us, that we now have an even greater obligation to deepen Anthroposophy.

At the end of a notebook entry on this theme, a draft letter to members and "fellow combatants," Ita Wegman wrote in relation to herself:

> Please be assured that my whole being is with all of you.
>
> My life has been given back to me anew; I feel the inner obligation to shape it in a deeper way than hitherto. For all of us a new period must begin and is announcing itself like the glowing light of dawn! Let us remain free in allowing what the higher worlds intend and what we yearn and petition for from below to work upon us.

≈

In the first few weeks of her recovery, in further draft letters to leading coworkers of her curative institutes, Ita Wegman struggled to formulate a sustainable concept of the Medical Section, and thus give shape to her own spiritual task, with which she had been deeply preoccupied in the previous nine-week period of her illness. To Franz Löffler, who had invited her to Gerswalde at the most severe period of her illness[184] ("*It was so kind of you to invite me to convalesce in Gerswalde. Unfortunately I was too ill to undertake such a long journey, and I would have been a very big burden for you, too*"), she wrote:

> The changes that have occurred in the Society have been painful for me; but at the same time I also have the sense of

*Ita Wegman: Notebook entry (draft letter)
about her inner situation, June 1934*

finally being rid of an undignified situation within the executive council and the Goetheanum, and of being exposed to personal affronts each day. One endured as long as one was able to, but now a new period is beginning

The only thing we have to be careful of now is not to rush too quickly into narrower forms again. We need an affiliation with free forms of work and collaboration, but our work must be differentiated. I mean by this, for example, that our medical tasks must be fully and completely sustained. The concept of the Section, with which Dr. Steiner wished to create a community of people working in medicine, with medical tasks he sought to deepen esoterically, must not be lost sight of, for otherwise we would lose the ground under our feet. It is these tasks after all that connect us so deeply with Dr. Steiner, and which also connect me with all of you. Esoteric medical tasks, specifically, became clearer in my awareness while I was ill, and I even think that this was the purpose of my illness. These tasks are different from those related to the Society.

And in a draft letter to Karl König she wrote: "Only if we do not forget what is intrinsic to medicine and what Dr. Steiner wished to esoterically configure, regarding this as our most sacred task, can our work be a source of blessing."

Finally, on June 18 (the anniversary of the founding of the first institute at Lauenstein, Jena, when Rudolf Steiner had visited and outlined its future form in 1924), Ita Wegman sent the following joint letter to all therapeutic institutes:

Hondrich near Spiez, June 14, 1934

Dear friends,

In celebration of the tenth anniversary of Dr. Steiner's visit to the Lauenstein, I'd like to say to the institutes and their directors and staff that I am thinking of them all with a warm heart. This anniversary evokes a special sense of earnestness when we look back to the same day ten years ago. So far, we have managed to hold together. Despite distinctions between institutes, differences in human character, we have succeeded in realizing and publicizing our curative work in a unified way, and have pursued higher aims with one accord. These higher aims have lived in our hearts as we sought to realize them: to realize what Rudolf Steiner saw as the esoteric nature of medicine. This is the task he entrusted to the Medical Section: to form a community of people in the Section with the will to extend esoterically the art of medicine and related fields. Sadly, Dr. Steiner was compelled to leave us alone in this most sacred work, and thus it remained only as a longing in our hearts—and in my view, this has found expression in the fact that those who felt this have held together out of the very depths of their being. Today we celebrate this tenth anniversary, a time most often associated with inner challenges and the decisions they necessitate. This day of remembrance may therefore be more significant than others are. Will we manage to keep on holding together despite all the difficulties we face owing to the crisis in the Society? Can something new dawn because we hold firm, so that a moment arrives when deepening of anthroposophic medical work and curative education can achieve a breakthrough for medical esotericism? If we will undertake this deepening as our sacred task, hold together and keep faith with the higher goal that Dr. Steiner invested in the Medical Section, a time of new and fruitful work will assuredly dawn for us.

Dear friends, these thoughts have been surfacing in me recently in my mountain solitude, and although the world looks a very grim place at present, my heart still beats joyfully when I think that I can rejoin our circles soon with new vigor, to work with you and to work toward receiving a new impetus.

My best wishes to all of you
With warm greetings,
Your I. Wegman, MD

In the draft version of this letter, Ita Wegman had written, very succinctly: "Here is my wish for this tenth anniversary: to hold together and to deepen our common work."

≈

Ita Wegman dictated her letter of June 14 to the curative institutes on the last day of her stay in Hondrich. Still weak (*"I am of course not nearly at the point yet of starting work again. My heart is still very weak, above all, but I do feel that I have got over the illness*"[185]), she was nonetheless now clearly facing forward, toward the future. The clinic car took her to Wengen, at a somewhat higher altitude but not far distant. Here she stayed briefly at a hotel (whose bills she was unable to pay) with her helpers, subsequently moving to a chalet in a landscape surrounded by mountains—a view in which she often immersed herself completely. In a notebook she wrote a text of rare beauty about this, testifying to the nature of her thoughts and contemplations during these days:

Radiant blue sky, Jungfrau Mountain and its eternal snowcap soar proudly aloft, its peak broad and its shape striking.

If, in all tranquility, you allow the mountain to work upon you, certain forms become apparent in its contours. High above, almost at the peak, the face of an Indian godhead, as one might call it: Brahma, the god of existence who comes to visibility in the finest substantiality, in the white mass of snow. He has slit eyes, a straight nose, and his skull is shaped like a tower. One level below him is a sleeping valkyrie, as if carved out of the granite. She wears a suit of armor, and her head bends backward.

Between these two is the face of Mercury.

These three continually appear and reappear. When the sky is bright, clear, and cloudless, one can easily see them. Wengen, from which one has the best view of the Jungfrau, is a plateau-like valley surrounded by mountains, so that one can feel protected by mighty beings. Here, in this valley, the elements play themselves out.

Mists rise from mountain crevices, slowly finding thjeir way toward light and warmth. They remain hanging within the forests, where they slowly settle, to be drunk thirstily by the dry trees. A whole cloud of mist can slowly vanish in this way and nourish the woods. The mists also rise higher, becoming ever brighter and purer, merging increasingly with the light, and so acquire a wondrous blueish-white tinge.

Oh, these clouds, which one would so like to stroke with one's hand, gather or fade; as you observe and unite with them, they fill you with universal powers.

Then the rushing water.

≈

In Wengen, Wegman's correspondence broadened again to encompass the whole spectrum of daily concerns in Arlesheim and of people in other locations connected with the work there. The Arlesheim clinic was in an economically very fraught and existentially endangered situation, greatly intensified as a result of the past year's political events (with the loss of many patients from Germany and other countries) but also due to Wegman's illness and the breakdown of relations with people connected with the Goetheanum since the general meeting. In Wengen Wegman began to write to people she knew who had financial means, asking them to support funding of the clinic, and accentuating the importance of the spiritual work in Arlesheim (*"The physicians are now in a situation where they are compelled to spend all their time in medical consultations, leaving little time for spiritual work. And you will, I'm sure, acknowledge what it means in the current climate to be unable to devote oneself sufficiently to spiritual work"*[186]). At the same time she offered the prospect of her return to the clinic and emphasized her personal commitment to its survival (*"As soon as I am completely well again, I will of course once again connect fully with the work at the clinic and the institutes. It was very burdensome that I fell ill at this difficult time. As soon as I start work fully again in the clinic, things will change too. For the time being, because of my state of health, I still have to remain absent from Dornach"*[187]).

By the end of June and beginning of July, Wegman was already engaging with difficulties at the Sonnenhof and also in London, doing so with great energy and complete resolve. For instance, when the plan for a vegetarian restaurant adjoining her London Therapy Center came to nothing again, she wrote in no uncertain terms to Madeleine van Deventer:

> I just cannot allow all these things to fall away. This really isn't possible. Nutrition is too important an issue for me to let the work initiated in this direction lapse again. Through nutrition we come to processes of healing, to a proper global pedagogy and to a healthy civilization and culture. If only a small, germinal beginning has been made here, it is still significant, and I cannot allow any stone to be left unturned in the attempt to save it—and certainly there are those who wish to do so.[188]

Near the end of June, Hilma Walter had to leave Ita Wegman to nurse her brother-in-law, who had suddenly become gravely ill, and then to return to England and the children in Clent. Wegman knew that she owed a very great deal to Walter's highly professional treatment of her during this time, and her whole, loving, and absolutely dependable loyalty and essential spirituality. After her departure, she sent her two handwritten letters, in the second of which she took very much to heart the fate of Walter's relative, who soon died despite her help (*"If you have stood close to death as I have, and have been saved; and then hear that another has had to leave the physical plane despite all the good help and nursing he was given, then you feel a strong sense of destiny at work. His destiny had come to an end, whereas I must begin anew. At the same time you gain a sense of being connected, of human belonging. And between us you yourself stand with your remarkable destiny: helping me to remain on the earth and at the same time standing by your dear brother-in-law and helping him as he*

Wengen 28 Juni 34
Hotel Belvedere

Liebe Dr. Walter,

Gestern hörte ich, dass Ihr Schwager Herr Rau gestorben ist. Es war dies zu erwarten nach den letzten Nachrichten, die ich bekam; Trotzdem wird es für Sie alle schmerzlich sein. Hoffentlich hat Herr Rau nicht gelitten und haben Sie ihm gütig etwas geben können. Wollen Sie Frau Rau und Schwester Hedwig so wie auch den jungen Rau meinen warm empfundenen Beileid mit diesem Verlust mitteilen. Wenn man selber wie ich am Rande des Grabes gestanden hat und gerettet wurde und hört, dass ein anderer den physischen Plan hat verlassen müssen trotz aller guten Hülfe und Pflege, dann kriegt man stark die Empfindung des schicksalsmässigen. Sein Schicksal war zu Ende und ich muss wieder neu anfangen. Zugleicher Zeit bekommt man das Gefühl des Zusammen verbundenseins, der menschlichen Zusammengehörigkeit. Und dazwischen sind Sie mit Ihrem merkwürdigen Schicksal: Mir helfen zu können auf der Erde zu bleiben und Ihrem lieben Schwager über der Schwelle

Letter from Ita Wegman to Hilma Walter, June 28, 1934, page 1

crosses the threshold into the world of spirit. My thoughts will be with you at the cremation" [189]).

After Hilma Walter's departure, from the end of June increasing numbers of visitors from Arlesheim (including Sidonie von Nostitz and her protégé Bendit Loeb) came to see Ita Wegman in Wengen, where she was also continually accompanied by Anni and Mien Viehoff and her English friend Kalmia Bittleston. Despite this increasing engagement with people, Wegman made clear in her detailed letters to Madeleine van Deventer—which referred to everything happening in Arlesheim—that there was as yet no chance of her returning there. She mentioned extended travel plans (including an invitation from Georg Moritz von Sachsen-Altenburg for them to visit Palestine together) and wrote to her young, down-to-earth Dutch colleague with unmistakable clarity:

> My soul still needs to see foreign lands, for otherwise I will have no powers of resistance. All sorts of things are still cramped in my ether body: old stuff that I have to shed and is still emerging with great force. Time and new impressions will have to help me here.[190]

Ita Wegman was increasingly longing to go South. In the second half of July, she left Wengen and the magnificent surroundings of Lake Thun with her companions and traveled to Valais to—as she wrote—experience Mont Blanc and the Great St. Bernard Pass.

≈

There, in a hotel in the woods near Lake Champex, news of another death reached her—this time of a young child who had been her godson since 1933, Martin Tobias Mirbt from Clent, whose parents were friends of hers. Deeply moved and inwardly agitated by this event, Ita Wegman took up her pen again and began her letter to the parents with these words:

My dear friends,

It was with real distress that I heard Martin Tobias had passed away. His coming and going had meaning—though the materialists may find none. What did his soul, his individuality seek? The purpose of it was to sample earthly incarnation, and when the Tobias individuality did not find his way into the physical body available to him, this led to pneumonia, and to his spirit distancing itself once more. Such "I"-beings sacrifice themselves to the world of spirit—they incorporate earthly forces that they carry upward with them, unused and undiluted. The mother will remain strongly connected to an individuality of this kind.[191]

Carl Alexander and Gertrud Mirbt had worked closely with Count Keyserlingk in the past and, after a lecture by Carl Alexander Mirbt at the London World Conference—which Ita Wegman had played a major part in—they had taken up an invitation from Daniel Nicol Dunlop to develop biodynamic agriculture in England, and had arrived in Clent at the beginning of the thirties. Wegman ended her letter to them by speaking briefly about her own situation, describing it in these words:

I am feeling much better, and have been convalescing in the mountains here—not knowing before how much strength they can emanate. Thus I am hopeful of regaining all my powers eventually so that I can get back to work. In the meantime, the situation in the Society and the world at large has completely changed, and so I will have to feel my way into it all again.

In Valais, Wegman was visited by George Adams Kaufmann, and discussed with him among other things the program for the next "Summer School" in England. She was considering returning briefly to the clinic in order to resolve—or at least collaborate in dealing with—its complex financial situation[192] ("*The clinic's financial situation must certainly be sorted out*"[193]) and in correspondence discussed changes of nursing staff as well as the need to sell a car. At the same time she immersed herself in and absorbed the influences of the surrounding landscape, the lofty world of the Matterhorn region,[194] and lived in her meditations.

An increasing need grew in Ita Wegman for the whole world and warmth of the South—especially for the familiar realms of Greece through which she had traveled with Ilse Knauer in 1932, again after a very difficult, stricken period in her life. But at the same time Wegman did not yet feel quite strong enough to embark anew on a reconnaissance of Greece. At the beginning of September therefore she traveled on to Italy, spending some time at Lake Maggiore in Ticino, and from there embarking on a trip to Milan and an intense exploration of the history and culture of the Renaissance. She finally reached Venice in the middle of the month, writing as follows to Fried Geuter on September 17: "I am preparing to undertake a big sea voyage, which will conclude in Palestine."

The letter continued:

I have completely recovered from my illness, and feel myself as healthy and strong again as before. It is a remarkable experience to have been close to death and then to be given back to life. Much has happened in my inner life during this period, but also outwardly in the Anthroposophical Society. I found it beneficial not to have to participate actively in these things, and to observe them from afar.... It is good that things are taking shape without me—this gives me the sense of being inwardly free, which is very good, of much importance for my progress.

Ita Wegman and Kalmia Bittleston in Venice, September 1934

In the few days of her second stay in Venice (which she had first visited on the way back from Greece in 1932) Ita Wegman immersed herself in its historical and spiritual significance, contemplating the "city's spirit" as Emil Bock had done six years earlier,[195] and attending in particular to St. Marks, the mood of early, eastern Christianity and Rudolf Steiner's comments on the Gospel of St. Mark. She wrote to Fried Geuter, in this connection, about her pleasure at the fact that the curative educators at Schloss Hamborn, threatened by political developments, had recently been giving keen attention to this Gospel. (She had learned this from Siegfried Pickert, who had also visited her in Valais.[196]) Of Venice she wrote:

> You know that Dr. Steiner said that the Gospel of St. Mark is the Gospel for our time. Of the Mark individuality he said that he worked both esoterically and exoterically: esoterically as far as Ireland, developing into the Grail stream and Roscrucianism; and exoterically here in Venice as patriarch, and as bishop in Alexandria where he was murdered. I am very pleased indeed to be able to trace his influence here in such a detailed way, since he is the patron saint of St. Marks and the whole history of Venice was very strongly connected with him in the early Christian era.

On Wednesday evening, September 19, the train arriving in Venice from Basel brought Werner Pache, Julia Bort, Georg Moritz von Sachsen-Altenburg (heir to the throne), Adam Bittleston, Margarethe Bockholt, and Erich Kirchner. With Ita Wegman and Mien Viehoff they boarded the ship *Vienna* the following day at noon. "I am preparing to undertake a big sea voyage, which will conclude in Palestine."

The voyage to Jaffa—interrupted by days ashore, visits to sights, and expeditions—lasted nine days, and took them to Monte Gargano, Brindisi, then to Corfu and along the western

Kalmia Bittleston and Ita Wegman on board the Vienna, *September 1934*

and eastern coastline of Greece to the landscapes and locations of Homer, to Piraeus and Athens, and also to the ancient initiation sites of Eleusis, Delphi and Thebes. The voyage continued through the Aegean Sea toward the western coast of Asia Minor—which they reached after a detour of great importance to Wegman to stay for five days in Constantinople. Then the voyage continued in a southeasterly direction through the Levant, stopping at Rhodes and Cypress, before finally arriving at the ancient, historical port of Jaffa, gateway to central and southern Palestine, on Saturday, September 29 at 6 a.m.: the day of Michael. This port, like the rest of Palestine, had fallen to Alexander the Great in 332 BC.[197]

As Wegman's colleague Margarethe Bockholt recorded in her account of the trip,[198] the port of Jaffa was full of lively, restless bustle in Oriental and Levantine style, and this, after the quietness of the night, the intensity of the ocean encounter with the islands of the ancient Greek world and an inner longing and expectation about the landscape of the Gospels (which Wegman

Old town and harbor in Jaffa

had been contemplating and meditating upon for weeks) surprised
the travelers and initially caused them problems:

> The *Vienna* anchored some way off from land. In a small
> motorboat we passed jagged reefs to enter the harbour, which
> presented an unspeakably colorful spectacle: endless barges
> piled high with their freight, costumes of all kinds, cries, and
> stench.

The further journey to Jerusalem led them through impressive
plantations of lemons and oranges but soon revealed a growing
desert landscape characteristic of Judaea, with camel caravans
and tents. At midday, Ita Wegman and her companions reached
Jerusalem, and took up quarters for six nights in the French
monastic hostel of Notre Dame de France, a quiet, cool place
with long corridors and small, cell-like rooms, where Emil Bock
had stayed two years previously, as well as in the spring of the
same year.[199]

After a brief pause, Ita Wegman and her friends started to study Rudolf Steiner's lectures on the Fifth Gospel, which were to accompany her throughout her Palestine trip, alongside other Christological lecture cycles by Steiner, the Gospels themselves, books by Anna Katharina Emmerick[200] and thorough, intense study of ancient Jewish history. In their discussions of Rudolf Steiner's first lecture in Kristiania [Oslo] (concerned with the spread of the Christ impulse), Ita Wegman for the first time spoke to the others about her experiences in Constantinople at the start of their trip together—inner impressions which Werner Pache noted in his diary as follows:

> She said she had been led to Constantinople since she had suddenly felt too ill to come with us to Greece—where she had really longed to go. She therefore had to go to Constantinople, for which she had previously always felt the greatest distaste. There, she said, she had experienced how many of the Turks had been destroyed, and this had given her a powerful impulse: the sense that this should be redressed. And in asking who in the world could do this, it became clear to her that it must be the Germans. She really doubted the possibility of this (1932–33, tendency to look toward England for everything). Through her illness, and this experience now, she had been guided back in this direction. And she wished to affirm this; and said that the way the discussion had turned to this today, the day of Michael, was grace for which one should be grateful. If only a few people, she said, would not lose this hope and confidence in the Germans—as I, after all, have done. But she said she had also experienced in Constantinople the *maya* of current events in Germany. Arriving in Constantinople she had immediately felt well again. Then the conversation continued in relation to the verse: "The German spirit has not yet fulfilled / what it is to accomplish in the world." Dr. Steiner, she said, had spoken of how we must repeatedly remember this.

According to this, despite the current state of Germany, and its dramatic and dangerous distortions and estrangements, Ita Wegman once more trusted in the possibility of bringing about a key change in civilization through anthroposophic Spiritual Science and thus through Rudolf Steiner's intention for the role and influence of Central Europe—a change that would orient culture toward Christ's future activity and impulse. She saw her recovery from her grave illness in recent months as a prompting to keep faith with her anthroposophic initiatives and efforts in German-speaking lands, and to strengthen these efforts despite the existing threats, and thus, in spiritual terms especially, preparing for the future.

That afternoon the companions went for a first walk together (accompanied by John P. Merezian, a young Armenian with a remarkable knowledge of the area, whom Emil Bock had met in 1932 and had chosen as his guide again in the spring of 1934[201]) through the Oriental-style streets full of bazaars near the Church of the Holy Sepulchre. Thus they explored the physical locality of Jerusalem but at the same time also gained a sense of the current condition of the Jewish people. Around 5:30 in the afternoon, as the sun was setting, Ita Wegman and her companions reached the Wailing Wall; and she later recorded as follows her impressions of this in a notebook:

> The Wailing Wall is a part of the remaining Temple of Solomon. The Jews stand before this wall and pray and lament, coming to an ecstatic state in their memory of lost greatness and in the hope of regaining this greatness once more when the long expected Messiah comes. It is very moving to see this. One is easily filled with compassion and may wonder why it is not possible for the Jews' strength of heart to be used better than in such fruitless lament.

Thereupon Ita Wegman wandered in the growing twilight through the Valley of Josaphat from Mount Zion to the Garden of Gethsemane, passing cypresses and many graves beside the rushing Kidron River: the path that Christ took on the night of Maundy Thursday after the Last Supper. Darkness had already arrived when Wegman reached the Mount of Olives, where she stopped for a longer while with her companions, looked toward Jerusalem and pondered deeply:

> When, in the evening, you let all these places rise up in yourself, you can gain a strong impression of what occurred there; but to begin with it is hard work to really confront the city itself, which emanates a strangely heavy atmosphere. (Margarethe Bockholt)

The following day, the friends visited the various stations of the Via Dolorosa in reverse order, starting with the Church of the Sepulchre and thus the historical location of the events of Golgotha;[202]

The Garden of Gethsemane and Jerusalem

and also reached the healing Pool of Bethesda where excavations were underway ("*Some of the old steps have been exposed again, and one descends deep into the earth: in those days, too, there were 25 steps down to the pool*" [Margarethe Bockholt]). They were also shown the house of Joachim and Anna, the traditional birthplace of Mary: a cave dwelling beneath a later basilica built by the Crusaders. In the afternoon they drove to Bethlehem, and saw the ancient Christian basilica of the Church of the Nativity, the birth cave concealed beneath this church, and the Cave of St. Jerome ("*The place of Christ's birth is in a cave connected with others, really a network of subterranean caves and passages. Bethlehem in general is full of caves and grottoes; and Dr. Steiner says that it was formerly a place where Adonis and Attis rites were celebrated, and that we should see 'world-historical karma' in the fact that it was precisely here that the birth took place.*"). They also visited dwellings in Bethlehem itself ("*They are like caves in the ground, divided in half but horizontally. One half, lying deep underground, is for the animals, and above them lives the whole family: sleeps and cooks. And seeing this you can understand much better why the stable would be offered if there were no room up on top.*"). From the little hilltop town they saw the olive field of the shepherds' annunciation in the glow of the setting sun. Monday was a rest day and no more was undertaken than a walk in the evening to the Mount of Olives. They took this path again at dawn the next morning (at 4:30) and explored the place carefully, after which they rode to Bethany on mules, on hard, stony paths. There they had a view back to Jerusalem, but also, further toward the East, to the grandeur of the desert landscape of the Dead Sea. And they finally reached their goal:

> Bethany, where Mary, Martha and Lazarus lived, and where the awakening of Lazarus also took place, is a small place with modest, square dwellings of stone.

Bethany

To reach the grave of Lazarus, you descend again deep into the earth. The doorway where Christ once entered has been walled up, but from there one crawls through a narrow crack into the grave that has been carved out of rock to make a fairly roomy chamber. A stone lay before it, and above this an opening; and we were told that Christ had spoken the words of resurrection through it. An atmosphere of great inwardness still hovers here, and one gains a sense of how the being of Lazarus John wishes increasingly to connect with the earth; also that this place was made ready in advance for this great mystery through many intimate conversations that may have taken place there, and through the inward devotion that holds sway in it. (Margarethe Bockholt)

On their penultimate day in Jerusalem, October 3, Ita Wegman went to visit Mount Zion in the morning, and especially the place of the Last Supper (*"Here much has been destroyed due to the position of the mosque: you don't get a very strong impression. Yet one does recognize the place precisely as Katherina Emmerich describes in her visions"* [203] [Margarethe Bockholt]).

The expedition group in the Dead Sea landscape,
October 3, 1934 (Ita Wegman, left)

In the afternoon there followed a trip in hired vehicles to the
Dead Sea, lying 400 meters below sea level, on narrow, winding
streets through the hot Judaean desert, passing former Essene settlements on the way. Wegman and her friends visited the ancient
city of Jericho and were as much surprised by the extent of the
rich, tropical vegetation of this oasis (with many banana trees,
date palms, and poisonous plants) as by the intensely arid and
dead character of the surrounding landscape of the Essenes, St.
John, and the Temptation.

They reached the Jordan and the region where Jesus was baptized,[204] observing its waters for a long time; and finally reached
the Dead Sea at sunset:

> Red and purple color tones in the desert and in the water.
> Colors like those one sees in mist: veiled, not luminous. The
> water is oily, viscous due to its great salinity, which makes it
> very buoyant. Even in the evening the air is still sultry and

The desert of Judaea and the Dead Sea

probably never cools very much: an atmosphere like being in a steam bath. The experience of this place is very strong; it changes your awareness; you are compelled to encounter very different ether forces, perhaps more of the quality of life and chemical ether. You feel your skeleton and it tastes like lead in your mouth. If one spent longer here one might start to grasp why all living things die in pure life ether, and how these forces are no doubt also active in the decay products of radium and such. Dr. Steiner once said that Christ came here before accomplishing great acts of healing; and likewise returned to the site of the Jordan baptism before the awakening of Lazarus. Here one inevitably gains the sense of a quite unique place on earth. It is the place where Sodom and Gomorrha once stood; they were destroyed by fire—probably a volcanic eruption. Into this breach entered strong earth activity and salinization. The change in atmosphere on this whole trip from Jerusalem to the Dead Sea and back is so strong that it asks much of the organism's powers of acclimatization. I returned quite dazed from the trip. (Margarethe Bockholt)[205]

On the last day in Jerusalem, Ita Wegman and Margarethe Bockholt once again explored the whole, mighty surroundings of the temple mount,[206] studying also the historical and spiritual history of its buildings. With their companions and John Merezian, they drove to Emmaus in the afternoon and were deeply moved—especially also in contrast with their experiences in the desert and at the Dead Sea the day before—by its lofty position and atmosphere, as well as by the monastery and gardens cared for there by a German monk of the Borromaean Order.[207] They took their farewell here from Judaea.

The next morning, from Notre Dame de France hostel, Wegman wrote to Madeleine van Deventer just before she left Jerusalem, saying she was no longer intending, as originally planned, to travel on from Palestine to Egypt. She also included a brief account of her impressions on the trip:

> It is hard to describe our impressions here. It was quite different from what we expected, especially to begin with. The intimate Christian atmosphere has been completely buried. All that is left are some material vestiges over which the diverse religions contend. That is a colossal disturbance. Nevertheless, a few places remain beautiful and untouched—for instance where no church has yet been built. The landscape is wonderfully beautiful. It is actually the case that you have a strong experience of geology here, whereas in Greece the meteorological aspect comes more to the fore—as the Doctor described it in *Christ and the Spiritual World*.[208]

As Emil Bock had done before her, Ita Wegman spent the second half of her time in Palestine—thus the remaining six days

†

NOTRE-DAME de FRANCE

JÉRUSALEM

✳

TÉLÉGR. ASSOMPTIONISTES-JÉRUSALEM
Téléphone N° 140
Boite Postale : N° 298

5ᵗᵉ October 34

Liebe Dr. v. Deventer

Ich habe Ihnen depeschiert, dass
ich die Reise nach Ägypten
aufgegeben habe, teilweise weil sie
zu ermüdend ist, aber auch weil
sie doch zu teuer ist.
Wir fahren dan̄ mit dem gleichen
Schiff, womit die anderen
die Rückfahrt antreten, mit
bis zu Brindisi und wir
ruhen dan̄ in Capri von unseren
Strapazen etwas aus. Der Eb,
Prinz ist hier leider krank ge-
worden, Fieber und Diarhöen.
Glücklich ist er wieder jetzt
hergestellt und können wir
weiter reisen. Er fährt dan̄ auch
mit nach Capri. Heute wollen

Letter from Ita Wegman to Madeleine van Deventer,
October 5, 1934, page 1

III

wir nach Nazareth.
Es ist schwer die Eindrücke
Ihnen zu schildern, die wir
hier haben. Es ist so ganz
anders als wir erwartet
hatten, hauptsächlich im Anfang.
Das intim christliche ist aber,
laut verschuttet und es bleibt
nur das materielle übrig,
um dem man sich unter den
verschiedenen Religionen streitet
Das stört kolossal. Schön sind
doch trotzdem einige Stellen
die noch unberührt geblieben
sind d.h. worauf man noch
keine Kirche gebaut hat.
Das Land ist wunderbar schön
und es ist tatsächlich so,
dass man hier das Geologische
stark erlebt während man
in Griechenland das Meteorologi-
sche erlebt, so wie der Doktor
es beschrieben hat in Christus und

Letter from Ita Wegman to Madeleine van Deventer,
October 5, 1934, page 2

die geistige Welt.

Wie geht es in der Klinik?

Ich habe schon gedacht ob Sie nicht Lust haben Ihre Ferien in Capri, Neapel vielleicht auch Sizilien zu verbringen mit uns zusammen? Es wäre doch sehr schön.

Es würde doch zu viel sein noch nach Aegypten zu reisen. Die Reise ist anstrengend Ich fühle mich sehr gut trotz aller Anstrengungen.

Wir fahren den 10ten October mit dem Jeruzalem nach Brindisi sind den 13ten dort und den 15ten wohl in Neapel Hotel Royal

Lassen Sie uns dort etwas von sich hören.

Mit vielen herzlichen Grüssen
Ihre I. Wegman

Letter from Ita Wegman to Madeleine van Deventer,
October 5, 1934, page 3

up to October 10—with her friends in Galilee, mainly at the Sea of Galilee. Late on Friday morning they passed locations of Old Testament lineage, drove through the land of Samaria and, via Sichem (Nablus)—where David's tabernacle and Joseph's grave were located, and where Christ spoke at the well—they arrived in Nazareth. Here they were again shown cave dwellings said to have been inhabited by the Holy Family. Here too, there was much that tended to divert one's attention from things of importance (*"In Nazareth everything has been built over in a terribly Catholic style"* [Emil Bock[209]]). However, Margarethe Bockholt wrote as follows about this former center of the Essenes, and the place where Jesus conversed with his mother: "Nazareth is really the only place where one can spiritually approach the being of Mary, and where this deeply veiled mystery of her being comes strongly before one's soul."

Immediately after visiting Nazareth, they ascended Mount Tabor, from whose summit Ita Wegman and her friends surveyed the land of Palestine as far as the Jordan, the Sea of Galilee, and the Mediterranean, deeply immersing themselves in the experience of the mountain itself:[210]

> Here, in this spot ascending above the surrounding land, occurs the transfiguration, the conversation with Moses and Elijah. Here, too, John, James, and Peter were able to reach a new level of development. In Nazareth, therefore, we have the subterranean dwelling, the "home" where the deepest conversations that can unfold between human souls took place between mother and son; and in Samaria the well where in conversation Christ gives the living water— that is, an understanding of the spirit working into life; and the mountain, where he rises out of life into the world of spirit and allows some of his disciples to participate in this. (Margarethe Bockholt)

After spending the night in Nazareth the group then went to stay for the next few days at a Borromaean hostel in Tabgha by the Sea of Galilee, between Tiberias and Capernaum—which Emil Bock had likewise frequented with his priest colleagues. In this very different atmosphere of "cosmic goodness" (Bock) Ita Wegman studied the healings described in the New Testament, and also the distinctive meteorology, vegetation and fauna of this region. She went to Capernaum—where two monks at a lonely monastery looked after the excavations of the old synagogue destroyed by an earthquake in AD 400—and also frequently went to the Sea of Galilee itself, where she watched glorious sunrises and sunsets, and found some cooler temperatures at this season of otherwise extremely hot, almost tropical weather.[211]

On Tuesday afternoon they drove further over the Heights of Sareph—where it started to rain a little for the first time on their trip, so that aromas of essential oils began to rise from the land—and through the Crusader town of Akkon to Haifa. They spent their last night at a hostel on Mount Carmel, familiar to Elijah and the Essenes. Early on Wednesday morning in Haifa, Ita Wegman visited the new settlements of Jewish immigrants from Russia, spoke with them about the future of the country, and then embarked on the waiting ship in a reflective mood. Margarethe Bockholt's account is as follows:

> A great deal of diverse life has arrived in Palestine: the various settlements are all different in character depending on their prevailing spirit or that of their leaders. But there is a huge amount of striving and also a sense that old, western forms of thought do not belong here, that they must be broken and that nothing new has as yet appeared. West and East clash strongly here. It is hard to imagine that no battle will occur here between Arabs and Jews; and perhaps it will also be a flash point between the Japanese and English since one

feels that these two powers also impact on one another here. There is so little here that is strong enough to act as balance between these polarities.

Therefore, leaving Haifa Wednesday evening at 10 p.m., one had a melancholy feeling and the great question: What will unfold here?

≈

Whereas most of her companions returned to Arlesheim after the ship docked in Brindisi (the place where Virgil died), Wegman headed for Capri and thus to the Gulf of Naples and the region of Vesuvius. In a letter to Madeleine van Deventer on October 5 she had first mentioned the possibility of continuing her trip there, and possibly also going to Sicily, inviting van Deventer to join her (*"It would be lovely if you came"*). Now Ita Wegman, accompanied by Mien Viehoff and Georg Moritz von Sachsen-Altenburg, spent several weeks on the island of Capri, staying in a guesthouse—like Emil Bock who had likewise ended his trip to Palestine two years previously in Capri (and Rome). Wegman's notebooks show that while there she reflected intensely on her experiences in Palestine (*"I have tried to write everything down so as not to forget the most important things, which are often very subtle"*[212]), going over the whole trajectory of ancient Jewish history and tracing the signs of Christ's approaching incarnation.[213] Thus, in a notebook entry dated October 21, she wrote:

> It becomes comprehensible why Jesus Christ cannot live longer than 33 years in the land of Palestine and among the Jewish people. One then experiences how the whole earth becomes his dwelling place so that he comes to belong to all the peoples of the earth. The Mystery of Golgotha had to occur to release Christ again for the whole world. And that is the redeeming thing that surfaces in one's feeling—that Christ is to be found everywhere; even, one might almost say,

Mount Tabor

that he can better be found everywhere else than specifically in Palestine where everything has been covered over by all the cultures and history that occurred there, so that today the legacy of such a sublime teaching as that of Jesus Christ and his life is only a decadent Christianity.

A sense of pain rises in one, as well as a strong impulse to become a true follower of Christ and truly to understand him. Yet the historical events, the fact of them, did occur in Palestine after all, and this is why Palestine is so interesting, and deserving of our love. And because the Jesus Christ events occurred in a country full of history, the archaeological remains to be found there can be extraordinarily stimulating. The archaeological remains really accord with the geology of the land. Wherever you turn in Palestine, you are confronted by geology.

The rock formations, the powers of the earth, played a major role in the history of the Jewish people. It was as if these earthly powers and rock formations were a preparation for the Mystery of Golgotha. And it is therefore supremely tragic for the Jews that—with some exceptions—they have no means of understanding Jesus Christ and his mission retrospectively. They were and are unable to raise themselves

Sareph, October 9, 1934

from their geology. Jesus Christ was understood within Greek culture, in Greece, when his life became known there. There one is not struck by geological earth formations but more by what surrounds and encompasses the earth: the aromatic, airy ether world. As Dr. Steiner said, the Greeks lived in meteorological qualities. And here, primarily, grew an understanding of the resurrected Christ, who can be found in the etheric world. The geological quality connected with the Jews provided Jesus Christ with his physical body; the meteorological, connected with the Greeks, made it possible to understand the Mystery of Golgotha.

Looking at the present and toward the future, Ita Wegman wrote further:

The fifth post-Atlantean cultural epoch has the task of approaching a true Christology. Dr. Steiner made a beginning with this, continuing what lives as quintessence in the Gospel of John, teaching what underlies the Gospel of Mark, bringing alive what weaves in the Gospel of Luke and rendering comprehensible what the Gospel of Matthew tells us.

In the concentrated repose of her time on Capri, however, Wegman was not just seeking a merely interesting landscape for her reflections and for working through her review of Palestine (*"The weather here is wonderful, and I can work very well, alternating this with going for beautiful walks"*[214]), but had quite intentionally sought out the realm it offered her. She studied early Greek colonization of this Italian peninsula including— after a brief respite—the rich excavations in Herculaneum and Pompeii in the Gulf of Naples. She eagerly visited museums and looked at the finds exhibited there. She studied the spiritual movements in the centuries before and after the Mystery of Golgotha, the cultural context and conditions in which its impulse was either taken up or rejected, along with further developments in the ancient Mysteries. Tiberius, the Roman Caesar at the time of Christ, had built his imperial residence on Capri; and there the luciferic and destructive cult of the Caesars—and thus the violation of the Mysteries—had its source and point of departure. (In 1932, Emil Bock had written of Capri as the "place where the counter-event to the Mystery of Golgotha occurred simultaneously with it"; and had himself traced the Caesarean impulses there.[215]) Ita Wegman sought out these traces of the past, exploring the obstructing activities of the wrongfully initiated Roman Caesars. Initially she intended including in her studies the Klingsor impulses in Sicily, certainly also with an ongoing sideways glance at twentieth-century developments, in particular the current events in Germany. On April 17, 1917, during World War I, Rudolf Steiner had said in Berlin:

> And consider this: that a Caesar thus initiated would have said: I will take up arms—something that one could do inwardly in the Mysteries—against what has occurred at the turning point of the world! You have to form a really clear idea of the will to power possessed by these Caesars. It never

Die 5te nachatlantische Kultur epoche hat die Aufgabe zur wahren Christologie zu kommen. Einen Anfang hat Dr Steiner damit gemacht Er sehl fort was im Johannes Evangelium als Quintessenz lebt, er lehrt, was im Marcus Evangelium zu Grunde liegt, er lebt was im Lucas evangelium webt, und er bringt zum Verständnis darjenige, was das Matheus evangelium sagt.

Ita Wegman: Notebook entry about the importance of Rudolf Steiner's Christology, October 1934

occurred to them that they might be powerless against the will of the gods but instead resolved—and that's why they had themselves initiated—to commence battle with spiritual cosmic impulses and, as it were, to oppose the course of evolution. *This has also occurred at other periods, and is happening today. It is just that people do not notice, do not know it is happening.*[216]

In letters she wrote to Arlesheim at the end of October,[217] without going into any further details on her spiritual efforts and questions—which focused continually upon the historical influence and future impulse of the events in Palestine—Ita Wegman stressed that she would still need a little time before returning ("*It would be too soon for me in psychological terms to return and start work again. My soul still needs more nourishment than*

Christ monogram on the lid of a grave,
Laurentius catacomb, Rome

it has yet received. My physical body is healthy"[218]). At the beginning of November, she traveled on to Rome, whose history she studied intensively, visiting the sites of early Christianity and of its hidden places of worship (and likewise the catacombs that Emil Bock and Robert Goebel had described in 1930). At the same time she sought out the monuments and documents of the Roman Caesars with their adversary intent, and again visited many museums to continue examining traces of Greek culture in the centuries around the time of Christ (*"One can really experience Greek art in Rome. And when you read that something is a copy of a work by Praxiteles, Skopas or Polyktet, you can be sure that the copy was made by a Greek. In fact, you can often get the sense that they aren't copies at all but original works carried off from Greece and labeled a copy just to safeguard them"*

[Notebook]). Ita Wegman was ready to return to Arlesheim via the Alps and to engage again with her own, immediate tasks only after bringing these explorations and inner clarifications to a provisional conclusion.

≈

In the end, she arrived back in Arlesheim after a six-month absence on November 18, 1934, to the great joy and relief of the whole clinic and many friends who had been told of her return. She now moved in to the bright, upper rooms of her wooden house, which Madeleine van Deventer had prepared and furnished for her. The children from the Sonnenhof came there to sing her songs of welcome, before they and their carers led Wegman down to a festive tea in the clinic (later she said that she was *"at home again in the clinic"*[219]). To Werner Pache, who immediately reported on existing urgent problems and decisions affecting the curative work, Ita Wegman said, "Yes, let us now get properly down to work, but everything must be carried inwardly."[220]

In the first three days back at the clinic, Wegman received detailed reports on everything, and gradually accustomed herself again to circumstances in Arlesheim. She then wrote a first, detailed letter to Hilma Walter in England—who had treated her in the spring and helped her to surivive—about her experiences over the past few months:

Arlesheim, November 22, 1934

Dear Dr. Walter,

I have been back for a few days now from my long convalescence trip. It was very good to undertake this journey; I feel much refreshed and really am as healthy now as I ever was; I can cope with a good deal and can work. The trip

KLINISCH-THERAPEUTISCHES INSTITUT
ARLESHEIM (SCHWEIZ)

TELEPHON ARLESHEIM 62.022
TELEGRAMME: CLINIC ARLESHEIM

POSTCHECK-KONTO BASEL V 8487
POSTCHECK-KONTO KARLSRUHE 70.104

ARLESHEIM, den 22. Nov. 1934.

Liebe Dr. Walter!

Seit ein paar Tagen bin ich zurück von meiner langen Erholungsreise. Es war aber gut, dass ich noch diese Reise gemacht habe, ich habe mich sehr erfrischt und bin tatsächlich wieder gesundheitlich so wie ich früher war, kann schon manches wieder aushalten und leisten. Die Mittelmeerreise hat mir ausserordentlich gut getan. Dann der Aufenthalt in Palästina war ein Erlebnis und weil dieser Besuch in der trockenen Jahreszeit stattfand und nicht im Frühjahr, in dem die meisten Menschen Palästina besuchen, hat sie ganz andere Resultate ergeben, als ich selber erwartet habe. Das Land ist ganz, ganz anders in der trockenen Jahreszeit als in der Regenzeit. Es ist in der Trockenzeit ganz dürr, und das was man verbindet mit der Wüste als solcher, kann man wirklich in Judäa - dem Teil, wo Jerusalem liegt - erleben. Wie es sein könnte im Frühjahr, davon hatten wir eine Ahnung, als wir einen ersten Regenguss mitmachten, wodurch geradezu die Erde neu erweckt wurde und man einen wunderschönen Duft emporsteigen fühlte, so als ob man Weihrauch anzündete und die ersten Keime sich mit der Erde verbanden. Dieses Erlebnis war für mich ausserordentlich wichtig und brachte mir zum Bewusstsein, dass es doch heilige Erde ist, diese Palästina-Erde, worauf der Christus gewandelt hat. Sonst ist es sehr schwierig, in dieser trockenen Atmosphäre wo die Aetherwelt sich zurückgezogen hat, die Christus-Jesus-Taten zu erleben. Es drängte sich einem vielmehr die alte jüdische Geschichte auf, und das ist eigentlich riesig interessant, dieses bewusst zu werden. Ich kann mir aber gut denken, dass im Frühjahr, wenn die ganze Vegetation wieder da ist, die Aetherwelt sich also wieder mit der Erde verbunden hat, dass dann auch das Christus-Erlebnis wieder zu finden

Letter from Ita Wegman to Hilma Walter,
page 1, November 22, 1934

123

to the Mediterranean did me a lot of good. Then my stay in Palestine was a powerful experience—and because my visit took place during the dry season and not the spring, when most people visit Palestine, its result was quite different from what I expected. The land is very, very different in the dry period from the rainy season—very arid—and the idea one has of the desert is something you can really experience in Judaea, the area surrounding Jerusalem. We got an inkling of what it might be like in spring when we witnessed one downpour, which awoke the earth to new life so that a beautiful fragrance rose from the earth: it was like lighting incense; you could sense the seeds making their first connection with the earth. This was an extremely important experience for me, and made me aware that this earth of Palestine where Christ wandered is, after all, sacred. Otherwise it is very difficult to sense the deeds of Christ in this arid atmosphere from which the ether world has withdrawn. Instead, the whole of ancient Jewish history was very present, and it is actually of huge interest to become aware of this. I can certainly imagine that in spring, when all the vegetation returns and the etheric world has therefore connected with the earth again, one can also rediscover an experience of Christ.[221] Therefore, I have a longing to go there again at that season.[222] The trip to Palestine has not really come to an end yet. Something remains open—but this lack of completion has a fruitful effect.

I did not go to Egypt. I was unable to connect these two things. And so I went to Italy on my return from Palestine, spending another fortnight there in Naples and Capri to acclimatize myself. I was very surprised to find that these climatic changes—from the temperate zone into almost oriental heat and back again to the temperate zone—did not have any negative effect on my physical state. I found I could walk very well again, perhaps even better than ever. I kept being astonished that it was possible to have been so ill as I was, finding it so difficult to walk from the house in Hondrich to the little

Von Neapel bis Cumä
das Phlegräische Gefilde.
Hier ist die Eingangspforte
griechischer Kultur nach
Italien. Die Gesänge Virgils
und Homers haben hier
ihren Schauplatz gehabt.
Der Golf von Neapel früher
ein Krater gewesen
Deshalb die verschiedenen
Insel, Halbinsel, Buchten
und Vorgebirge vulkanisch.
Auch jetzt noch vulka,
nische Umwälzungen
merkwürdig was hier
alles statt gefunden hat.
Das Zusammen spiel von
Wasser mit steinigen Felsen
von Luft mit Licht in tiefe
Grotten. In den Klüften mit

Ita Wegman: Notebook entry about Capri and Naples

hill and back, but then later to undertake long walks that would have been arduous even for a perfectly healthy person. I experienced Italy as very salutary indeed; and I made the wonderful discovery that this region of Naples, in the Phlegraean landscape, was a doorway through which Greek culture entered. Here one could find one's way back to Homer, and Virgil was at home. I was able to trace the full extent of this Greek cultural influence in the extensive museums there, and in what has been brought to light by excavations—finds from Pompei, Herculaneum and Stabia.

Capri is a jewel. The island is bathed in sunshine and enjoys a glorious climate. Then I traveled from Naples to Rome, because I wanted to end my trip by exploring how Christianity continued, how it spread and what became of it later. There, too, I had some rich experiences. There, you can find everything necessary for studying early Christian history and art, along with the impact of the Caesars who lived at that time and received an initiation they themselves forcibly took. It is *this* Rome that I wished to study in particular.

Having been there, too, for another fortnight, it was time for me to return home, and I did so with joyful gratitude because I myself felt a sense of completion, and at the same time had a feeling that my presence was also needed here. I was received with the greatest warmth here, and was much moved. Having been away for 9 months like this, it is easy to think people will have forgotten you; and then to find that this was not so did me a great deal of good inwardly, helping to make my return easy and joyful. Therefore, I have engaged fully here again with my whole being, and I do hope that a period of fruitful work can begin for me. In the near future I will have to go to Holland to visit my mother, who also became very ill during my absence. Although she is now better, I don't want to postpone my visit to her. I will visit Hamborn on the same trip—that would be on December 1 and 2—to speak with the curative educators there. I received a telegram from Zeylmans today asking me to meet with the committee of working groups during my visit to Holland. Thus things are coming toward me again and I will gradually have to find my way into all the changes that have occurred while I was away.

From Kalmia I have heard that there has been much to do in Clent. You also wrote to me about this. Hopefully a calmer period has arrived now and you can rest a little. I'd be grateful if you can pass on my news in this letter to Herr and Frau Geuter and Wilson. I will write to everyone soon. Warm thanks to you for your bouquet of flowers that Sister Hedwig brought me on your behalf.

Very, very warm greetings, dear Dr. Walter,

Your Ita Wegman

P.S. It would be wonderful if you could come here for Christmas, but I presume it would be difficult? I have a great longing to celebrate a warm, deeply reflective Christmas, especially now after my illness and travels. Do consider it. It would be so lovely if you and your sister could be here.

Your I.W.

That week, Ita Wegman drove to Holland to see her gravely ill mother (who celebrated her 83rd birthday on November 27 [223]) and to hold conversations with Willem Zeylmans. Then she went on to Hamborn and—at the urgent request of Heinrich Hardt— also drove further to the curative institute in Altefeld near Jena, and finally to Eisenach. Back in Arlesheim she renewed her correspondence with the anthroposophic physicians and curative educators, encouraging them individually to persevere and to maintain their capacities for social community (*"The memory I have [of Gerswalde] when I got there was of such a strong and vital fullness of life that it seems inconceivable to me that no solution to the problems can be found"*[224]). She concerned herself with the clinic, the patients there, and the numerous social and financial difficulties. "And so I have engaged fully here again with my whole being, and I do hope that a period of fruitful work can begin for me."

A letter Ita Wegman wrote in the second week of December to one of her experienced and much-valued nurses—who had temporarily left the clinic while she was away and whom Wegman was very keen to bring back as soon as possible—shows how intensively she engaged with the concerns in Arlesheim very shortly after her return:

Dear Sister Hedwig,

I have been back at home, in the clinic, for a few weeks now, and was very sorry to find you are not here. When I asked about you I was told that you had taken on the nursing of your sick mother, but that it might be possible for you to return here. Since I value your work very highly, I am going to ask when you could come back to us. If you can't leave your mother alone there, I would even suggest that you might bring her with you when you return. We might find a way of arranging things so that this would be manageable for you. On the other hand, if this suggestion is impossible, I wonder if your sister could take over there for a little, while you give an intensive induction for one or two nurses here in the clinic. Your absence here has actually had catastrophic repercussions for the outpatients coming from Basel; and here one sees how vital a nurse is as a physician's assistant, continuing the latter's work by taking on some treatments and by proper understanding of how to relate to patients. Thus, good results arise from their collaboration.

Please give serious consideration to what I write here, which is closely connected with the very life of the clinic— and especially important now that many patients are no longer able to get here from Germany. If we do not take things strongly in hand, grave times may dawn for the clinic. My long absence, changes of physicians and nurses, and the difficulties in the Society have naturally all combined to threaten our very existence.

I hope you are well and that your parents are also feeling better, and I would be pleased to hear from you soon.

Warm greetings,

Your I. Wegman, MD

On the following day, too, December 13, Ita Wegman sent another long letter to a member of staff she valued highly and who was no longer working in Arlesheim. This was the physician Ilse Knauer, one of the former "young doctors" and part of the esoteric core of the Medical Section, who had left the clinic primarily because of her own illness, to seek treatment from her brother Siegfried Knauer, a physician in Berlin. Ilse Knauer and Ita Wegman had embarked together on a trip to the Greece Mystery sites in the spring of 1932. Knauer was an outstandingly knowledgeable and skilful physician, and possessed an original, distinctive faculty of judgment. In the letter to her, Ita Wegman again described the situation in Arlesheim—though now in clear and nuanced detail—and spoke of her recent experiences in Palestine and Italy, as well as of her altered stance toward the Goetheanum:

Dear Dr. Knauer,

It feels very strange to me to be here and not to find you among the physicians. I am really very sorry indeed about this. I would be so glad to hear how you are and what you are doing in Berlin. Might you like to come to us here at Christmas? You are warmly invited, and we would all be pleased if you could accept this invitation.

Thank God, I am fully restored now. I recovered my physical health in the Swiss mountains but then had a great longing to forget the bitter experiences of recent times that still weighed on my soul, and to absorb new ideas and outlooks. I was only able to do so by not connecting too quickly with Arlesheim again, but to embark on a long trip following

Mattheus sie daran erinnernd
das Jesus von gleichem Blute
ist, seine Generationen bis zu
Abraham verfolgt werden
kann. Er richtet sich zugleicher
Zeit auch gegen sie, dadurch das
er ihnen den Vorwurf herunter
schleudert das sie den Herrn
nicht erkant haben. Es ist
natürlich der Jesus Christus,
der so handelt, aber es ist
Mattheus der diese Leute von
Jesus Christus sieht und es beschließt
Es wird kräftig gegen dem
Pharisäertum gekämpft.
Es ist immer wieder das
Mattheus Evangelium, das man
in Palästina auf Schritt und
Tritt begegnet. Den Unverstand
den die Juden dem Christus Jesus
e zeigen.

Ita Wegman: Notebook entry about Christology

my convalescence. Therefore, I traveled to the Mediterranean, a journey made possible by dear friends from England. I was able to conclude these travels with a stay in Palestine—as you know, I had long wanted to visit this land—where I stayed for a fortnight; and then returned home via Italy. I was welcomed back with the greatest warmth. After this I had to go to Holland to visit my elderly mother whom I had not seen all this time, and I included a visit to Hamborn in this trip; and then returned here again. That was about a week ago; and now I'm sitting here and am glad to be back among dear, old friends. The way we're working has changed, much more focused, and unified—no doubt due to the grave events that we experienced. In the future it seems my work will be no different from before except that I will focus more on Arlesheim. I am well disposed toward the Goetheanum and the executive council, and always have been; nor will I look for conflict with it. It has always been my view that the Christmas Foundation Meeting had to be realized with five executive council members and I was therefore always in favour of this complement of five. But if the majority does not accept this there's nothing to be done but go along with that and look for ways to work fruitfully. I have no wish to fight. I want to try to think and act in a Christian way. Despite all difficulties the clinic is usually full. There are fewer out-patients, which is not surprising since you, Suchantke, and I have not been there. Now, however, numbers are increasing and so I hope that the work will proceed energetically and we will have overcome this crisis.

I would be most interested of all to hear how your health is—has it improved? Was your brother's treatment successful? I have been thinking of you often, remembering the lovely trip we took together in Greece. This time in Greece I only visited Athens, then traveled to Constantinople and visited Rhodes—very interesting as there are many traces in Rhodes of the Crusaders and Knights of St. John. Rhodes itself is enchantingly beautiful. The climate is wonderful, and many people come there from all over the globe to relax and convalesce. Palestine was also a powerful experience— so very different from Greece. You are really in the Orient, and encounter very ancient history at every step. Besides this, contemporary life there is also interesting: Mohammedans, Jews, and Christians live cheek by jowl, without any mutual understanding. Then also, sadly, the Christians do not understand each other either, and so one finds a caricature of true Christianity; and in Mohameddanism and Judaism an opposition to this Christianity.

On my way back I stayed in southern Italy, on the island of Capri, in order to acclimatize myself as preparation for returning to a European climate. In the Phlegraean region you can once again experience Greek culture, which flowered there after it had faded from Greece itself under Roman dominion. It was actually a wonderful experience to meet this unexpectedly. There was much to discover of that era from the excavations of Pompeii and Herculaneum, and Capri itself is a beautiful jewel.

You will know that coral grows close by, near Sicily, and the coral industry has grown up around it. I was reminded of an old belief connected with coral—that it benefits the blood, hematosis, if you wear it. Therefore, it occurred to me that you ought to wear a necklace of it; and I indulged myself by bringing one back for you. I enclose it with my warm greetings. I do hope this old belief is true! Perhaps you will have time to write to me at some point; and it would give me even greater pleasure if you could get away at Christmas and come to visit us here.

With very many warm greetings, in friendship and love,
Your I. Wegman

In further letters written during the second week in December, Ita Wegman stressed the fact that after her long illness and her travels she felt ready for a really new beginning ("*For my part, I am fortunate to be well again, and there was no doubt significance in my enforced withdrawal from everything for a period. I experienced this as benevolent grace, as I did, likewise, the chance to fill my soul with impressions of distant lands, which soothed my recent bitter experiences in the Society. And so I am now able to begin afresh."*[225] *"I wanted to see before me a clearly marked path that I must pursue in the future. And I was unable to return until I could see this path"*[226]). On one occasion she gave Eleanor Merry a hint of the spiritual turning point during her recent illness (*"Although I thought that my illness marked the end of my work on earth, an experience I had showed me that this was not so"*[227]), and suggested that, despite all the conflicts in the Society, there was a continuing possibility of "connecting in the spirit directly with Rudolf Steiner" and thus working for the spiritual continuity of anthroposophic endeavor. In this context, Wegman also spoke of her specific task in Arlesheim, which had become clearer to her in the past months as she recovered from her illness, and to which she wished to devote herself exclusively in the future:

> It is absolutely necessary for there to be a place here in Arlesheim where Rudolf Steiner can continue working as he intended, so that through us the continuity of this intention can be realized. This is, surely, a task for which I must go on living. Whatever may cohere around this work must gradually become evident and will do so quite naturally.

In these letters to a few of her trusted companions within the anthroposophic movement, Wegman repeatedly mentioned the ongoing, strengthening effect on her of her travels, without ever really detailing or revealing the spiritual nature of her experiences (*"I can say that I am really very grateful to have had this opportunity. The wealth of experiences I was granted has been hugely valuable for my further path. The verse 'Practice spirit recollection,' which Rudolf Steiner gave us at the Christmas Foundation*

*Meeting, really is true. One can practice this on a journey; and
so a trip of this kind becomes, more than recuperation, a voyage of knowledge and increasing insight, so that traveling itself
acquires a greater purpose"*[228]). Finally, six days before the Holy
Nights began, Ita Wegman sent a last, lengthy and subtly var-
ied account of her travels to Walter Johannes and Nora Stein in
London. Wegman knew that Stein—who had a profound knowledge of history and had himself often worked on related themes—
would understand and appreciate the spiritual background to her
studies on Capri, Naples, and Rome. Here too, though, Wegman's
warm, detailed letter offered only hints of her spiritual experiences, remaining silent about the hidden depths of her own being,
and refraining also from accentuating the political aspect of these
years (*"My letters are often opened at present"*):

Arlesheim, December 18, 1934

My dear friends Dr. Stein and Frau Nora,

The distance from England seems very great when one
would so like to see and speak with one another! It was easier
of course when you were in Stuttgart and we could reach
each other by car in a couple of hours. I was hoping to see
you all soon after my return but this hasn't been possible, and
now I will have to wait until February, when I'm coming to
England.

I really am well again now. It seems to me almost a mira-
cle that this is possible. When I was ill I did indeed think that
my work on earth was at an end. But a spiritual experience I
had told me this was not so; and from that moment on I was
able to get a grip on myself again and take my own recovery
in hand. My time in the Swiss mountains did me an enormous
amount of good. I really found the healing there that I needed.
But at the same time my soul was longing for new impressions
in order to push recent bitter experiences into the background,
and even to forget them. At this point, in a wonderful way, I

was given the chance to travel to the Mediterranean, followed by a visit to Palestine. I have to say that this trip and my visit to Palestine were extremely rich in impressions. Inwardly, I experienced some very important contrasts: impressions one could absorb in the high mountains and others, again, on the plains and the water; and then also to travel from the temperate zone to the Orient—for one can regard Palestine already as part of that. Contrasts between wet and dry, cold and hot—I passed through all of these consciously in my soul. I was able to experience whole cultures on this trip, and I found it really valuable to let everything rise anew inwardly in me through Anthroposophy. In Palestine at this season—I must stress that this was the dry season, when a desert character comes to the fore—you experience things very geologically. And this was why the Old Testament was much more vivid there than the life of Jesus Christ—I encountered traces of it everywhere. In the arid atmosphere, the experience of Jesus Christ seemed to have withdrawn from the earth. And since this dry, desert heat also shrank one's ether body, the connection between the etheric within one and the etheric in the cosmos seemed to be broken. Dr. Steiner also speaks of how one ought to go to Palestine in the early spring in order to experience something of the Christ through the ether realm's first contact with the earth. That is the only moment when you can still get hold of it—whereas in midsummer, fall and winter this is no longer possible. But the other aspect, the generations leading to Jesus Christ, is something one can especially feel at this time of fall. My experiences there were so rich that I did not go to Egypt afterward as I had originally intended.

I felt the need to experience how Christianity spread through the influence of Rome. Therefore, I traced these historical developments by traveling to Brindisi in Italy after Palestine, and from there to Naples and Capri. I also wished to experience the contrast between a majestic and tranquil mountain such as the Jungfrau, enthroned on high in white snow, and Vesuvius, where all is destructive beauty and one has the sense that it could at any moment wreak the most incredible havoc. The whole region is volcanic, and the experience of it indescribable—for instance in the region called Solfatara, which is said to be a burned-out crater. Here and there are places where the ground has caved in and you find yourself in a sort of crater basin where fluid earth bubbles in great heat, hissing and boiling; the stink of sulfur and sulfur smoke was everywhere. If you touch the ground with a flame, it starts smoking where before there was nothing at all to be seen; and at the same time everything round you also starts smoking due to the volcanic connections forming under the ground on which you're standing. It is really incredible to experience this. I also found this area extraordinarily interesting because of the influx of Greek culture on the Phlegraean coast. Homer still walked here, and Virgil lived here. There are sacred places such as the cave of the Cumaean sibyl, and above it the temple of Apollo—a kind of echo of Delphi, and yet also different again. Greek culture, Greek finds in the rubble of Pompeii and Herculaneum: the museum is full of these excavated artefacts—you feel as if you're in Greece. In fact, there is a greater wealth of treasures here than in Greece itself. These were all wonderful experiences. In Capri you are plunged into a quite different atmosphere. Here, where Augustus and Tiberius had their pleasure palaces, the Roman Caesars awaken in one. The difference between Capri and the Phlegraean coast is really very striking. Capri is a jewel in its beauty, its geology very interesting, and its climate extremely pleasant and beneficial. From Capri I went to Rome to witness the spread of early Christianity there. I have been to Rome several times, but have never before had such a rewarding visit. I wanted to seek out signs of early Christianity and the Roman Empire, and was extremely well rewarded in this; and returned from my trip with deep satisfaction. It is true that by traveling one can really practice the Christmas Foundation Stone verse

Ita Wegman's notebook

Solfatara
ist eine vulkanische
Gegend nicht weit von
Pozzuoli eine ½ Stunde
von Neapel entfernt.
Solfatara ist der Krater
eines noch nicht ganz
erloschenen Vulkans
Der Boden des
Kraters klingt hohl, wenn
man darauf geht.
Ein merkwürdiges Gefühl
man geht also auf dem
Boden eines Kraters;
von Zeit zu Zeit bricht
irgend wo der Boden
durch und es entsteht dann
eine art Öffnung wie ein
Becken mit siedendem
flüssiger ... die rauch...
und brodelt
überall durch kleine Öff...

"Practice spirit recollection." In this sense my convalescence vacation was also a journey of deepening insight.

Now I've told you a lot about me, and yet at the same time I'd like to hear all your news. I know that both of you are very busy in London, that various things have been worked through and you have achieved a great deal. I have gained the impression that things in England are generally going well. I heard that there are good developments in Clent and that Kent Terrace is improved by the new staffing and seems to be consolidating. Dr. Nunhoefer is getting an English degree [in medicine]. The Society is able to expand. So one gets the sense that everything there is progressing extremely well, and I'm very pleased about this. At present it seems to me

Ita Wegman:
Notebook entry
about the Caesars

that the focus of my work has to be more intensively here in Arlesheim. I will have to engage in battle with the demons here, and safeguard a small spot where Dr. Steiner's work can continue as he wished it to, so that the thread of connection with his intentions does not break. If too much is relinquished here then it won't be possible to ensure this. There has to be some continuity with Rudolf Steiner after all, and a part of this continuity—though naturally only a small part—I also see as residing in me.

What are you doing at Christmas? No doubt your plans have already been made? Wouldn't you like to come to us perhaps? That would be really lovely. You would be welcomed here with much joy and warmth. Since I have no idea what time you have available, you'd have to write and let me know, and then I would try to sort out funding for your travel. Although things are difficult here it seems to me nevertheless that a great deal of spiritual help is shining down upon us; and with this hope, too, I am entering Christmastide. I hope things are looking good for you too! Is Frau Nora's health better now? And how are you Dr. Stein, and dear little Clarissa Johanna—who no doubt is no longer so little but a young lady by now.

Very warm greetings to all three of you. I remain, in friendship and love,

Your

Ita Wegman[229]

≈

In this way Wegman invited many of her friends and acquaintances to come to Arlesheim to experience and celebrate Christmastide (or *"consecration-tide"*[230]) together. Back in November she had already expressed this desire to Hilma Walter (*"I have a great longing to celebrate a warm, deeply reflective Christmas, especially now after my illness and travels"*[231]).

Ita Wegman wished to give the whole period of the Holy Nights a Christological form, and make this accessible to the community as active Christ principle. While this was similar to all the previous years,[232] it was now informed by still greater resolve, embedded in the deeper context of her experiences in Palestine, and at the same time wholly future-oriented ("I want to try to think and act in a Christian way"[233]). Thus she wrote to the most diverse people and invited them to attend spiritual-scientific study on every evening of the Holy Nights, despite the very tense political situation: "Although things are difficult here it seems to me nevertheless that a great deal of spiritual help is shining down upon us; and with this hope, too, I am entering Christmastide."

KLINISCH-THERAPEUTISCHES INSTITUT
ARLESHEIM (SCHWEIZ)

ARLESHEIM, den 14. Dez. 1934.

TELEPHON ARLESHEIM 62.022
TELEGRAMME: CLINIC ARLESHEIM

POSTCHECK-KONTO BASEL V 6487
POSTCHECK-KONTO KARLSRUHE 70.104

Lieber Herr Geuter!

Ihrer Einladung, aus Holland nach England zu kommen, um
Sie zu besuchen, konnte ich nicht Folge leisten, nicht nur deshalb, weil ich den Brief zu spät bekam, sondern auch deshalb
weil doch, nachdem ich so lange Zeit weg gewesen war aus der
Klinik, nun jetzt eine längere Anwesenheit hier selbstverständ-
lich war. Der Besuch nach Holland zu meiner Mutter war ja eine
absolute Notwendigkeit, weil sie nach meiner Krankheit mich doch
gern wiedersehen wollte. Auf dem Rückweg war ich dann noch in
Hamborn, wo einige Heilpädagogen zusammengekommen sind. Dann
fuhr ich wieder nach Arlesheim und hoffe hier einige Zeit ruhig
arbeiten zu können.

Ich habe mit Freude gehört, dass die Arbeit in Clent
immer weiter gut vorangegangen ist. Das ist ja ein grosses Glück,
dass in England dieses noch möglich ist. Deutschland hat ja schon
mit ungeheuren Schwierigkeiten zu kämpfen, um wirtschaftlich bestehen zu können. Die Arbeit in den Instituten in Deutschland
geht auch gut von statten, nur haben doch verschiedene jetzt mit
wirtschaftlichen Schwierigkeiten zu kämpfen. In der Weihnachtszeit
werden wohl verschiedene der Heilpädagogen auch hierherkommen.
Bei den Meisten ist das natürlich mehr nach Weihnachten gedacht,
weil sie sich sonst nicht freimachen können. Und da richte ich
auch die Frage an Sie: Wie steht es mit Ihnen? Wird niemand von
Ihnen sich freimachen können, auch einmal hierherzukommen? Wir
würden uns sehr freuen, wenn das möglich sein könnte. Man kann
dann auch manches noch besprechen, was per Brief vielleicht nicht

*Letter from Ita Wegman to Fried Geuter (a curative educator
in Clent), inviting him to join the Christmas meeting in
Arlesheim, December 14, 1934, page 1*

so leicht geht und auch zu Missverständnissen führen könnte.

Zu meinem Bedauern habe ich von Dr. Walter gehört, dass
es Ihrer Frau nicht so ganz gut geht und dass sie eventuell
sich einer kleinen Operation unterwerfen sollte. Für Ihre Frau
sind bestimmte heilgymnastische Widerstands-Uebungen heilsam,
die mit den Beinen zu machen sind und die Dr. Walter, wenn sie
sie ihr noch nicht gegeben hat, einmal zeigen sollte. Ich er-
innere hiermit nur Dr. Walter daran.

Was mich selber betrifft, so bin ich in der glücklichen
Lage, wieder gesund zu sein, und hat es wohl eine Bedeutung gehabt, dass ich eine Zeit lang von allem durch force majeure
entfernt wurde. Dieses habe ich als eine grosse Gnade empfunden,
ebenso die Möglichkeit, meine Seele mit Eindrücken zu füllen,
die ich von weiten Ländern holen konnte, wodurch die bitteren
Erlebnisse innerhalb der Gesellschaft wieder verdrängt wurden.
So kann ich jetzt wieder neu anfangen.

Mit den besten Wünschen für ein schönes Weihnachtsfest
verbleibe ich mit herzlichen Grüssen an Ihre Frau, an Michael
Wilson, Mr. und Mrs. Wilson, Dr. Walter, und die vielen lieben
Mitarbeiter

in Freundschaft

Ihre
I. Wegman

*Letter from Ita Wegman to Fried Geuter,
December 14, 1934, page 2*

*"One picture shows Jerusalem. You can see the great temple—
it used to be the temple of Solomon and is now a mosque."*

In all these letters there was great tranquility and assurance in
and around Ita Wegman, and also a Christian composure regarding the events of the last general meeting of the Anthroposophical
Society, the attacks and slander she had experienced and the
ongoing processes of collapse. This transformed stance comes
to expression not only in the pre-Christmas letter to Ilse Knauer
already quoted (*"I am well disposed toward the Goetheanum and
the executive council, and always have been; nor will I look for
conflict with it. It has always been my view that the Christmas
Foundation Meeting had to be realized with five executive council
members and I was therefore always in favour of this complement of five. But if the majority does not accept this there's nothing to be done but go along with that and look for ways to work
fruitfully"*) but also in one to Jules Sauerwein. Here, for the first
time, Ita Wegman connected this new outlook directly with her
experiences and studies of the previous months, explaining:

> There is still conflict in Dornach no doubt, but I am no longer
> in the least bothered about this. For me, conflict and battle

"The other shows the Mount of Olives; and the path you see there is the one Jesus Christ often took at sundown. If you ascend the Mount of Olives and go farther, you arrive at Bethany, where Martha, Mary, and their brother Lazarus lived."

in the physical world are maya. Spiritually things look very different, and I adhere to this spiritual stance and arrange my life with a sense of faithful connection to Rudolf Steiner. Christianity is still far from being understood. You gain a deep realization of this from being in Palestine, from seeing that there is nothing left there of what occurred—no understanding; and that the spread of Christianity outward from Rome has not been accomplished in the spirit of Jesus Christ either. Nor can one expect, therefore, that anthroposophists who now hear something of esoteric Christianity for the first time will already have the strength and courage to live this esoteric Christianity, which after all is very strongly related to Anthroposophy. We can also see the conflicts and battles in this light, since souls are in fact dissatisfied with themselves, and then project this outward in dissatisfaction with others, and in battling with others instead of battling with themselves. One can always work on behalf of Anthroposophy and Rudolf Steiner, also in outward life—there is no need to work alongside these anthroposophists to do so.[234]

On December 20, still, Ita Wegman sent Hilma Walter two photographs from her Palestine travels ("*One picture shows Jerusalem. You can see the great temple—it used to be the temple of Solomon and is now a mosque. The other shows the Mount of Olives; and the path you see there is the one Jesus Christ often took at sundown. If you ascend the Mount of Olives and carry on further you come to Bethany, where Martha, Mary and their brother Lazarus lived*" [see page 142]). Four days later she stood before the bright candles of the Christmas tree, and after waiting a long time in silence and stillness while the community gathered, began her address at 9 p.m. This was to be the spiritual and Christological foundation for future Christmas gatherings in Arlesheim. In her introductory words, Ita Wegman reminded her listeners that the forthcoming year 1935 would bring with it the thirty-third recurrence of the spiritual impulse that Rudolf Steiner had initiated in 1902 in his work *Christianity as Mystical Fact* and had continued to elaborate throughout his life. Then she went on (according to her preparatory notebook entries):

We therefore bear a great responsibility, not just for our own self-development, which should proceed without pause or inhibition, but for ensuring also that the spiritual stream is not extinguished. This means that what Rudolf Steiner created should remain connected with him so that this knowledge works to kindle light in us, to shine within us, and forms a bridge with the world of spirit.

And speaking these words to you I would like them to be understood in the sense of our standing before a new beginning. We must experience the Christmas period as filled with spirit, intensely connecting ourselves with the spiritual wealth

die restlos und ohne Hemmungen vor
sich gehen sollen, sondern wir haben auch
dafür Sorge zu tragen, dass der Geistesstrom
nicht erlöscht. Dass das, was von
R. Steiner geschaffen worden ist mit ihm
verbunden bleibt, dass dieses Wissen
in uns wirkt die Brücke bildet
zur geistigen Welt.
Und wenn ich jetzt diese Worte zu Ihnen
spreche, dann möchte ich es in dem Sinne
verstanden haben, dass wir vor einem
neuen Anfang stehen. Wir müssen
die Weihnachtszeit geisterfüllt erleben
uns innerlich verbinden mit R. Steiner's
Geistesgut,
... zu verstehen was er gewollt hat
...
... Mögen wir zusammen einen Bund
bilden von Menschen, die aufrichtig
dieses wollen, die bewusst diese
mögen die Früchte gute sein! Möge die geistige
Welt uns erhören, die Bitte, die ich jetzt aus...

Notebook entry by Ita Wegman, December 24, 1934

145

given by Rudolf Steiner. We must let this come to new life again in our hearts, seeking to understand what he wished: seeking to inwardly experience anew the Mystery secrets of South, North, East, and West and bring them into synthesis. In doing so, we can again experience Anthroposophy illuminating our hearts.

Let us form together a bond between people who honestly desire this (who consciously take up this work). May the fruits be good! May the world of spirit hear the petition that I now speak at this Christmastide, asking that it mercifully accept our efforts and encompass us in its wise light. May we succeed in bringing together the building stones of this work to construct the edifice of work that will become better and more intense each year as our powers grow. If we consciously intend this, we will unite to realize it freely and without compulsion.

Thus, spiritual community building was, in a sense, inaugurated "anew" in Arlesheim.[235]

3

"Willing, Selfless Sacrifice"

1935

"*I am very well once more. I have found my way back to myself from severe illness and will now remain unerringly loyal to Rudolf Steiner, as well as doing what I consider would be right in his eyes.*" (January 10, 1935)[236]

"*Spiritual beings need nourishment, spiritual sustenance that only human souls can give them, which can proceed from a certain stance of soul with a selfless will for sacrifice. When souls can affirm the severe trials that approach them, something good can develop for the future. This, I believe, is the test we must prevail in and upon which much may depend in the future.*" (April 10, 1935)[237]

As a conclusion to the spiritual-scientific and Christological studies and gatherings of the Christmas and New Year period, anthroposophic friends of Ita Wegman in the Dutch, English, and German Societies arrived in Arlesheim on January 5 and 6 for talks and meetings. The conversations focused on world events and developments since 1902, but also the last period of Rudolf Steiner's life, the weeks and months since March 30 of the previous year, and the beginning of the severe conflicts in the Society.[238] On January 6, the intention was to agree and fix on a strategy for future action with Ita Wegman—in the sense of developing a purposeful and organized way forward. However, Wegman was not comfortable with this idea despite her real joy at seeing everyone again and all the hopes and expectations that were being invested in her. More than ever before she felt herself very distant from this "closed group,"[239] sensing that she did not belong to it. Wegman had not led any resolute battle for the Goetheanum and the General Anthroposophical Society since 1934; nor had she done so, really, in all the preceding years, despite her dynamic offensive and her world-oriented commitment since Steiner's death, and her consistent efforts to perceive and realize the tasks personally entrusted to her by Steiner.

Wegman was aware of having behaved in some ways too quickly and decisively after 1925, with too much will and too little circumspection, albeit—despite all allegations—with the best of selfless intentions. It had also long been apparent to her that she had repeatedly found herself in difficult situations in which, ultimately, she had been compelled to defend and loyally support particular individuals' efforts that she herself considered to be mistaken and inappropriate—both in form and sometimes also in essence. While much (though not all) in her own thinking and actions had been characterized by purposeful necessity and consistency, after all the events and experiences of recent years Ita Wegman was no longer willing to participate further in the conflicts surrounding the Goetheanum.[240] On the feast of Epiphany, when the English Society presented its detailed proposals for an offensive, she inwardly withdrew,[241] suffering heart problems and other renewed signs of illness. Ita Wegman felt deeply connected, as she did with few other companions, with Daniel Nicol Dunlop, George Adams Kaufmann, Walter Johannes Stein and Montague Wheeler, and knew that these people had pure intentions. Nevertheless she refused to work further on the English proposals, and after a short pause for reflection telegraphed on January 7 to decline attendance at the general meeting in London and a reading of Class Lessons as she had been requested. On January 9, after Walter Johannes Stein had left, she wrote to him in explanation as follows:

> Something lives in me that is entirely different from what was proposed, and so I am unable to resolve to work further as if nothing had occurred—as if I had just gone for a little holiday trip. I was granted a glimpse into the world of spirit, and encountered Christ and Rudolf Steiner who sent me back to earth and expected me to act different from how I had done hitherto. I experienced great disappointment when I gathered from Dunlop's talk that the movement in England is after all seeking to assume an outward form without distinguishing the soul qualities of the diverse people in it. This means that the Christmas Foundation Meeting has really been abolished. The karmic connection between Rudolf Steiner and me is truly an essential part of the Christmas Foundation Meeting. Many people at the Goetheanum know this very well, and

Draft letter from Ita Wegman to Walter Johannes Stein,
January 9, 1935

it has given rise to the hatred consistently practiced against
me. The hatred will remain until the Christmas Foundation
Meeting has successfully been erased from members' memories. This would allow a falsification of history to be undertaken, to *prevent* people from experiencing karma. It would
have been enormously valuable if England had grasped this
and undertaken not to forget the Christmas Foundation
Meeting at any cost. Though it cannot be perpetuated in its
totality, it can continue to work if we give serious credence
to each and every member of the executive council in terms
of his karma with the Doctor, or with the Society, or other
karmic connections.

Although we do not know exactly what was proposed to Ita Wegman in the first week of January, her further letters show the extent to which, for esoteric reasons, she rejected any reconfiguration within the given executive council (*"I will not go along with reconfiguring the Society. I feel an inner urge to remain true to Dr. Steiner's intentions. This is how things presently appear spiritually to me"*[242]). Instead she held firmly to the form and meaningful spiritual entity that Rudolf Steiner had created at the end of 1923. As on certain occasions after her recovery in 1934, at the beginning of 1935 Wegman repeatedly emphasized the specific karmic relationships of the separate executive council members in their overall significance for the General Anthroposophical Society (*"Now I have often told members why the executive council back then, when newly founded, was chosen by Steiner as it was. It was for this reason alone: because he wished to reach new people with each new executive council member he appointed. Through the karma of each individual—which thereby comes into effect— many people can be reached"*[243]). This was a spiritual reality which she wished to be consistently observed, irrespective of the fact that this reality had been put out of action at the last general meeting, if not before (*"The movement at the Goetheanum can run on as smoothly as anything, but it has nevertheless sundered itself from what the Doctor intended with the Christmas Foundation Meeting"*[244]). Reviewing her annoyance and renewed bodily crisis in the days around January 6, Ita Wegman wrote a little later to Daniel Nicol Dunlop:

> Having been ill and not attending any meetings, I found myself in the presence of something that was new for me, and brought me into a new situation. This was the realization that the idea of the Christmas Foundation Meeting—which is no doubt broken on earth but still exists in the world of spirit— was no longer at the forefront of consideration by you and

the other members. While I can certainly understand this, it was a new situation I was meeting, one I found myself in for the first time.[245]

The proposal that English members had evidently once again made to her—to edit and publish documentation of her karmic work with Rudolf Steiner[246] and thus to present an account of the central karmic connection that was a "key aspect of the Christmas Foundation Meeting"—was one she decisively rejected; at the same time she regarded her work in England as being provisionally at an end, in spiritual terms. As she wrote to Walter Johannes Stein on January 9, in the future she wished to wait and see whether the "karmic orientation is seeking to take root somewhere else or kindle anew," adding in a passing remark: "I hope you understand me, and will remain faithful to me; I mean, to my being."

Ita Wegman's stance, once again, bore no trace of resignation or passivity. She had grown further through the inner developmental movements of the previous year, and reached an ultimate certainty ("*We often have to battle endlessly before things stand clearly before us*"[247]). She demonstrated the signs of great renunciation and of extraordinary focus on her own spiritual life task, independent of majority views and strategic considerations. Wegman was sustained by what she experienced as inner loyalty to the process at work in the Christmas Foundation Meeting, wishing to preserve this for the future irrespective of the current situation at the Goetheanum ("*What I have to do, in fact, is to gather around me*

*the people who still bear within them the right, true connection
with the Christmas Foundation Meeting. Their number may be
small, but I also feel that if this does not happen then something
of spiritual value will go under: a spiritual stream that I must
safeguard and that I wish to carry onward in a pure form*"[248]).
That Ita Wegman did indeed regard the legacy of the Christmas
Foundation Meeting as spiritually inextinguishable, and that she
thought it might be realistically possible to realize it again in later
times, is clear from various hints in her letters at the beginning of
1935. For instance, as part of more extensive comments she wrote
to Gerswalde:

> When I returned after being ill, I pondered for a long time
> on what might still be done with the desperate anthropo-
> sophic situation. The following solution suggested itself:
> that the Christmas Foundation Meeting no longer functions
> as a totality but that the fact remains—whether or not one
> wishes to acknowledge it—that the executive council mem-
> bers are united with Dr. Steiner though a ceremonial deed
> [and] within the Anthroposophical Society must under-
> take the work they are responsible for. If each individual
> accomplishes their work in the right way, as Rudolf Steiner
> intended, and the people who have a karmic connection with
> this work collaborate and really safeguard the right unfold-
> ing of these things, then despite all the difficulties a time
> will eventually come when a unity arises once more, even if,
> perhaps, in our next life.

A few weeks later she wrote in a similar vein to Herbert Hahn:

> With the Christmas Foundation Meeting Dr. Steiner prefig-
> ured a work of the future that it was not possible to real-
> ize because old powers did not allow it. This is an insight
> one must come to. Perhaps this future work will only happen
> once some people have been made free of the Society.[249]

In addition to her esoteric mission to lead the Medical Section, the tasks that Ita Wegman continued to regard as intrinsically hers included primarily her responsibility for the First Class, and thus for the future of what Rudolf Steiner called the spiritual "School of Michael."[250] Wegman's refusal to attend the English general meeting at the beginning of February and to give Class Lessons there (*"I have written to Mr. Dunlop in as kind and tactful a way as possible so that he does not take offense at my refusal. I remain connected with him as ever"*[251]) was, not least, an expression of her increasing awareness that the impulse of the Class should not be confused with the destiny of the Anthropophical Society, but should instead be seen, preserved and realized in its pure, intrinsic nature.[252]

Ita Wegman's continual references to the "impulse of the Christmas Foundation Meeting" implied that the whole executive council had esoteric significance in its karmic connection with Rudolf Steiner; but equally and especially it suggested a duty and obligation toward the Class, whose founding the spiritual world had made possible.[253] Only a few of those in close proximity to Ita Wegman were sufficiently aware that this duty and obligation was one which Rudolf Steiner had entrusted to her in a very comprehensive and binding way,[254] and, indeed, that it was connected to a very great degree with Wegman's karmic awakening in 1923, and thus with her whole destiny. On January 27, Ita Wegman invited responsible colleagues of hers in Arlesheim to an intimate meeting, during which she spoke for the first time of processes of inner clarification that she had undergone in recent weeks, and announced that the Class Lessons would begin again. Werner Pache subsequently noted in his diary:

> [She] spoke of the spiritual fraternity and the Christmas Foundation Meeting, of keeping complete faith with this. She

herself wishes this, she said—had finally decided to give the Class Lessons again, but in free form. A beginning was made with this.

Two days later, Ita Wegman wrote a detailed letter about all these things to Gertrud Goyert in Cologne who, along with her husband, had hoped Wegman would visit Cologne following her trip to Holland and Hamborn in the first half of January, to hold intensive discussions about processes at work in the Society. In her letter, Wegman made it clear that she was not yet in a position, or willing, to extend her working travels—but instead had a sense that she needed to focus her spiritual work in Arlesheim (*"I also have a great need to focus my work intensively at a particular place rather than traveling around everywhere and doing one thing here, giving advice there. Instead of this I need to unfold my powers entirely at one specific point, and gather around me the people who also think this"*[255]). At the same time she stressed the need for her to adopt her own, intrinsically "neutral" position in the further disputes in the Society: a stance that would allow her to fulfil her specific esoteric task, which had grown clearer to her inwardly during 1934 and in recent weeks. She wrote:

> I say this with all love...that I do not wish to ally myself with any party in a way that might give rise to a particular form. The old Society expelled me, and so one naturally cannot expect much from that quarter. The others, who have regrouped, are strong and will I am sure work in the right way, too. But there are a great many who do not wish to bind themselves to one faction or another in this way, but who hold a picture of Rudolf Steiner deep in their hearts, and do not want to commit themselves already to an existing form.... I wish to unite as a free human being with all who value working with a colleague of Rudolf Steiner's. The moment I enter into an express form that does not originate

directly with Rudolf Steiner, I have the feeling that I am distancing myself from him. These are hugely subtle thoughts that I am expressing now, which can also be misunderstood. People may say I want to keep something special in reserve for myself. However, none of that is true. I am speaking from my deepest, inmost being. By seeking not to ally myself with a particular party, I will be able to try to give the Class Lessons again here and there; and this is in every respect an absolutely neutral spiritual treasure. If one party regards this spiritual treasure as a power impulse and another faction thinks that its members also should have a Class, it will not be possible to give the Class in a pure form. One cannot pull esotericism out of shape in one direction or another: it must flow through one as inner necessity and remain in direct connection with the world of spirit.

In writing all this, at the same time I have to say that I am wholeheartedly in agreement with the united working groups amalgamating and trying to help one another. That was also necessary, and I will assuredly always work hard to help these people who have formed alliances, in whatever way I can. But I myself feel that I have a different task from them. And it is for this task I wish to live, for it has gradually ripened in me to clarity. Through a spiritual experience I had while I was ill, I found that I have a task to fulfil, and that I had to return to the earth for this purpose.[256]

In other long letters at the end of January and beginning of February, Ita Wegman explained her stance to astonished and disappointed friends and members.[257] In these replies she was very assured, clear in her position and at the same time discreet: she was seeking a language for processes that could only be communicated with difficulty, whose spiritual dimension belonged firmly to the future. They concerned each individual's biographical karma and evolution but also the future of the *specific* community of human beings that Ita Wegman continued to link closely with the real idea of the Anthroposophical Society: a community which, despite all present estrangements, she was firmly resolved to embrace:

> I have the strong need to distance myself from all disputes and conflicts, and only do what is directly connected with Michael and the impulses of the Christmas Foundation Meeting. There is not a great deal to say about this. I wish to carry it in my heart and try to feel myself directly connected with the spiritual fraternity in the world of spirit—since the mirror of this union, the Anthroposophical Society, can no longer form the vessel for what can flow from this spiritual unity. Slowly, very slowly, one has to rebuild things—and perhaps this can only happen in the heart—so that this vessel arises in purity again.[258]

It was in this way that Ita Wegman sought to continue discerning and keeping faith with the language of destiny implicit in her absence from the last, extraordinarily destructive general meeting, her own illness, and her experience in the world of spirit. In a letter that in some ways summarized this stance, she wrote on February 1 to the physician Klara Zupic-Dajceva, who was practicing in Zagreb and worked publicly for Anthroposophy:

> I have decided not to enter the fray but to withdraw from combative collisions. This stance was more or less given me by destiny since illness kept me away from the last general meeting when the really terrible things were happening. I therefore had no involvement in the resolutions that were passed there, on either one side or the other. I will therefore continue to adhere to this stance that has, really, been assigned me by destiny: keeping myself distant from these things and trying to return to the originating impulse of Rudolf Steiner, which is connected with the Christmas Foundation Meeting and consisted of his aim to make the Anthroposophical Society a vessel into which a wealth of esoteric wisdom from Michael

and the Michael School could pour. As you know, Rudolf Steiner established the so-called First Class, which was later to be expanded into three classes. He linked me very strongly with this Michael School. But now of course, things are such that when two sides do battle with each other, the Christmas Foundation Meeting is no longer intact; and at the same time the vessel upon earth into which Rudolf Steiner wished this wisdom to pour is now broken. Yet in the spiritual realm things are still as they were; and my very strong impulse is to adhere to this domain of spirit and to regard these earthly conflicts and impossible deeds as unreal. If some people can resolve to work together to keep faith with what I regard as this originating impulse of the Christmas Foundation Meeting, to work together with heartfelt accord, then perhaps it would after all become possible at some point for things to improve. And if not, then I have the task at least of carrying the purity of Rudolf Steiner's intention in my heart and bringing it back with me to the world of spirit.

I do not know if you understand me, but this is the stance I will adopt, and as far as possible keep myself removed from the battles. Of course, it is possible that some things must be put right, but I will always do this without conflict. That is what I wished to say about Society matters.

~

Ita Wegman was trying to keep herself "as far as possible at one remove from the battles"; nevertheless, soon after her return to Arlesheim, in mid-November 1934, she had once again found herself the target of severe and extremely hurtful attacks. Carrying within her entirely different outlooks and perspectives, she had been surprised in December by Hermann Poppelbaum's text "From the History of the Anthroposophical Society since 1925" and had then also heard about a meeting at the Goetheanum where steps were prepared for the final dismissal of herself and

Draft letter from Ita Wegman to Albert Steffen, January 1935

Elisabeth Vreede, and for further action against members in Holland, England and Germany ("*We received news of this dubious meeting by strange chance—which is perhaps not chance, since it was supposed to remain secret. You see how sadly things have declined*"²⁵⁹).

Hermann Poppelbaum, with whom Ita Wegman had been in friendly contact for many years, with much mutual esteem, had accentuated in his indictment—written "with the agreement of the Dornach executive council"(!)—that Wegman had immediately laid claim after Steiner's death to being his successor and director of the School at Dornach, and in subsequent years had built up an empire with international "bases" working in intentional opposition to the Goetheanum. Furthermore he stated that she was endangering the existence and substance of the anthroposophic movement and Society through her willful seizure of power and her "non-methods" in both science and finances. These, he said, were part of a comprehensive strategy, and supposedly exerted manipulative and suggestive effects on members.

During that same period, Hermann Poppelbaum was negotiating with the leadership elite of the Nazi party on behalf of the Anthroposophical Society in Germany. His accusations against Ita Wegman not only overlooked the reality of the years since 1925, absurdly misinterpreting them or ascribing grandiose designs to her actual intentions, but, paradoxically, mirrored the political situation of Adolf Hitler's increasing ascendency (in diametric contrast to Wegman herself). On February 1, Ita Wegman wrote to Klara Zupic-Dajceva about the accusations once again made against her:

> It is astonishing to witness how so much hatred can be invoked;[260] and here I agree with you completely: I, too, believe that those who find such degrees of hatred within them are not the originators of it, but that powers stand behind them who are working to weaken the Anthroposophical Society.[261]

Eleven days later she wrote as follows to Poppelbaum himself:

> I have read your slander against me, and am astonished that it is possible for someone who is a pupil of Rudolf Steiner to judge another, also a pupil of Rudolf Steiner, in such a one-sided way, and to view the events from such a one-sided perspective. The tone and attitude of your text is so extraordinarily trivial, so unloving, that I will not give it any further attention. I cannot and will not defend myself against such accusations. As you have presented them, they are absurd. I know you from former times and I would prefer to keep in mind this other picture that I have of you rather than to engage in an unedifying battle. You will eventually come to see that things in fact are different from the one-sided accounts you have heard.[262]

In her reply to Hermann Poppelbaum, Ita Wegman only corrected a single point, relating to Rudolf Steiner himself,[263] also
requesting him to read out her reply at his Hamburg branch of
the Anthroposophical Society. Poppelbaum did so but left out
the passage quoted above (*"You will understand that I did not
read out the whole of your letter"*).[264]

~

Ita Wegman tried as far as possible to base all her further steps
and words on the stance with which she had returned from
Palestine, which she had acquired and then developed and consolidated through her experience of being ill and her recovery.
She safely maintained this spiritual stance through the weeks
of January and February, protecting herself through spiritual
work, with complete conviction that the tragic events at the
Goetheanum were destined to occur (*"This will probably be
the final act of the Christmas Foundation Meeting, and what
comes after this will be quite different. I have the feeling that
these things are inevitable, a matter of destiny, and so I am
tranquil and await what is spiritually intended"*[265]). Yet we
should not ignore how much she suffered from the acutely hurtful claims and aggressive accusations in January, February and
March, and how surprised,[266] injured and exposed she felt herself to be on occasion:

> It is really the case, too, that one copes worse here in
> Dornach than anywhere else. I haven't yet been back for two
> months and already have the old cares and worries: you get
> up with them in the morning and go to bed with them at
> night. And yet I had been quite free of all these things, was
> able to work well and fruitfully, and think clearly. That is,
> after all, karma, which you have to accept with all compo-
> sure and tranquility.[267]

Ita Wegman took these events in a spirit of "tranquility" and "composure" and focused her efforts on Arlesheim or on the specific intention of the clinic and its spiritual, geographical surroundings, connected as these were with St. Odile and the Grail.[268] She not only tried to let the destructive forces of the conflict wash harmlessly over the clinic's therapeutic impetus but even sought to create a healing counterweight with her work—ultimately a Christian and Christological impulse. Ita Wegman had long seen the events in Germany and the shadow cast by them at the Goetheanum as a battle and resurgence of powers fiercely opposed to esoteric Christianity; as a hate-driven resistance focused on Rudolf Steiner and anthroposophic Spiritual Science, and thus also in stark enmity to the spiritually progressive evolution of human beings as embodied in the new Christian mysteries. The blindness and estrangement at work in the General Anthroposophical Society were, in her view, the perfidiously intelligent work of powers seeking to use, for their demagogic purposes, the egoism, psychological frailties, and pathological tendencies of individuals. With great effectiveness such powers were proving capable of initiating processes and dictating opinions to which large majorities almost helplessly succumbed, losing all individual power of judgement and discernment. With her clinic at Arlesheim Wegman wished to oppose these powers resolutely, though not by engaging directly with the emotions they were invoking. On February 14, with this in mind she wrote to Bernard Lievegoed in Holland about the current situation in the vicinity of Dornach:

> The crisis in the Society has affected us here far, far worse
> than anywhere else further away from the Goetheanum. One
> has to find a great deal of strength to stop these huge waves
> of hatred and misunderstanding that assail us, and stand
> firm against them. Nevertheless I have a strong sense that we
> must not let ourselves be weakened, and that the work must

continue especially here in Arlesheim—which has after all played a major part in the history of anthroposophic work after we were led here by destiny when permission for a building in Munich was turned down. Dr. Steiner said certain things in this vein. I have a great sense of responsibility not to let the seed planted here in Arlesheim just wither away, which is no doubt the intention of certain dark powers; but instead to stand our ground and try, merely through our presence here, to create a counterpoise in the battles that are occurring spiritually.

One week later she wrote in another letter to England:

I am sure you can imagine that 1935 is a deeply serious time for all of us; and I keep trying to find ways of giving people an experience of this, so they can properly evaluate the events that can be expected. But when one sits here in the strange atmosphere of Dornach and Arlesheim, where attacks of demonic character continually disturb the peace, it is not easy to maintain one's equanimity; and one easily starts yearning to go somewhere far away, to hold oneself at one remove from the unedifying events occurring in the Anthroposophical Society. Nevertheless, I want to try to keep this battle, with which I am no longer otherwise concerned, at a distance from our work.[269]

≈

At the end of March, exactly ten years after Rudolf Steiner's death and three weeks before the general meeting of the General Anthroposophical Society at which Wegman and others were expelled, yet another text was published in Dornach to augment and dramatically intensify Poppelbaum's first account. This was a 154-page "Memorandum on matters of concern in the Anthroposophical Society from 1925 to 1935," which had been authored by 12 people (or "submitted" to the Anthroposophical

Society). Again, like Poppelbaum's recent "pamphlet," this spoke
the language of accusation, allegation and innuendo but had now
been developed and systematized. It purportedly traced with
compelling logic the activities pursued by Wegman since Rudolf
Steiner's death and the means she employed—her intended occu-
pation of the Goetheanum by developing an international spear-
head against it, in which prevailed a "sectarian spirit," and uncon-
ditional subjection to Wegman's "infallible authority in all words
and deeds." She was accused of gathering colleagues around her
and misusing those who supported Wegman's "sole dominion"
within the Anthroposophical Society, based on "mystic intentions" and pseudo-esoteric pretensions. All this supposedly aimed
to remove the other executive council members, beginning with
Marie Steiner, whom Ita Wegman had intentionally informed too
late of Rudolf Steiner's imminent death, thus preventing her from
attending his deathbed and bidding him farewell from the earth.
In its "documentation," the "Memorandum" traced these developments year by year, integrating them into a coherent picture at the
absolute center of which stood Wegman's now exposed attempt at
seizing power (*"It is my karma to stand at the very center of these
things, and also to be the focus of all attacks"*).

We do not know how Wegman reacted directly to reading this
"work," publication of which was announced in the newsletter's
epoch-making issue on March 17, 1935, alongside the full text of
the dismissal and expulsion motions,[270] explanation of these,[271]
and an accompanying article by Marie Steiner (entitled "Current
News"[272]). During the period when the "Memorandum" was published in Dornach, or directly after she had studied it, Wegman
fell ill and was confined to her bed for several days with severe
neuralgia (*"It was impossible for me either to speak or work"*[273]).

Bizarre powers held sway and were at work in this pseudo-
historical "documentation"—ultimately brutal powers of

solche Wiederholung gar nicht vorausgesetzt zu werden brauchten.
Dennoch entstand das Streben, Frau Dr. Wegman als die alleinige Leiterin
der Hochschule anerkennen zu lassen. Auch sie selber stellte solche An-
sprüche. In dem erwähnten Reisebericht sagte sie darüber vorläufig
schon das Folgende:

> „Als Dr. Steiner diese I. Klasse der Freien Hochschule für Geisteswissenschaft be-
> gründete, setzte er mich als Mitarbeiterin ein. Es versprachen damals die neuaufgenom-
> menen Schüler, diejenigen Schüler, die noch keine Esoterik von früher gehabt hatten,
> treue Mitglieder der Schule zu sein. Deshalb fühlte ich mich nach dem Tode unseres
> Lehrers Dr. Steiner nicht gelöst von diesen Verpflichtungen, im Gegenteil, ich empfand
> diese mehr denn je, da ich die Einrichtungen, die Dr. Steiner getroffen hat, als Reali-
> täten der geistigen Welt anzusehen habe. Und so fiel mir die Aufgabe zu, die Wieder-
> holung der von Dr. Steiner gegebenen esoterischen Stunden der Freien Hochschule für
> Geisteswissenschaft aufzunehmen. Und dazu konnte zu meiner großen Befriedigung in
> Paris der erste Schritt getan werden."

Trotz der stilistischen Verworrenheit dieser Sätze wird darin doch
der Standpunkt klar, den Frau Dr. Wegman damals und auch später
immer einnahm. — Bei der Gründung der I. Klasse aber wurde Frau
Dr. Wegman in keinem anderen Sinne als Mitarbeiter Rudolf Steiners
bezeichnet als die anderen Vorstandsmitglieder, sie sollte jedoch
als Schriftführer die Anfragen vermitteln, die gestellt werden sollten,
wenn ein Klassenmitglied einem andern den Inhalt von Klassenvorträgen
mitteilen wollte, bei welchen dieser andere nicht hatte anwesend sein
können. (Diese vermittelnde Tätigkeit wurde übrigens bei auswärtigen
Klassenstunden, bei welchen die Schriftführerin nicht anwesend war, von
Dr. Steiner von Fall zu Fall auch anderen Vorstandsmitgliedern über-
tragen.) Von einer „Einsetzung" war nie die Rede gewesen. Das Sich-
berufen auf „Einsetzungen" und „Missionen" wurde überhaupt charak-
teristisch für die Haltung Frau Dr. Wegmans und ihrer Mitarbeiter, sowie
für Frl. Dr. Vreede. Herr Steffen, Frau Dr. Steiner und Herr Dr. Wachsmuth haben es immer ganz entschieden abgewiesen, daß sie selber von
Rudolf Steiner in irgend einer Weise eingesetzt worden wären oder mit
irgendwelchen Missionen betraut. Dr. Steiner hatte immer nur von Auf-
gaben, Pflichten und Verantwortungen gesprochen. Die Auffassung, daß
Frau Dr. Wegman im Sinne der von ihr gemeinten Mitarbeiterschaft als
der Überlebende von ursprünglich zwei Leitern der Hochschule zu be-
trachten sei, wurde von ihr selbst abwechselnd ausgesprochen und dann

14

"Memorandum" with Ita Wegman's marginal note: "Lie"

distortion and destruction. The content of the accusations for-mulated there had nothing to do with the truth of Ita Wegman's real intentions and activities. Nevertheless they stirred up highly emotionalized responses, and in doing so even drew on an inten-tional distortion of the last hours of Rudolf Steiner's life, or of Ita Wegman's conduct during them. In the weeks and months after the "Memorandum" appeared, Ita Wegman sought only to cor-rect one thing that related indirectly to Rudolf Steiner himself, as she had done in her response to the document by Hermann Poppelbaum at the end of the previous year. In doing this she asked, among other things, for help from an eyewitness at the time, Hilma Walter.[274] Otherwise, Wegman again declined to defend herself any further, let alone take offensive action, aware of the pointlessness and hopelessness of such action in view of the prevailing opinions. At the same time, more importantly, this stance accorded entirely with the inner path she had been pursu-ing for months now. It is possible that, on one occasion only, she decided to address her colleagues at the clinic in regard to these issues (in Arlesheim some time around March 30, 1935), for in her notebook she outlined some words in this context. Here, for the last time, she described her real sense of shared responsibility for the Class Lessons:

> For ten years now, I have been the target of accusations and slanders that never cease; and today, the tenth anniversary of R. Steiner's death, the final act must conclude in which, at the next annual general meeting, motions will be passed that dismiss Dr. Vreede and Dr. Wegman from their posi-tion as executive council members. To justify this action, a thick document has been written, entitled a "Memorandum," which enumerates all our "evil" deeds. Here events within the executive council and at meetings of the General Secretaries are described by people who were not even present. That is

angelegenheiten gesprochen worden ist
muss ich auch öffentlich darauf
antworten,
Als die Klasse eingerichtet wurde
wurden alle ältere Mitglieder, die in
Dornach wohnten und die Dr Steiner schon
Jahre lang kannte ohne weiteres aufge-
nommen, sie konnten sich per Brief an-
melden, Die Klasse fing in Februar an
und setzte sich mit kleinen Unter-
brechungen bis August fort. Dan kam
eine grosse Veränderung in den aufnahmen
Es kamen jetzt viele Menschen von
ausserhalb Dornach und es wollte jetzt
R Steiner die Menschen auch sehen
die er aufnahm und einige Worte mit ihnen
sprechen, Mir sagte er, dass die Menschen
jetzt wissen sollten, dass die Klasse die
Michaelschule sei in der geistigen Welt
Von dieser Michaelschule sei er der Leiter
und ich seine Mithelferin. Ich hätte
zu hüten die Mantrams, man musste sich
an mich wenden wer ein Mitglied die
Mantrams weiter geben wollte. Dies sei
ein esoterischer act, der Anfang einer neu
einzusetzenden Esoterik. Zugleicher Zeit wurde
es bei der aufnahme so eingerichtet das
der Doktor neu aufnehmende die Worte hatte
Dies ist die Michael Schule die von mir und
Dr W geleitet wird.

Notebook entry by Ita Wegman (draft of a lecture), March 1935

already very strange; and when one reads the Memorandum carefully, ultimately all blame is laid at my door.

Wherever I turn and whatever I do, there isn't a single good hair on my head; and my last letter to the executive council, or to Albert Steffen, gives most cause of all for outrage. This letter is blown up out of all proportion. But members must start to reflect on what is going on here, for it conceals a mystery: such great hatred against me, cultivated and nourished for ten years now.

A memorandum has been published with the aim of justifying the expulsion from the Society of two executive council members, Dr. Vreede and myself, along with 6 other leading individuals. The document relates ten years of history leading up to this.

When I picked up this Memorandum, my heart started racing a little and the thought surfaced in me—"Now you will be tested as to how you react to this attack." However, I myself was very surprised indeed after reading it to find that I felt nothing at all. I was neither angry nor sad. The whole thing was alien to me. I found that I had distanced myself entirely from the matters dealt with in the Memorandum. I was extremely pleased at this, and see that it concludes 10 years of suffering, and that my illness has also played a part in this.

I have not decided to speak to you about my situation in the Society in order to defend myself, but because I have a sense that the people who work with me have the right to know what is going on with me. It is important to repudiate the accusations and set things straight; but often this is not possible. For ten years the same accusations or slanders have kept coming, naturally with variations. I am said to be seeking power. After the death of R. Steiner I am said to have proposed myself as the sole leader of the School of Spiritual Science. That really is crazy. How could I ever think of being sole leader of the School since it consists, after all, of all the sections and the Class?

As far as the Class is concerned, I do have to make a public reply here since the Memorandum openly discusses Class matters.

When the Class was established, all older members who lived in Dornach and whom Dr. Steiner had known for years were admitted to the Class without further formalities, registering their attendance by letter. The Class started in February, and continued, with brief interruptions, until August. Many people came from outside Dornach, and R. Steiner also wanted to see the people who were admitted and say a few words to them. He told me that people should know that the Class was the Michael School in the world of spirit. He was the leader of this Michael School and I his assistant. My task, he said, was to safeguard the mantras. And anyone wishing to pass them on to someone else must address themselves to me or to him. This, he said, was an esoteric act, the beginning of a new form of esotericism. At the same time, admission to the Class was arranged in such a way that the new member was told: "This is the Michael School, which is led by Frau Dr. W[egman] and me."[275]

≈

Otherwise, even after the "Memorandum" had appeared, Ita Wegman repeatedly emphasized that the only stance that would help in the current situation was a seemingly passive, long-suffering and patient one; and indeed that this was the only way to spiritually overcome the threat of these powers and forces. At Easter she organized a study gathering at Schloss Hamborn with a primary focus on Christological themes,[276] and on April 10 wrote with further clarification to Paris:

> This is how I see it: spiritual beings need nourishment, a spiritual nourishment that only human souls can give them, which can proceed from a particular inner stance, one which contains the selfless will for sacrifice. If souls can affirm the severe trials that come toward them, then this can result in

positive effects in the future. And I believe that this is the trial which we must surmount, and that much in the future will depend on this. By this I do not mean that one should not defend oneself, not put the record straight; that has little to do with it, and may well even be necessary to weaken the power of the demons. What I'm speaking of is an inner stance of soul that we need to take toward these things.[277]

In addition, Wegman was already clear in the days and weeks preceding the general meeting on April 14 that she would continue her medical and esoteric tasks, and would in no way spiritually accept the forthcoming majority decisions of the general meeting (*"It is not my intention at all to accept resolutions by a general meeting. Only Rudolf Steiner could appoint or dismiss me, and I know without any doubt that things look different in the world of spirit than most people in the Anthroposophical Society think."*[278] *"As far as I am concerned myself, I will never allow a general meeting the right to dismiss me, whom Rudolf Steiner appointed. Only he could do this. I understand very well of course that this is of no use in relation to the majority of members; yet a small minority will perhaps see its validity if they wish to continue to give Rudolf Steiner any serious credence at all"*[279]).

Count Polzer had come to Wegman in the second half of March to tell her of his intention to undertake a final effort to avert the threat of these decisions by the general meeting[280] (*"Since it is scandalous if people can later say of the Anthroposophical Society—which is really after all an international movement— that it succeeded in expelling, like criminals, people of international standing such as Dunlop, Zeylmans and also myself, who were also personal friends of Rudolf Steiner"*[281]).

Ita Wegman supported Polzer's initiative (*"I could only reply to him that I would have done something similar in his place"*[282]), although she never felt that Polzer would be successful (*"The*

Anthroposophical Society has so thoroughly lost any sense of freedom and justice that it has really fallen asleep in relation to higher moral laws."[283] "*I have the feeling that these things cannot be averted, that they're destined; and so I am tranquil and await what is spiritually intended*"[284]). Wegman's support for Ludwig von Polzer-Hoditz was motivated by purely spiritual considerations, untinged by any tactical or strategic aims, and based only on the substance of his words.

Ita Wegman (like Herbert Hahn for instance[285]) was convinced that future times would take note of the historical protest by Ludwig Polzer-Hoditz[286]—and also of the fact that he was more than entitled to warn many members of the Anthroposophical Society about their shared responsibility for the outcome of the vote, which would be inscribed irrevocably in their continuing destiny. Ten days before the general meeting at Dornach, which was to affirm and enact the dismissal and expulsion motions on Palm Sunday 1935 by an overwhelming majority, Ita Wegman wrote again to Wilhelm Goyert[287] in Cologne—who was likewise in opposition to these developments:

> Personally I would not care at all if the Anthroposophical Society expels me from the executive council and/or the Society along with various other individuals. I feel all such things to be maya. Things look different in the world of spirit, and it may also be true that the destruction of a particular form must be seen in the same way as the Goetheanum fire: it is sad, but what was burned down was an earthly thing. The spirit is inviolable, and will be able to act all the more powerfully. One might even speak of a symbolic burial that could be followed by a resurrection.
>
> Karmically, however, it will have grave consequences for the members if they just allow this Society to be destroyed without doing anything to prevent it. Therefore it is to some extent my duty to draw the members' attention to these

Easter telegram from Ita Wegman to Clent;
"I look courageously to the future."

things. Nothing need be done for my sake or that of the 7 other individuals, but every member ought really to do something for himself.[288]

～

After April 14, 1935,[289] Ita Wegman did indeed carry on her work, no longer in the great room at the Goetheanum in Dornach, or as official leader of the Medical Section, but at her clinic and in the cultivation of her international connections with all spheres relating to anthroposophic medicine, whose key figure she unmistakably remained (*"We have a great deal to do here, and everything is continuing as it did before. The resolutions of the Anthroposophical Society have nothing to do with our work"*[290]). She never relinquished the intrinsic idea of the Medical Section at the Goetheanum, whose full esoteric and spiritual shape had become especially clear to her while she was ill in 1934. Shortly after the decision at the general meeting, she wrote to her medical colleague Gerhard Suchantke in Berlin:

It has become very clear to me that the tasks that Rudolf Steiner gave me have nothing to do with the resolutions of the general meeting. The School, with the sections, was actually a spiritual initiative founded by Rudolf Steiner, and one he connected with the Anthroposophical Society. He himself and the executive council members he appointed were part of this School. To a certain extent the Society had to accept the executive council as a given. The Sections were then appointed by Rudolf Steiner himself, and the Society had nothing at all to do with this. Thus I cannot feel myself to have been dismissed from this School, and the tasks within the School that were connected with two people who have been expelled by the Society cannot be extinguished by this means. While the Society has of course been fragmented, we remain in a sphere in which the Society cannot intervene. The fragmented School can no longer work together as a unity, but perhaps the separate parts can still work effectively, and the people who belong to each other by destiny can gather together.[291]

As Ita Wegman told Hilma Walter, she wished to keep faith with the Medical Section "within Rudolf Steiner's Spiritual Science,"[292] not only maintaining the intensity of this work but, if anything, increasing it even further.[293]

If one surveys her whole correspondence and diverse areas of work after April 14, 1935, there is little doubt that after the dismissals and expulsions, despite the trauma and tragedy of these processes, Wegman was in some respects relieved and released, freed from huge pressure and an ultimately almost unendurable tension and exertion of effort (*"A path of unspeakable suffering that has gone on for ten years for a number of people within the Anthroposophical Society has thus come to a conclusion. Looking back on this we can have a sense of relief that these things are finally at an end"*[294]).

KLINISCH-THERAPEUTISCHES INSTITUT
ARLESHEIM (SCHWEIZ)

ARLESHEIM, **im Juli 1935.**

TELEPHON ARLESHEIM 62.022
TELEGRAMME: CLINIC ARLESHEIM

POSTCHECK-KONTO BASEL V 6487
POSTCHECK-KONTO KARLSRUHE 70.104

Liebe Freunde!

Wir laden Sie zu einer dreitägigen Arbeitszusammenkunft in der Zeit vom 27., 28. und 29. September 1935 ein, um uns über folgende Fragen ein tieferes Verständnis zu erarbeiten:

a) Die Heilmittel der verschiedenen Naturreiche in ihrer Beziehung zum Menschen

b) Die Bedeutung ihrer Zubereitungsprozesse

c) Die Elemente Feuer, Wasser, Luft, Erde in ihrer Wesenhaftigkeit und therapeutischen Verwendung

d) Das Krebsproblem, die Viscumtherapie, die neue Maschine (als Thema eines speziellen Nachmittags gedacht).

Wir bitten um Referate über die Anwendung einzelner spezieller Heilmittel.

Die Zusammenkunft wird stattfinden im Klinisch-Therapeutischen Institut.

Mit freundlichem Gruss

Invitation to a physicians' meeting in Arlesheim, Michaelmas 1935

No lethargy or stagnation could be discerned in her medical and spiritual work in Arlesheim, despite the aggravated financial situation of the "Clinical-Therapeutic Institute" and a temporarily unclear situation in which Ita Wegman herself considered it possible that the institutions connected with her might have to close.[295] Already in the second half of May, however, she said that the work was going "from strength to strength,"[296] and that "new life" was burgeoning in Arlesheim ("*It seems as if a new lease of life has come after the events at the Goetheanum, and is starting to make itself felt everywhere"*[297]). This was a life "in accord with Rudolf Steiner,"[298] in which she gave many people the opportunity to participate in unpressured freedom. In letters to her physician colleagues, Wegman offered to continue their previous medical collaboration, without any moral pressure and in absolute respect for the freedom and individual responsibility of each of her correspondents.[299] When she eventually came to organize an initial study conference of anthroposophic physicians in Arlesheim again, Ita Wegman opened her address on Michaelmas 1935 with these future-oriented words:

> I greet you very warmly, really very warmly, since I am so pleased that you have come; that, despite all difficulties, you have not allowed yourself to be diverted from coming.
>
> You see, every year we used to work together here as physicians at Michaelmas; and so it seemed to me that we should do it again this year, that we had to do it. We have had many difficulties, but despite this we have to ensure that this ongoing work continues. These difficulties—I need to briefly refer to them and give you my point of view so that nothing obstructs us, and so that you understand what I meant by a continuation of this work.
>
> When one is entrusted with a task by Rudolf Steiner, one cannot let it slip from one's grasp or allow it to be wrested away; one cannot distance oneself from it either. It is simply a reality. If difficulties arise because one acquires a different view of these tasks given to particular individuals by Rudolf Steiner, this still doesn't amount to proof that the person who received a specific task ought to relinquish it. On the contrary, those who have received such tasks must keep inner faith with them as rigorously as possible, must commit themselves with all their powers to the tasks they have been entrusted with, even if these powers are not adequate to fulfil them. It is for this reason that I have undertaken to use all my strength to continue these studies

that Rudolf Steiner initiated, with the physicians who wish this; but I also have to say this can only be modest in its range and compass. The only option is to begin again from the beginning, on a small scale, yet bearing in our hearts the seed that Rudolf Steiner planted there. Having once committed ourselves to Rudolf Steiner, as you know my dear friends, no power in the world can do anything to sunder this connection with the person who gave the world a very great gift.

There has of course been a change in the nature of the work to be accomplished here, which ought really to have been undertaken in collaboration with Rudolf Steiner. But despite this change, the warmth we carry for it in our hearts is and remains the same. And this also is how you should understand it and—if you are able—connect with what we seek to realize here. Though we now do not have the scope and space—I'm saying this for your ears only—which we ought to have for this work in the Goetheanum, we are nevertheless still working for the Goetheanum since we cannot sunder ourselves from Rudolf Steiner. This is self-evident. We cannot sunder ourselves from his work. There is room for all people at the spiritual Goetheanum. I need to explain my position to you here since it is the first time we have met since all the unpleasant events and difficulties occurred. For my part, I view these as very great misunderstandings that I hope will eventually be cleared up. I hope a time will come when we can once again work together with each other in love and tranquility (notebook).

≈

Despite the broad positivity she expressed, Wegman was at the same time aware that key processes at work within the General Anthroposophical Society had come to a provisional conclusion in 1935. The task of the shared ideal of the School and the karmically based executive council had been gravely violated, thus further injuring the spiritual Goetheanum. Ita Wegman now lived in continual awareness of the failure this represented, and the sense of having let Rudolf Steiner down—a failure in relation to the overall development of culture and civilization, whose fatal destructiveness was ever more in evidence as events headed inexorably toward conflict and warfare.

The death of Daniel Nicol Dunlop, which came out of the blue just six weeks after his expulsion from the General Anthroposophical Society, struck Wegman as highly symptomatic and indicative of the situation. Ita Wegman had witnessed encounters between Rudolf Steiner and Dunlop, and knew how highly Steiner had esteemed this anthroposophist of international standing and charisma, with whom she had collaborated very closely for many years.[300] Dunlop died in London at the age of 66 on Ascension Day, 1935. Wegman had rushed to England to attend him as he lay ill.[301]

Two years earlier, on April 17, 1933, she had written to him in a letter:

> We are extraordinarily grateful to the friends in England that we can turn our eyes from here toward England as if to a kind of stronghold that stands firm against commotions in the world and within our Anthroposophical Society; and I would ask that you, Mr. Dunlop, regard this as extremely important. I see in you someone with whom we can all be connected in our efforts to improve the lot of humankind.

Now she stood at his grave, deeply shaken yet with great inner certainty about the workings of destiny. Willem Zeylmans van Emmichoven and Montague Wheeler spoke at the cremation. Ita Wegman herself gave a short address to a group of anthroposophists in London a few days later, which she had prepared with the aid of a few pages of notes in English:[302]

Telegram wording
by Wegman about
Dunlop's death

My dear friends,

It is a long time since I last visited you in London. Glad as I am to see you again, the cause of my visit is a very sad occasion, for we have lost our dear friend Mr. Dunlop. To stand here and to see that chair in the corner standing empty fills me—and you also no doubt—with great grief. It is almost impossible to grasp that he has gone. Yet this is so, and we must face this fact.

The question arises in our mind as to why this must be so. Inexorable karma has been at work. Only a few days ago he was still well, then suddenly he fell ill—an illness so strange in its symptoms that the doctors were unable to help him despite their efforts. It was as if he was not meant to receive the help needed, and one hindrance after another presented itself. The spiritual world had, so to say, already laid its hands upon him, claiming him as its concern now; and so it happened that our beloved friend passed through the gate of death. He was sundered from all who loved him; but this had to be, and was thus ordained by the world of spirit.

He told me that he had seen Rudolf Steiner by his side before his operation, though did not recall whether Rudolf Steiner had spoken any words to him. This reminds me of an experience I myself had. It is a remarkable fact that I, too, was standing at the threshold of death not long ago during my grave illness, and that I, too, encountered Rudolf Steiner—who sent me back into earthly life. Here, in the case of Mr. Dunlop, Rudolf Steiner welcomed him to him. A re-encounter had taken place, followed by a new togetherness. Rudolf Steiner is in the process of gathering all those who have completed their task. If we judge by earthly reason, we might have the impression that Mr. Dunlop had not completed what he began, but this is maya. Our higher being will never consent to leave the earth until all has been completed in a higher sense. Ultimately, our higher being stands above life and death and holds sway over them. Beyond our conscious awareness we feel whether we must stay or go; and in this awareness we can feel or say remarkable things. In addition, I wanted to tell you about my own experiences, in an attempt to approach a deeper understanding of Mr. Dunlop's last hours. I visited him on the morning of the day he died. This was my second visit, the first being on the previous day when I had found him looking good, with a strong pulse, and I was full of hope. However, he himself said to Nunhoefer, "It is not so easy; I cannot get through." The next morning the whole situation had changed. His pulse was worse, and he said with much greater emphasis: "I cannot get through. I don't understand what the surgeon has done." I clearly recall my own feelings at a similar moment in my grave illness. The patient is very well aware when the actions and ideas of the physician are at odds with his own situation. In my own case I knew that the consultant, who held out little hope for me, was mistaken. The opposite view lived in my soul. I knew that I would recover after a while; and no one can deprive

my dear friends
It is a long time since I
see you here in London. I am glad
to see you again, but at the same
moment every sad that it must be
in this time, in which
we have lost our dear friend
mr Dunlop. Staying here and
not seeing him sitting there on
that chair in the corner is for me
a great grief. It is not to believe
that he has gone away. And still it
is so, we have to face it.
The question raises in our mind
why it has to be so. Inexorably
Karma has worked. For a few
days still healthy, then suddenly
an illness came, but so strange
in its symptoms, doctors were not
able to help him. Although longing
to help him, there was hinderance
on hinderance as right help might
not be. The spiritual world
has so to say lad his hands on
him, it was her affair, and so
it came that our beloved friend
passed away through the gate of
death alone. It
separated from those who loved him, but
it so, this was the language
of the spiritual world

Draft of the memorial speech for D. N. Dunlop, June 1935, p. 1

one of this inner certainty. Now I was hearing Mr. Dunlop say these words: "I cannot get through." This was an inner knowledge, and gave him the sense that the doctor had acted in a way inappropriate to his situation. In our subconscious both of us had a feeling of pivoting between departing or remaining on the earth.

Ah, my dear friends, at such moments a mighty chasm opens up between those who think in a scientific mode and patients who are already halfway into the world of spirit. And the deepest abyss of all exists between ordinary nurses who do not believe in a world of spirit and patients who are in the process of crossing the threshold of death. There is no understanding of this, and not the least help therefore. This, too, must become one of the tasks of anthroposophic physicians—to redress the discrepancies in such a situation. This won't happen overnight, but I am sure that it will come eventually.

Thus it was his karma that he had so many friends yet was left alone to meet the world of spirit. Here all earthly feeling had to fall silent. Here the individuality itself held sway. And then, after Mr. Dunlop had departed, an extraordinary change came over his countenance, revealing his most intrinsic being. The signs of the spirit in its true form became visible, uninfluenced by nationality and education or the effort of daily struggles. This countenance was like a revelation, and I must say that it seemed to me the word TAO was resounding from his head, and an image appeared suggesting this countenance belonged to someone who attended to the revelations of the Great Spirit: a person who hearkened with all his might to the rushing of the wind. He seemed to be one with all that is concealed behind nature; and then I recalled the words of Dr. Steiner who told me once, after a conversation with Mr. Dunlop, that he was the right man to lead the Anthroposophical Society in Great Britain, and that his task would be to instruct others about cosmic dimensions for he possessed all western knowledge. These words by Dr. Steiner, my dear friends, give substance to the image so that, in standing before this transformed countenance—which revealed a great mystery—no one could have said he knew Mr. Dunlop in his true nature. He continually showed only one aspect of his nature. The other aspects were concealed, and it is possible that he himself had only an inkling of his true being in his dream life or when he was alone with himself, unburdened by the troubles of mundane reality and the well-meaning influence of others.

I would like to end with a short anecdote, something that occurred between Dr. Steiner and Mr. Dunlop when they first met one another. Dr. Steiner, who could speak no English, and Mr. Dunlop who knew no German, were to have a conversation, an exchange in the physical world. It was Herr van Leer who initiated this meeting. He spoke a great deal. Van Leer was a good man, devoted to Dr. Steiner, and very pleased that Mr. Dunlop had found his way to Dr. Steiner.[303] He talked and talked.... And what did Dr. Steiner do? He took hold of Mr. Dunlop's hand under the table and squeezed it, thus showing there was no need of any words of explanation between them, and that he already knew him very well.

Yes indeed, Dr. Steiner knew him very well and this was why Mr. Dunlop loved him so devotedly. This, my dear friends, is our greatest comfort, for we now know that they will meet each other again, that they have already done so as Mr. Dunlop crossed the threshold. Rudolf Steiner gathers all those who have completed their earthly task, to found with them a community for future work in the world of spirit. We can be connected with this community if we so desire. A bridge can arise between Earth and Heaven.

In the days, weeks and months after Dunlop's death, Ita Wegman did not manage to write an obituary for him as she had intended. She was, instead, profoundly struck by his continuing spiritual presence which made his departure from the earth seem to be of only superficial importance and made a retrospective "obituary" seem more or less obsolete (*"You see, I did not write the article in the end since I keep experiencing Mr. Dunlop's living presence everywhere, and am now almost unable to write about his demise"*[304]). Nevertheless, Mr. Dunlop's death marked an irrevocable break in many ways for Anthroposophy in England; and shortly after Wegman returned to Arlesheim from London, Walter Johannes Stein wrote to her to say:

> Yesterday, with the remark that my services would no longer be needed after Dunlop's death, I was dismissed from the World Survey and World Power Conference. I will try to hold on here, and hope I manage to.[305]

Despite all the diplomatic and mediating activities involving Hermann Poppelbaum, the end of 1935 brought with it finally a prohibition on the Anthroposophical Society in Adolf Hitler's Nazi Germany. Ita Wegman looked upon this turn of events, which scarcely surprised her, with a sober appraisal and without any satisfaction [Ger.: *Schadenfreude*]. As far as she was concerned it was implicit in current developments. The efforts she had focused on England in 1933, and her whole internationalist outlook had been little understood and still less supported in anthroposophic circles. It had, rather, been the object of defamatory cynicism (*"And she had a great deal to do with 'these people' who wished to conquer the world on her behalf by means of world associations, world conferences and youth camps"* [Memorandum][306]).

From April 1935, far-seeing cosmopolitan individuals capable of working in the international arena (such as the deceased Daniel Nicol Dunlop, but also Willem Zeylmans van Emmichoven, George Adams Kaufmann, Eugen Kolisko, and Karl König) were now émigrés expelled from the "General Anthroposophical Society." At the same time, though, people in Dornach now found themselves faced, to their surprise, with a situation that left them little scope for activity and further constricted their own effectiveness within a wider cultural context. In the wake of the Reichstag fire act, prohibition of the Anthroposophical Society—which Heinrich Himmler and Reinhard Tristan Heydrich had already resolved upon in June 1934—came into effect on November 1 when the decree was signed by Heydrich with the agreement of Rudolf Hess and Wilhelm Frick. It was announced by order of the Gestapo in Berlin on November 15. The same day, Ita Wegman wrote to the curative educator Gustav Ritter whose work in Sweden she had been supporting:

> Things in Dornach have in the meantime gone very quiet, since the victorious act which people there were so proud of initially has elicited a reaction. Difficulties have arisen in all the branches and in the schools, too. People are even talking about a closure of all private schools in Germany; branch meetings [of the AS] are being summarily shut down by the police, and eurythmy performances are prohibited, and so on; one therefore gets a sense of creeping disintegration in Germany; and it now seems likely that we can, at some point, expect all outer anthroposophic activity to be prohibited.

Naturally, Wegman deeply regretted these developments, but at the same time she saw in them a task and opportunity—a prompting to be honest and uncompromising in relation to clearly delineated anthroposophic contents (which were diametrically opposed to Nazism in *every* respect) but also to thoughtfully and carefully examine all the Society's forms and structures (*"and so the moment may have arrived when this must be done"*[307]). She herself was firmly resolved to carry her clinic in Switzerland safely through the escalating crisis despite all obstacles and hindrances (*"Here we are working feverishly at least to maintain what we have here, since our clinic may be the only remaining place still with a personal connection to Dr. Steiner"*[308]). She also saw it as a possible point of new departure for future developments at the Goetheanum, though she was aware that this might only occur after other, cathartic processes had run their course:

> The Goetheanum has not conducted itself as it should have. Nevertheless, they have not yet begin to recognize this. Steffen speaks only of the great injustice that has been done to them. They do not know what to do at present, and are pretty downcast.[309]

At the end of 1935, Ita Wegman lived in some anxiety about the continued existence and security of her curative institutes in Germany, which she had last visited during the summer of that year. She was not depressed however, but extremely confident that the spiritual strength of the people working there, and the powers protecting them, would stand firm in the face of all threats (*"I myself cannot say that I'm feeling downcast; although I am prepared for the worst.... I still have a sense that the world of spirit is once again embracing Anthroposophy, and that, despite all difficulties, we can be sure that spiritual guidance will lead us where we need to go"*[310]).

In both social and spiritual respects, she supported the people working in these institutes, at the end of the year also intensifying her parallel efforts in England, at the same time supporting the work of Weleda there (as Dunlop had done so energetically) and the activities of Rudolf Hauschka in London. On December 17, she wrote to Eleanor Merry:

> The thing of chief importance is to maintain the true form of Spiritual Science. At present, evil powers have gained the upper hand in Germany; but as anthroposophists we have already reached the stage of being able to move elsewhere the activities that can no longer be realized in Germany, as seen always from the higher perspectives of humanity.

In pursuing these aims, she advised Merry to keep in touch and maintain contact with Dornach-oriented circles, and to respect them. As on frequent previous occasions, Wegman again emphasized the need to link new developments to past ones, without seeking to ignore, let alone abolish, the latter:

> The Society as such ought not to be dissolved in England: this would be quite wrong. But all kinds of opportunities should be created for people to approach the Society and freely receive what they yearn for, quite freely, without becoming members. It seems to me that generosity should prevail here. And these people, as "free members" throughout the world, should really form in the near future a fraternity of people such as Dr. Steiner spoke of, who look to Christ as their exemplar and guide.[311] Yet if a core of the Anthroposophical Society does not survive, it will be impossible to create a fraternal alliance of this kind. Something new can never arise without continuity connecting it with the old. In England people should simply go on working in calm and composure as they have done hitherto, but allow a free spirit to stream in like a fresh breeze.

During December Ita Wegman was also keeping an eye out for further useful ways of expanding and relocating. She returned more intensively to her old ideas of establishing an affiliated clinic and a curative institute in Ticino, Switzerland (both of which were successfully inaugurated the following year, 1936[312]), supported Gustav Ritter's curative work in Scandinavia, planned the founding of a curative affiliate in Paris (which opened its doors in 1937) and also helped Walter Johannes Stein plan a longer trip to America and his activities while there. On December 16, Wegman wrote in this regard to Madeleine van Deventer, who was then in London:

> I always feel that he [Stein] should go to America, accompanied by someone who will arrange it all for him.... There is

not a great deal of time left. If we do not make some efforts
here, we will lose all the friends we still have in America.... I
always remember what Dr. Steiner said: *"I'm saving Stein for
the great undertakings"*—and where else can these be accomplished if not in America?

Two days later she turned to Walter Johannes Stein himself,
and wrote:

> It strikes me that this is important. After all, we must think
> of opening up America in some way to your activities. In the
> past I always regarded England as a transitional country for
> you, but pictured the way you work as being really suited to
> America. I have sometimes spoken of this with Mr. Dunlop,
> and if he were still alive you two would have attended the
> World Power Conference there together. His death has
> changed things, but I believe it would not be a good idea sim-
> ply to drop this plan. Please don't forget about it but instead
> turn your thoughts in this direction. After all, we have to
> seek out all kinds of other opportunities now.

≈

In the second half of December—after and alongside all her
renewed efforts to save and support anthroposophic medical
impulses in a contracting and darkening world—Wegman turned
her focus to the spiritual shape of Christmas study and work at
Arlesheim. For the second time since her recovery and trip to
Palestine, she wished to base the period of the Holy Nights on
shared awareness of the working of the Christ being, this time
drawing on the Gospel of Luke and Rudolf Steiner's comments on
it. Wegman could look back at this point on an exhausting year,
yet one whose challenges she had met undaunted. She had waged a
largely successful battle against powers and forces intending—in
vain—to extinguish her activities. The "losses" in Dornach were
in her view and in her words just "maya." Against all adversities

Ita Wegman's notebook, December 1935, pages 1 and 2

an inner, Michaelic stance had won through, along with the spiritual substance of esotericism. Ultimately the spiritual connection with Rudolf Steiner and the intentions of a future Christianity had been upheld. In a notebook draft for her opening address for Christmas Eve, Wegman wrote:

> Introduction: speak about the right to celebrate festivals, even in grave times. Forming centers of light where a bridge can be built to the suprasensory world in which the souls of the dead reside, and meet with newborn souls who have resolved to descend [to earth]. Souls should bear upward to this world not just the horror [of their experiences] but also the warming rays of love that have been kindled by just judgment and an understanding of human evolution. Each and every day these rays of love should ascend; and every soul on earth is capable of sending these upward. In community with each other, people will be able to make such rays of love stronger and more luminous. Then the Christ power in these

souls, which slumbers or sleeps in them, will be re-awoken; and they will perceive Christ who receives them at the gate of death, so that they can feel: we die with Christ: *In Christo morimur.*

And the souls that seek to descend, to incarnate in the phys.-eth. [physical-etheric] body that awaits them, will sense these loving rays as warmth that gives them courage and confidence to fulfil their mission on earth. They will know that they are born from the divine, and have descended to earth: *Ex deo nascimur.*

Moreover, human beings on earth who grasp the secret of birth and death will be awakened by the spirit, will reconnect with the spirit they have lost: *Per spiritum sanctum reviviscimus.*

Therefore, we can answer as follows the question that has arisen in us as to whether or not it is fitting to celebrate festivals at this time of such affliction and adversity: not only are we entitled to do so, but also we must. Thereby we create centers that can shine out—upward, downward and on all sides; and these centers are created by the sacred fire that flares within us.

Epilogue: A Letter
from Ita Wegman to Maria Röschl

February 22, 1935

"All old forms, including the ultimate and final form of Anthroposophy, have been fundamentally destroyed; it now seems to me as though we can no longer seek a suitable form for anthroposophic life, but that each and every person becomes this form, and that Anthroposophy tries to unite with it. Wherever this happens, people will find one another and join together to become part of a true union and fraternity in the spirit."

Arlesheim, February 22, 1935

Dear Dr. Röschl,

I would gladly have written to you sooner if I had not been prevented firstly by my mother's grave illness and subsequent death, which meant that I had to go to Holland, [313] and secondly by all the work I found waiting for me here.

It was a great shame that we didn't speak while you were here, but twenty minutes, as you yourself said, was too brief for a conversation. I was very pleased to hear from you that the little conference in Tuebingen went so well. It really seems to me that this kind of work in small groups will bear the most fruit at present.

I was deeply moved by the feelings you expressed to me in your last letter. Like you, I have a great need to speak with you, and I will certainly make room for this as soon as I see that the work here, which I neglected for so long, is properly back on course. However, I'd already like to say a few things here about my position in relation to the Society.

I have long pondered on what stance I should take toward the Anthroposophical Society that Rudolf Steiner forged into a unity at the Christmas Foundation Meeting. As you know, it has not been at all possible to realize what Rudolf Steiner intended with the Christmas Foundation Meeting. The resistance was very great from the outset, and he was aware of this the moment the ritual act had been accomplished at the Christmas meeting. We then fought for ten years so that the Christmas Foundation Meeting principles might make headway. Nevertheless, sadly, the opposition was so great that we could not get anywhere, and now, in fact, a split has occurred within the Anthroposophical Society. Strangely, as things reached their crisis point, I succumbed to illness and was unable to participate in any of the meetings and decisions. I experienced this as a remarkable sign that I no longer, in fact, had anything to do with these earthly things; and as I grew more ill it also seemed to me that I had no further task, either, on the physical plane. Yet an experience in the world of spirit told me something different.

In an encounter I had there with Rudolf Steiner, at which the Christ being was also present, I learned that I was not expected in the spiritual world but that I still had things to do on earth. From this moment on, I also found the strength to take full responsibility for my own recovery again. I was not told what my precise tasks were, and I also understand that this is for me to discover by my own strength. While I stayed far away from Dornach I always had the feeling and the assurance that, undeterred by everything that was happening, I must keep faith in my heart with everything that Rudolf Steiner had intended to bring to the world with the Christmas Foundation Meeting. Yet I also knew I must not succumb to the illusion of lamenting what was no longer possible and remain in a mournful mood about it, taking no further action; but that instead I needed to form a particular resolve that would make it possible for my work to continue.

Thus it eventually became evident to me that I must return to the founding impulse that Rudolf Steiner had intended to give the new Society by drawing down from the spiritual fraternity in the world of spirit (school of Michael) still more than before of what Michael taught there. I have heard many things about this school from Rudolf Steiner, including his and my connections with it. I want to return to this impulse as the thing of prime importance that occurred during the Christmas Foundation Meeting, connecting very strongly with it and acting out of it. I am as yet unable to say how this may develop. I am preparing for it and awaiting what comes, and have no wish to push myself forward at all, nor to ally myself anywhere. If anything good lies in this impulse and people are found who can feel enthusiasm for it, then it will find its shape. It bears a seed for the future within it and is the last thing that Rudolf Steiner entrusted to human beings on earth. What was given as the First Class, and is now in many people's hands, has not yet been exhausted by any means, yet it must be treated in a different way from hitherto. I sense around it slowly, and in this cautious sensing, things illuminate themselves.

All old forms, including Anthroposophy's ultimate and final form, have been fundamentally destroyed; and it now seems to me as if we can no longer seek a fitting form for anthroposophic life, but that each and every person is this form, and that Anthroposophy seeks to unite with it. Where this happens, people will find each other and join together to become part of a true union and fraternity in the spirit. The Society is no longer necessary, because Anthroposophy is already on earth. Individual human beings are the important thing, and together, through each person's own inner development, they must form a higher fraternity with its roots in the world of spirit. This will preserve the full, distinctive nature of each individual's path. Thus, each person's freedom is assured, and each will feel connected with this spiritual fraternity or school of Michael through one's own insights. This is what resounded within me. What counts here is for me to stand strongly within this impulse. Everything else will then take care of itself.

As far as the group is concerned with which you are connected, dear Dr. Röschl, I would like to have said a few words to you about it before the new people were admitted. But since destiny took a different course, I prefer to remain silent on this now. At a later point when we see each other again in person, we may be able to talk further about this.

I heard that you are going to England and will stay in Clent for a while. These visits by Germans to England feel to me similar to the Greeks arriving in Rome. May they have the right outcome for both parties! What already once existed in world history can then arise again at a new and higher level.

With warm greetings I remain

Your I. Wegman, MD

Notes and References

1   Letter from Ita Wegman to Erna Benthien, 3.31.1933. Ita Wegman Archive, Ita Wegman Institute (Arlesheim, Switzerland). All unpublished letters and documents quoted in this book belong to this archive.

2   Werner Pache noted the following in his diary (clearly after a conversation with Ita Wegman about Rudolf Steiner's last birthday on 2.27.1925, and his illness): "He wished to be quite alone. Frau Dr. Steiner was away. It is likely that Wachsmuth was there as usual, since he came regularly every day at 5 a.m. with a folder of business to be dealt with, and Steffen may have looked in briefly, and Dr. Noll. Otherwise he was alone. He was sitting on the chair and reading letters that had just arrived. Now and then there was a knock at the door and someone came in with flowers. Frau Dr. Wegman would go to fetch them in and show them to him, at which he would look at them through his glasses and say, 'Very nice,' and then carry on reading. Then Dr. Wegman gave him a leather briefcase, a very useful one with many pouches. He liked it very much and he immediately began to pack letters away in it and to use it. He was already very tired yet he must still have had some hope that things would improve. This expectation was there right up to the last moment. No doubt that is also why he always spoke of things continuing. It would have made no sense otherwise when he said, I think on Dr. Wegman's birthday, 'It would be lovely for us to take a trip soon to Palestine'" (Werner Pache's diary, Ita Wegman Archive). Ita Wegman herself spoke of Rudolf Steiner's planned trips to Greece and Palestine in her London lecture on 2.27.1931 (cf. Emanuel Zeylmans van Emmichoven, *Wer war Ita Wegman* [in English: *Who Was Ita Wegman? A Documentation*, vols. 1–4, Mercury Press, 1995, 2005, 2005, 2013], vol. 1, Dornach, 2000, p. 316).

3   Emanuel Zeylmans van Emmichoven, *Who Was Ita Wegman?*, op cit; Zeylman's account of Wegman's Palestine trip and her preceding illness was based largely on the brief summary by Madeleine van Deventer in *Who Was Ita Wegman?*, vol. 2, pp. 194–195, whereas surrounding events between 1933 and '35 figure on pages

187–209, and in vol. 3, primarily on pages 105–135 (all page numbers in this note refer to the German edition, hereafter "[G]").

4   Letter to Maria Roeschl, 2.22.1935 (see epilogue).

5   As Emanuel Zeylmans has previously emphasized, Ita Wegman's decisive trip to Greece took place in the spring of 1932, exactly at her third "moon node" and thus at the point of new impetus of a specific biographical phase (Zeylmans, *Who Was Ita Wegman?*, op cit, vol. 2, p. 177 [G]). At this point, Wegman was already in existential need of this journey to the ancient Greek Mystery sites ("I, too, have come to see that I am neither physically nor psychologically capable of attending the Annual General Meeting at this time, seven years after Rudolf Steiner's death. I hope this recuperative trip will allow me to gain some distance from all that has happened over the past few years." Letter to Albert Steffen/Marie Steiner/ Elisabeth Vreede/Guenther Wachsmuth, 3.10.1932). She returned from her travels with new strength and resolve ("Like a healing balm the marvellous ancient world has worked upon me, and I feel as though newborn, and strong enough to carry on with Rudolf Steiner's work, as I carry it in my heart, without being led astray. And if all of you help, we will be able to realize the part of R. Steiner's intentions that relates to myself, to my entelechy, at least as far as our powers allow it, or to the extent that is necessary in saving this work for the future." Letter to Fried Geuter, 5.25.1932). Two years later, but now at the very end of her capacity to deal with the conflicts, Wegman again fell dangerously ill. She was then 58, and thus at an age which the Kabbalah of Jewish esotericism regards as the "absolute summation of life," and the precise scope of a bodily existence ("Under its sign, at the Messianic Meal of the end-time of the Leviathan, the earthly body will ultimately be consumed. Then the Saturn period of our life will commence, when judgement is made." Diether Lauenstein, *Der Lebenslauf und seine Gesetze*. Stuttgart, 1992, p. 76). Having overcome this illness, in the summer of 1934 Ita Wegman resolved to travel to Palestine, and here came to inner experiences and outlooks that were of decisive importance during 1935 and for the whole of the rest of her life up to her death on March 4, 1943.

6   Cf. Rudolf Steiner's key comment about Christ becoming perceptible in the etheric from the 1930s on (or the development of the human capacities required for this perception) *and* about the risk to this new phase of humanity's evolution from materialistic and anti-spiritual powers that might distort or even prevent it. These comments were made in lectures as early as the first half of 1910

(for instance in CW [Collected Works of Rudolf Steiner], vols. 116 [*The Christ Impulse and the Development of the Ego-Consciousness,* New York: Anthroposophic Press 1976], 118, and 125. In his lecture in Strasbourg on 1.23.1910, and two days later in Karlsruhe, Steiner highlighted the special significance of the years following 1933. In Karlsruhe he said, "1935 and 1937 will be particularly important. Quite distinctive capacities will become apparent as a natural endowment in people. At this time great changes will occur and Biblical prophecies will be fulfilled. Everything will change for the souls on earth then, and likewise for those who are no longer physically embodied." Rudolf Steiner, *Das Ereignis der Christus-Erscheinung in der ätherischen Welt,* [in English: *The Reappearance of Christ in the Etheric,* Great Barrington, MA: SteinerBooks, 2003] CW 118. Dornach, 1984, p. 25). See also Sergei O. Prokofieff, *The Appearance of Christ in the Etheric: Spiritual-Scientific Aspects of the Second Coming,* London: Temple Lodge, 2012, and Sergei O. Prokofieff and Peter Selg, *The Creative Power of Anthroposophical Christology,* Great Barrington, MA: SteinerBooks, 2012, ch. 3, "Christ's Reappearance in the Etheric in Relation to the Fifth Gospel."

7 Cf. Gundhild Kacer-Bock, *Emil Bock. Leben und Werk.* Stuttgart, 1993.

8 Cf. Ellen Huidekoper, *In silberner Finsternis. Eduard Lenz (1901–1945), ein Leben in den Umbrüchen des zwanzigsten Jahrhunderts.* Stuttgart, 2003.

9 Notebook entry by Ita Wegman, April/May 1935.

9a Cf. Peter Selg, *The Last Three Years. Ita Wegman in Ascona, 1940–1943,* Great Barrington, MA: SteinerBooks, 2014.

10 Letter from Ita Wegman to Madeleine van Deventer on 2.25.1933.

11 Letter from Ita Wegman to Madeleine van Deventer, undated (9.1933).

12 In a letter (to Alice Wengraf) dated May 8, 1933, Ita Wegman wrote, "We have now again launched energetically into giving courses etc. Currently there are 30 unemployed people here in Dornach/Arlesheim who were attending Stegmann's workers' college in Essen, working there throughout the winter and attending preparatory courses in Anthroposophy. Now they're here at the Goetheanum and have been receiving courses from all the sections; from us, too. We're involved in this right now and it really is fine work since these people have a remarkably strong relationship to Anthroposophy, and also the capacity to judge events in the world in an open-minded way. There are many Germans among them;

many who no longer have any work in Germany or no longer wish to be there at all and are now seeking refuge, and have also found it in various other countries."

13 Letter from Ita Wegman to Heinrich Hardt, 5.12.1933.

14 In Stuttgart Ita Wegman took part in the public conference on "An anthroposophic orientation to the world"—organized by the "Anthroposophic Working Group"—and between January 4 and 9 attended lectures by Willem Zeylmans van Emmichoven ("The world situation in the Far East"), Maria Roeschl ("Poland's spiritual connections with Central Europe"), Herbert Hahn ("The Scandinavian people"), Karl Heyer ("The French character and the contemporary world"), Elisabeth Dank ("Misunderstandings between America and Europe"), Alfred Heidenreich ("England at the threshold of a new era"), Karl König ("Illnesses of our age"), Walter Johannes Stein ("Is there a task for Europe as a whole?") and Eugen Kolisko ("An anthroposophic orientation to the world"). On her return to Arlesheim Ita Wegman wrote to Wilhelm Goyert in Cologne on January 10 as follows: "I was interested to participate in the conference in Stuttgart, and once again felt how strong the anthroposophic movement is there despite all the unpleasantness that surfaces within the Society. It was a lovely experience."

15 Letter from Ita Wegman to Madeleine van Deventer, 5.29.1933.

16 Cf. Ita Wegman, "'We fight for Each Soul,' Letter to Ernst Lehrs Concerning the Education of Adolescents," January 20, 1931, in Peter Selg, *A Grand Metamorphosis: Contributions to the Spiritual-Scientific Anthropology and Education of Adolescents,* Great Barrington, MA: SteinerBooks, 2008, pp. 83–85.

17 Letter from Ita Wegman to Fried Geuter and Michael Wilson, 1.15.1933.

18 André François-Poncet, quoted in Johannes Ebert/Andreas Schmid, *Das Jahrhundertbuch.* Munich 1999, p. 420.

19 Letter from Ita Wegman to Erich Kirchner, 2.5.1933. In the Berlin *National-Zeitung,* a 14-part series attacking Rudolf Steiner and Anthroposophy began on 2.1.1933, detailing Steiner's supposed occult influence on the German Chief of General Staff Helmuth von Moltke, as contributory cause of the lost battle of Marne. In relation to the contemporary press campaign against Steiner and Anthroposophy, see Uwe Werner, *Anthroposophen in der Zeit des Nationalsozialismus (1933–1945),* Munich, 1999, pp. 23ff; in relation to the "attack" on Rudolf Steiner by Nazi circles on 5.15.1922 in Munich, cf. Christoph Lindenberg, *Rudolf Steiner. Eine Chronik,* Stuttgart, 1988, p. 486, and the eyewitness reports cited there.

20 Letter from Ita Wegman to Hilma Walter, 4.28.1933.

21 Letter from Ita Wegman to Fried Geuter and Michael Wilson, 3.24.1933.

22 Letter from Ita Wegman to Erna Benthien, 3.31.1933.

23 Letter from Ita Wegman to George Adams Kaufmann, 4.29.1933.

24 In his account of the initial official anthroposophic responses to the situation in the spring of 1933, Uwe Werner summed up as follows: "They sought to give explanations and present an account of themselves. Since false, misleading and defamatory assertions about Rudolf Steiner and Anthroposophy had been circulating for many years, they took this opportunity to focus attention on statements by Steiner in which he propounded a German spirit. Anthroposophy was even presented as the loveliest blossom of true German identity. In this way they hoped to have solved the problem—and thus henceforth to be left in peace" (op cit, p. 10). In his monograph, Werner then outlined the various means by which leading representatives of the Anthroposophical Society (in particular Hermann Poppelbaum) had sought to practice diplomacy. These involved discussions with and submissions to the new rulers, and refutation of defamatory attacks on Steiner, repeatedly highlighting ways in which anthroposophic Spiritual Science could be reconciled with the German National Socialist view of the human being and the world, and the mission of Germany it emphasized. Answering a question from a Nazi regional leader in Hamburg as to the significance of Anthroposophy for the future of Germany ("What does the Anthroposophical Society do that benefits the German people?"), Poppelbaum replied in a written statement: "Its connection with the German idealism of the classical period means that it is already rooted in German identity. It teaches a deeper view of German nature and of the historical mission of the German people within humanity. According to Rudolf Steiner, the task of Germany is to bring the nature of the eternal (or our unegoistic ego) to exemplary realization in us, whereas other nations primarily realize and develop other aspects of the human being's overall nature" (quoted by Werner, op cit, p. 71).

25 "The available sources do not easily tell us how National Socialism was judged by the Anthroposophical Society. It is certain, however, that different members saw it in very different ways. Some believed that National Socialism was primarily a movement for cultural renewal, for instance expecting that Hitler's 'reform' would lead to realization of the threefold social order. Similarly the national executive of the German AS were urged to draw the attention of these

'best-intentioned people'—that is, the Nazis—to the spiritual treasures of Anthroposophy so that the latter might be 'incorporated into the new Reich'" (Werner, op cit, pp. 26f.). Cf. also note 119.

26 Erna Benthien, an anthroposophist and former patient of Ita Wegman, wrote to Wegman in Arlesheim on 4.23.1933 (and received no reply from her): "It seems also as if all of Europe is unable to understand Germany. The present leaders know exactly what they want, and are working out of intuition. The greater guidance of the world had to take this step for otherwise we would have Bolshevism in Germany now.... It is probable that you will not be able to properly assess what's happening in Germany as you are still thinking of the attack on Steiner in Munich by nationalists. If I look back on these events in calm reflection, I have to say that the attack was probably less directed at the Doctor himself but more likely against some of his colleagues from Jewish circles.... All I can say in a letter is that I am resolved to work with the current government of Germany—how and where is in the lap of the gods." Wegman also received letters from (a few) other people she was on close terms with in the Anthroposophical Society, who expressed approval of the 'spiritual turning point' in Germany. She usually replied only briefly and succinctly (or not at all): "I have a different view of the events in Germany from those you expressed, but some experiences cannot be discussed further" (To Luise von Zastrow, 5.14).

27 Letter from Ita Wegman to Karl Nunhoefer, 6.21.1933.

28 Letter from Ita Wegman to Dorothy Osmond, 6.22.1933.

29 Letter from Ita Wegman to Pieter de Haan, 3.13.1933.

30 Letter from Ita Wegman to Willem Zeylmans van Emmichoven, 3.13.1933.

31 Letter from Ita Wegman to Bernard Lievegoed, 3.7.1933.

32 Letter from Ita Wegman to Herbert Hahn, 3.13.1933.

33 Letter from Ita Wegman to Albert Strohschein, 3.5.1933.

34 Letter from Ita Wegman to Eberhard Schickler, 3.19.1933.

35 Cf. Emmanuel Zeylmans van Emmichoven, *Who Was Ita Wegman?*, op cit, vol. 2, pp. 188f [G]; and Peter Selg, *"Ich bin für Fortschreiten." Ita Wegman and die Medizinische Sektion* (in English: *I Am for Going Ahead: Ita Wegman's Work for the Social Ideals of Anthroposophy*, SteinerBooks, 2012), Dornach, 2004, pp. 139ff.

36 On March 7, as one among many instances of a similar vein, she wrote in a letter to Fried Geuter and Michael Wilson in England: "The situation in Germany is really very grave indeed, and it is extremely important for people to concern themselves in detail with these things, also sending friends the supportive thoughts that

they now have such need of in this very difficult situation. It seems highly probable that we will soon have a great battle on our hands to preserve the freedom all our institutes have had until now. And once again I'd like to...ask you very, very warmly to preserve the unity of our work in your thoughts, where possible letting your thoughts dwell on this whole, since it is only through unity—even as unity emanating from England—that anything can be accomplished of our tasks in medicine and curative education." In a parallel letter sent the same day to Holland (to the curative education physician Bernard Lievegoed) she wrote, "No doubt a difficult situation will now arise, chiefly for our German friends, so that we must indeed consider everything and try to create a united front of people who really have the will to understand and help each other." Six days later, in another letter to England, she stated, "The world situation is growing ever more difficult, and we must make every effort to ensure that our international work is not endangered; the planned gathering will also play an important role here" (to Fried Geuter and Michael Wilson, 3.13.1933).

37 Letter from Ita Wegman to Willem Zeylmans van Emmichoven, 3.22.1933.

38 Letter from Ita Wegman to Fried Geuter, 3.29.1933.

39 Contrary to the note by Emanuel Zeylmans in his biography—"We do not know whether this gathering actually took place or not"— various letters from Ita Wegman during the first half of April (and also the clear recollection of participant Walter Johannes Stein, cf. note 40) show that the meeting not only did take place but was productive ("The meeting we held in Stuttgart had a very good effect." Letter from Ita Wegman to Daniel Nicol Dunlop, 4.17.1933). According to a last preparatory note in Wegman's hand dated 4.17.1933, the following, at least, participated in the Stuttgart meeting (and/or the subsequent gathering in Berlin): Michael and Theodora Wilson, Fried Geuter, George Adams Kaufmann and Dame Florence (from England), Bernard Lievegoed, Pieter de Haan, Herbert Hahn and probably Willem Zeylmans van Emmichoven (from Holland), and Eugen Kolisko, Walter Johannes Stein, Albrecht Strohschein and Karl König from Germany. In addition, after arriving in Stuttgart, and following discussion with the other participants, Wegman also wanted to invite some younger anthroposophists from the group of friends and colleagues surrounding Helene von Grunelius.

40 A letter from Walter Johannes Stein, writing on May 8 from Holland in recollection of the meeting in Stuttgart, shows that many

of Wegman's friends and colleagues had not previously understood the extent of the German catastrophe. He writes, "Only now that I have got out of Germany again can I see why I found it so hard to understand you in Dr. Schickler's flat. It simply isn't possible to see things properly from inside Germany. You had the view of someone who comes from abroad. Only now do I, too, have this view. There is no doubt that people are being completely lulled and ensnared" (see note 60, with the assessment by curative education physician Heinrich Hardt, who also took part in the meeting in Stuttgart).

41 Letter from Ita Wegman to Hilma Walter, 4.28.1933.

42 Letter from Ita Wegman to Michael Wilson, undated (end of April, beginning of May 1933).

43 Letter from Ita Wegman to Fried Geuter and Michael Wilson, 4.28.1933.

44 Letter from Ita Wegman to Fritz Schimpf, 5.9.1933.

45 Letter from Ita Wegman to George Adams Kaufmann, 4.29.1933. In his reply to Wegman's letter George Adams Kaufmann wrote of the situation in England among other things: "I am pleased that you will come here soon, for these things will be much easier to discuss verbally. Times are changing extremely quickly. Here people are—I'd say almost unconsciously—particularly sensitive to what is happening in Germany. While current events are regarded as despicable, many circles do not remain entirely uninfluenced by them. Ruthlessness is infectious. Increasingly one sees what a terrible catastrophe this is for Germany, of all places, to take this path. In their subconscious, people expect so much from Germany. In purely pragmatic terms, we will have to proceed very carefully [with this campaign]. You know the terms and conditions that restrict immigration and residence permits for foreigners; right now, as we hear from many sides, these are being applied in a fairly strict and narrow way. Despite this, possibilities *do* remain here and, especially if we are courageous, will bear good fruit" (5.12.1933).

46 Various medical colleagues of Ita Wegman also asked her in 1933 how their work could continue in the changed political conditions and spiritual atmosphere. In May, Heinrich Hardt received from her a reply that—at first glance—seemed surprising. "As a physician we should work as hard and as much as possible at present; and my advice would be to do this as tangibly as possible. Of great importance, too, would be dietary remedies, bread and so forth, so that healthy nutrition becomes widespread. The clinics and healing centers should lead the way here. And in terms of Spiritual Science all that is necessary is to maintain an unshakeable awareness that

we are connected with one another, and to feel ourselves to be true seekers of the spirit. It is important to read—since you ask me—the esoteric observations on Rosicrucianism" (5.9.1933).

47 For instance, at the request of Hanna Lissau, a graduate of Jewish origin from Vienna, Wegman immediately offered an opportunity to come to the Sonnenhof (see facsimile on page 17) where Lissau began her training in curative education (and later eurythmy therapy) on 10.15.1933. Her tragic fate nine years later—when she was forcefully removed from the small curative education home of Roubiche—as well as Ita Wegman's fruitless battle for her release, have been outlined in my monograph *The Last Three Years: Ita Wegman in Ascona, 1940–1943*, Great Barrington, MA: Steiner-Books, 2014. In the meantime, further research with the help of the Archive director in Auschwitz, Krzysztof Antończyk, has revealed that Hanna Lissau died there as early as 10.14.1942, six weeks after her arrest in southern France.

48 Letter from Ita Wegman to Karl Nunhoefer, 4.30.1933.

49 Letter from Ita Wegman to Emmy Giesler, 3.17.1933.

50 Cf. Peter Selg, *"Ich bin für Fortschreiten."* *Ita Wegman und die Medizinische Sektion* (in English: *I Am for Going Ahead: Ita Wegman's Work for the Social Ideals of Anthroposophy*, Great Barrington, MA: SteinerBooks, 2012), Dornach, 2004, pp. 74ff.

51 This also included introduction of the children's services and reading of the Class Lessons by Wegman in curative education homes. We should not underestimate the importance and efficacy which these spiritual enactments—undertaken with the greatest faithfulness and commitment—had for the consciousness and continued existence of these places after 1933. On Feb. 12, 1933, Werner Pache wrote to Ita Wegman from Schloss Hamborn: "We want to ask you to come through Hamborn again on your way back from England to give a Class Lesson again. The day before yesterday, standing in the evening at Wittenbergplatz [Berlin], where, as in many other public places, Hitler's speech reverberated through loudspeakers, and the power of Ahriman felt almost overwhelming, I suddenly had a tranquil, confident sense of being released from the power of this evil force. A feeling that our cause will not founder. And then a boundless longing for the School [for Spiritual Science] came over me. Please make it possible! It is a help to us, right into the decisions we make relating to public policies."

52 Cf. Emanuel Zeylmans van Emmichoven, *Who Was Ita Wegman?*, op cit, vol. 2, pp. 51ff [G]; Peter Selg, *I Am for Going Ahead*, op cit, pp. 67ff [G]; and Peter Selg, *Der Engel auf dem*

*Lauenstein. Siegfried Pickert, Ita Wegman und die Heilpäda-
gogik.* Dornach, 2004.

53 Cf. Ernst Klee, *"Euthanasie" im NS-Staat. Die "Vernichtung leb-
ensunwerten Lebens,"* Frankfurt, 2004, pp. 36ff.

54 Letter from Ita Wegman to Heinrich Hardt, 5.9.1933.

55 Cf., for instance, the monograph survey by Arno Klönne, *Jugend im
Dritten Reich. Die Hitler-Jugend und ihre Gegner.* Cologne, 1982.

56 Letter from Ita Wegman to Mathilde Enschedé, 4.12.1933.

57 After spring 1933, Wegman and her colleagues in the curative homes
only communicated via letters brought in person. Everything else
was discussed face-to-face and was therefore not recorded in writing. On June 20, 1933, when Erich Kirchner had the opportunity to
get a letter taken to Arlesheim via Weleda, he gave Wegman a singu-
lar and exemplary report on the situation they were already facing.
He wrote, "In Pilgramshain the most diverse machinations are at
work in relation to Dr. König [the institute's physician], seeking to
identify him as a Jew and a foreigner. He has already been deprived
of his doctor title because he qualified as a physician abroad. The
regional president has demanded a report—from which one can see
that preoccupation with his person and with Pilgramshain itself
is now the region's prime concern. Bert Keyserlingk told me that
König has said he can only endure this assault on him for a few
more weeks, and would prefer to leave. He was prevented from giving a talk in a town nearby when the National Socialists informed
him they would disrupt it halfway through, and said he should no
longer be permitted to speak. While it might be possible for König
to remain here, even under current conditions, through the connections we have managed to establish with government departments
in Silesia, I can't see how he can continue to work. Apart from this,
it seems very likely that his continued presence will cause a great
deal of problems for the institute" (see facsimile, page 23).

58 Letter from Ita Wegman to Erich Kirchner, 6.21.1933.

59 Letter from Ita Wegman to Fried Geuter, 4.11.1933. Uwe Werner
stressed the good sense and relative success of the restructuring
initiated by Wegman as follows: "These changes must have helped
to ensure that in the first few years these institutes were largely
left alone by central Nazi authorities, although they were aware of
them. A whole series of reports by police informers and the police
reports themselves from 1934 and 1935 were left in Gestapo files
without further action.... The lack of any wider organizational
connection between the institutions and the Anthroposophical
Society, and the fact that they were not apparently affiliated with

each other, made the institutes of relatively little interest for the Gestapo" (Werner, op cit, pp. 162, 165).

60 Letter from Ita Wegman to Heinrich Hardt, 7.27.1933. Just two weeks later (on 8.14.1933) Wegman pushed Hardt—who probably saw the situation in much more positive, and therefore naïve, terms than she did—for further information: "Have you been able to find out more about the sterilization law?" After the meetings in Stuttgart on Mar. 31 and Apr. 1, Hardt had tried to cautiously express his more optimistic view of the situation and developments in Germany ("I do not see the current situation in Germany as hopeless because—so far at least—it is clear that Hitler is focusing on the political domain as such, since there was in fact great need for this due to [the country's] inner and outer weakness. But recovery of strength must of course not lead to abuse of the powers regained. Hitler experienced the horrors of war at first hand, and so I do not think he is frivolous about such things. I am not uncritical in regard to the opportunities I see in how things are going at present. But a certain degree of trust will help, while fear makes things worse"). Two days after Joseph Goebbels summoned journalists to announce that Germany was leaving the League of Nations and the Geneva disarmament conference, Hardt wrote, "It would be very good and important, dear Frau Wegman, if you would give your particular attention to the German physicians at this time, *especially* the German ones. You see, Germany is now the country in which decisions are being prepared in *one way or another;* it is also the country that stands most *alone* at present, and in which therefore *much,* also of a spiritual nature, can more easily break through. However one judges Germany's resignation from the League of Nations—it came as a great surprise to me—the League was after all a setup, a collusion of egoistic, routine representatives who think and act in outmoded ways. My hope is that here (in Germany) adversity may create receptivity for the innovative outlooks of Anthroposophy!" (10.16.1933). It was also Hardt who, immediately after the Berlin federation of Waldorf School representatives was formed—as the "Reich Association of Waldorf Schools"—wrote to Wegman (on 5.29.1933) asking for guidance regarding an "affiliation" of curative educators as part of the prevailing "conformity" activities [translator's note: This term (*Gleichschaltung*) was used in the Third Reich to denote enforced alignment with the status quo; it required uniformity of outlook and, specifically, a favorable view of the regime].

61 Letter from Ita Wegman to Emil Drebber, 2.8.1933.

62 Letter from Ita Wegman to Erich Kirchner, 2.5.1933. At this time (beginning of February 1933) Wegman was clearly still uncertain whether all her colleagues in the curative institutes would share her view of the Nazis' rise to power; she therefore wrote in a questioning and somewhat provocative way to Erich Kirchner: "But perhaps things have now reached the point where all of you are fervent about Hitler, and who knows whether I am alone in my view?" (ibid). Kirchner replied by return mail, in absolutely clear terms, fully agreeing with Wegman's assessment of the Nazi threat, and adding, "Above all, there will no longer be any certainty of any kind. While the government may have no time in the immediate future to pay us any attention, sooner or later they are likely to do so. We can see the sort of means they employ by the measures of the last few days.... We also see that the only possibility is to form islands, and to gather people here" (2.7.1933).

63 Letter from Ita Wegman to Erna Benthien, 3.31.1933.

64 In this regard see the letter of 3.23.1925 by Hilma Walter to Eugen Kolisko which I quoted in *Helene von Grunelius und Rudolf Steiners Kurse für junge Mediziner. Eine biographische Studie*, Dornach, 2003, pp. 181f. This letter, clearly, was written on behalf of Ita Wegman and Rudolf Steiner.

65 Letter from Ita Wegman to Walter Johannes Stein, 2.4.1935.

66 Letter from Ita Wegman to Mien Viehoff, 5.5.1933.

67 Letter from Ita Wegman to Karl Nunhoefer, 4.30.1933.

68 "On the twenty-seventh, I am to speak about Dr. Steiner" (ibid.). Ita Wegman's important lecture draft for this in her notebook was published by Emanuel Zeylmans van Emmichoven in 1990 (Zeylmans, *Who Was Ita Wegman?*, op cit, vol. 1, pp. 294ff and 117ff [G]).

69 Letter from Ita Wegman to Madeleine van Deventer, 6.18.1933.

70 Letter from Ita Wegman to Karl Nunhoefer, 4.30.1933.

71 On one occasion Ita Wegman wrote to Mien Viehoff with an explanation of and deeper perspective on her actions: "It is good to try everything possible in these times to give a human example of being on good, warm terms with all nationalities as a true spiritual scientist" (5.12.1933).

72 Letter from Ita Wegman to Mien Viehoff, 5.12.1933.

73 On April 20, Walter Johannes Stein, writing from a guesthouse by Lake Starnberger, reported in much detail to Ita Wegman (who was still trying to support him financially) on the difficulties he was experiencing in relation to his public lecturing work in Germany. He ended the letter—after describing his ongoing publishing plans—with the following: "If all that I have described cannot

be realized here, I will have to go to England. I am almost convinced that this will happen now. As an Austrian I can do this without difficulty. But I regard it as a matter of honour to have tried my utmost here first. Frau Doctor, you have conducted yourself similarly in other matters, and will understand my stance. This step would become necessary if changes happen in the [Waldorf] School, which I do indeed expect now. I thank you for your loyalty in adversity, at a time when others are acting differently."

74   Letter from Ita Wegman to Madeleine van Deventer, 2.25.1933.

75   Letter from Ita Wegman to Madeleine van Deventer, 5.29.1933.

76   Letter from Ita Wegman to Julia Bort, 5.31.1933.

77   Letter from Ita Wegman to Madeleine van Deventer, 6.5.1933.

78   Cf. the excellent biography by Thomas Meyer, *D. N. Dunlop. Ein Zeit- und Lebensbild* (in English: *D. N. Dunlop: A Man of Our Time,* Temple Lodge, 1996), Basel 1996, pp. 209ff.

79   Explaining the need for daily Class Lessons, Ita Wegman wrote to George Adams Kaufmann on 7.31.1933: "In any event, I consider it important to be consistent in realizing this, so as to have a spiritual foundation upon which we can rely, especially in a summer school." In general, though—apart from the spiritual dimension of the Class Lessons—Wegman was in favor of an event in Bangor that would be markedly different from classic anthroposophic lecture courses, and had responded with great disappointment when she received the final program for the event: "Oh dear, the Bangor program is so old-fashioned. Such a thing was fine seven years ago, but is now outmoded. Something different is needed now. This program would have been right for R. Steiner House in London, with big posters and publicity. But for Bangor it lacks verve; it lacks verve for a summer school. Here we need a spiritualized enlivening of nature, immersing oneself in nature, with joyfulness, playfulness, dance. Summer schools are for the young" (Letter to Mien Viehoff, 4.28.1933).

80   Letter from Ita Wegman to Fried Geuter and Michael Wilson, 3.13.1933.

81   Letter from Ita Wegman to Herbert Hahn, 3.13.1933.

82   Letter from Ita Wegman to Heinrich Hardt, 5.12.1933.

83   Letter from Ita Wegman to Karl Nunhoefer, 4.30.1933.

84   The initiative for this came from the Munich students Eugen Berthold, Wiltrud Feitig and Iris Seebohm; on behalf of the three, Wiltrud Feitig wrote to Wegman on June 13, "My dear Frau Dr. Wegman, we have heard that a summer school is to take place in England in September, and would very much like to have a course

for medical students there either before or after that event. The work has now reached a point where we might benefit from going somewhere other than Dornach: we need new impulses and greater breadth so that we do not become creatures of habit. The only thing that might prevent us doing this—the matter of money—is something we are firmly resolved to overcome, even though we only have 5 marks between us at present.... I believe that it is now time to read the Pastoral Medicine Course (in English: *Broken Vessels: The Spiritual Structure of Human Frailty*, Great Barrington, MA: SteinerBooks, 2002 [CW 318]) in a quite different set of circumstances, in England. Or should we first study 'Initiate Consciousness'? We really wish to cultivate this Pastoral Medicine Course in the same way that we did with the courses for young doctors, and let it live among us."

85 Letter from Ita Wegman to Anneliese Feitig, 6.27.1933.
86 Ibid.
87 Letter from Ita Wegman to Fried Geuter and Michael Wilson, 8.11.1933.
88 Letter from Ita Wegman to George Adams Kaufmann, 7.9.1933.
89 Letter from Ita Wegman to Hilma Walter, 7.18.1933.
90 Letter from Ita Wegman to Fried Geuter and Michael Wilson, 7.18.1933.
91 Letter from Ita Wegman to Hilma Walter, 7.18.1933.
92 The letters were sent to Hermann Keiner (Dortmund), Hans Mothes (Essen), Werner Gutsch (Karlsruhe), Heinrich Stickdorn (Paderborn) and Rudolf Röchling (Bochum).
93 Letter from Ita Wegman to Heinrich Hardt, 8.14.1933.
94 Letter from Ita Wegman to Anneliese Feitig, 7.13.1933.
95 Letter from Ita Wegman to Fried Geuter and Michael Wilson, 7.18.1933.
96 Ibid.
97 Wegman herself wished mainly to visit the British Museum and the National Gallery in London with the students (letter to Mien Viehoff, 8.15.1933). She had gone there with Rudolf Steiner in earlier years, receiving from him numerous, thought-provoking pointers relating to spiritual and cultural history (cf. also note 104).
98 Only very rarely did Ita Wegman show in her letters in 1933 how much all the destructive events in the world were weighing on her, how much she personally suffered from them and how, despite all her creative, optimistic work and initiative, she was often at the very edge of exhaustion and despair. On one occasion, however, she wrote to Fried Geuter, Michael Wilson and Hilma Walter in

Clent: "There is such great need in the world, and everything cries
out for a state of spiritual balance, so that when a group of people
does not do something in just the right way, the equilibrium will
also become unsettled. *And it is this that torments me day and
night, making me almost sick at heart with the worry and tension
in me*" (7.18.1933; author's emphasis).

99   Letter from Ita Wegman to George Adams Kaufmann, 7.18.1933.
100   Letter from Ita Wegman to Fried Geuter and Michael Wilson,
      8.11.1933.
101   Letter from Ita Wegman to Mien Viehoff, 8.11.1933.
102   Letter from Ita Wegman to Fried Geuter and Michael Wilson,
      8.11.1933.
103   Wegman sent several letters in advance of the trip to her friends in
      England relating to the need for Lothar Marx to stay in England.
      In a message to Fried Geuter and Michael Wilson, she mentioned
      that several other members of the group of students might be con-
      sidering emigration, and wrote, "As I told you already, one of them
      is Lothar Marx, a very fine lad, who cannot return because of his
      Jewish origins, and whom we must help. But we can speak about
      this in person in England. A few others may also stay, but volun-
      tarily. For instance Holtzapfel, whose mother is a friend of Frau
      Plincke, is likely to be thinking of doing his whole medical studies
      in England rather than Germany; and then also Alex Leroi and
      Gisbert Husemann. If these people stay for a year in England, or
      perhaps altogether, this would naturally be a huge support for the
      work there" (8.15.1933). Cf. Peter Selg (ed.), *Anthroposophische
      Ärzte. Lebens- und Arbeitswege im 20. Jahrhundert* (Dornach,
      2000), p. 413, in relation to Lothar Marx, who was the only par-
      ticipant to realize plans for emigration, and later worked in Clent
      and Birmingham.
104   "She [Ita Wegman] took us on a tour through the museums in Lon-
      don that she had visited with Rudolf Steiner, telling us what he had
      said about each artwork. We also undertook our own excursions,
      having intense encounters with the elemental forces that are espe-
      cially strong in this country. In a boat on the Thames we made a
      trip to the countryside upstream from London. The boat capsized
      and we fell into the water but were all saved though not everyone
      could swim. We spent a few days at a large curative institute in
      Birmingham. We took part in an English summer school at Bangor
      in Wales and climbed to the Druid circles at Penmaenmawr. We
      visited Manchester. The whole trip was done in several cars which
      English friends had generously provided.... On our return we had

imbibed such a breadth of world air that it sustained us through the coming years" (Walter Holtzapfel, quoted in Zeylmans, *Who Was Ita Wegman?*, op cit, vol. 2, p. 334 [G]). After they returned to Germany, some of the students, at least temporarily, considered emigrating to England (or at least studying or working there for a while in anthroposophic contexts). On Oct. 5, for instance, Ita Wegman received a letter with a request for advice from the Berlin medical student Gerhard Schumacher, who clearly intended interrupting his studies in Germany to work in curative education at Clent but had met with great resistance to the idea from his parents. Ita Wegman replied to him a few days later with the following forthright and sympathetic words: "Dear Herr Schumacher, I'm sorry I was not able to reply to your letter immediately, since it arrived in the middle of the medical conference. I also allowed myself a little time to reflect on it, picturing your situation in much detail and that of your parents. My conclusion is as follows: If you really have the sense that you cannot study well in Germany as things currently stand (and I believe that this is indeed true for you, since you would suffer greatly psychologically) then it is necessary for you to make a change in your way of life. Your parents ought not to oppose this; and reproaching you, even threatening, as a way of blaming others, is something I consider quite unjustified. As anthroposophists, your parents must understand, after all, that all individuals have their own destiny and are led toward it. What gives your parents the right to think that you will remain dependent on others at a later period? If one is competent and industrious, one is never dependent; and what you are seeking, after all, is great human competency and commitment, which you wish to inform your medical studies. You are not in fact giving up these studies, but postponing them due to the current circumstances. This is something you really ought to make clear to the people around you, that we no longer live in times when, as in the past, people pursue the traditional tranquil path of studies from one term to the next, abiding by their parents' views. The times have changed; and one's studies do not have to remain so narrow in scope. In these changed times of ours, we can allow ourselves to structure our studies differently from the old, traditional way. This will not diminish your love for your parents. You must just make this clear to them, since it would not be good if your father held a grudge that might end up making him ill. You must do whatever is necessary so that your parents understand and can even let you go with their blessing. I can also understand your parents, and I believe the whole problem is due to the fact that they so much want to see you qualify as a physician. It is hard for parents to give up such an idea. But I also have to say that there is absolutely no need for you to relinquish these studies. You can plan things so that this is only a postponement of something you will take up again in the foreseeable future, but for now you plan to leave Germany for a while. This is something we need to embark on now. I hope with all my heart that you can find the right words and tone to tell your parents all this in a way they understand. What you must not do is to cease your studies because of *us*. I am very aware that many parents will find fault with me for alienating their children from them as a result of our trip to England. With warmest greetings, your I. Wegman MD."

Another student, Eugen Berthold, who had high expectations of his trip to England, returned to Munich disillusioned with his social experiences there. Writing to Wegman about this on 12.22.1933, he said, "What I experienced there was difficult. I found myself looking into human abysses, and never before have I experienced so strongly the powers of fragmentation at work in humanity. Nor have I previously experienced so clearly the fact that the Doctor is no longer among us; he would have understood what we wanted. We found ourselves thrown back on our own resources." Wegman wrote an encouraging reply in response: "I am very sorry to hear this. I'd like to be able to talk to you in great detail about many things at some point. I am firmly convinced that you see things in this way due to certain misunderstandings, which mean that you don't have the *full* picture. You write that you put all your efforts into taking this trip and had the highest expectations of it. But, dear Herr Barthold, isn't it possible that the trip will still bear its fruits? They may be concealed for now because the time is not yet ripe. Perhaps you should regard your experience in a different country, with different people, and the fact that the friends you have had so far now perhaps appear differently to you, more as something that was necessary. Perhaps you should try a little to forget the bitterness that is connected with this experience, and make a new beginning here with your old, loyal connection with us and also with the Medical Section. You can remain sure of my old, faithful friendship to you and of my sense of gratitude toward you, for you have always been one of those who helped sustain the courses, and always did everything you were able to for the Medical Section. I do not underestimate this, and nor will I forget it" (1.1.1934).

105 In the spring and summer, Ita Wegman and her colleagues in Arlesheim, with other invited physicians, had worked through the

available shorthand notes and transcripts of the course (and also those of the Curative Education Course). ("We are currently in the process of thoroughly revising the Pastoral Medicine Course (in English: *Broken Vessels: The Spiritual Structure of Human Frailty*, Great Barrington, MA: SteinerBooks, 2002 [CW 318]), which, as you know, contains a great many errors. If you are here I'd also very much like to go through it with you" [letter to Karl König, 7.7.1933].) Ita Wegman wanted to discuss this revised version at the Michaelmas gathering with the priests, before it went to print. Thus, on 7.12.1933, she wrote to the chief coordinator of The Christian Community, Friedrich Rittelmeyer: "The Medical Section intends giving a course after Michaelmas that will concern itself more with the Pastoral Medicine Course. The time to do this has arrived now that we have worked through the rest of the medical material and can therefore devote detailed attention to the field of pastoral medicine. We have now worked through Dr. Steiner's course and have remedied errors in the transcript to the best of our ability. But before we finally publish this work, we would like to meet with the priests of The Christian Community so that this edition can be properly prepared for publication. Even though it may not be possible for all the priests to participate in this course, it may hopefully be feasible for a smaller or larger group of them to attend.... I can assure you that I could not possibly have held this course any sooner, despite enquiries from the priests and physicians, since I felt very serious responsibility regarding interpretation of this course; and it is therefore only now that I dare issue it in print." Wegman's letter ended with the words: "I very much hope, dear Dr. Rittelmeyer, that things will be well for you during these grave times, and that you can continue your work despite all difficulties."

106   In the conference due to take place from Oct. 4 to 7, only the mornings were devoted to the shared work on the Pastoral Medicine Course ("We will start at 9.30 a.m. in the Medical Section's premises at the Goetheanum with reading and revision of the Pastoral Medicine Course" [in English; see note 105], Ita Wegman to Albert Steffen, 10.3.1933); the afternoons were given over to medical seminars (for instance on cancer therapy); and in the evenings there were interdisciplinary—and public—lectures by Willem Zeylmans van Emmichoven ("Threshold states of soul life"), Karl König ("Ferdinand Raimund and his destiny"), Gerhard Suchantke ("Illness, healing and the evolution of consciousness") and Eugen Kolisko ("Sacramental life illuminated by an anthroposophic view of the

human being"). Cf. also the facsimile of the conference program on page 39; according to Wegman's report on the conference, it all went "extremely well" (letter to Fried Geuter and Michael Wilson, 10.14.1933).

107 Letter from Ita Wegman to Madeleine van Deventer, undated (September 1933).

108 Letter from Ita Wegman to Madeleine van Deventer, 11.15.1933.

109 Letter to English friends in Clent and London, 12.18.1933. On the same day Wegman wrote expressly again to Fried Geuter and Michael Wilson: "I really want to say again that I have only acted in response to a necessity, one that clearly arose before me. But I am aware that others beside myself must have insight into this need, for otherwise it might easily acquire a personal tinge; and this would not be right. At this point misunderstandings begin to arise. A huge number of misunderstandings do encircle my person. I have to bear with this and wait calmly until they are cleared out of the way." Five days later, on 12.23.1933, she wrote to Dorothy Osmond in her last review of her travels of that year, at the same time looking back on the whole year: "I also have to say that, unwittingly, I do not bear England within me in as luminous a way as has been the case previously. There too, there seem to be powers at work that seek to sunder it from a certain path it has taken so far. It really seems as if something is seeking to come about in England that can have grave consequences for the future—as if more death forces have gained entry there than was the case a little while back."

110 Oskar Schmiedel noted the following about a conversation he had with Rudolf Steiner in Dec. 1923: "The phrase he [Steiner] used fairly near the end of our discussion was important—how important became apparent in the years after he died—when he spoke of the opposition to Frau Dr. Wegman. Because of their significance, these words were ineradicably engraved in my mind, and I can therefore give them verbatim. Dr. Steiner said, 'If the campaign against Frau Dr. Wegman continues, the Society will be blown asunder by it.' And then he added these words that shocked me deeply: 'And this tendency is apparent in my closest vicinity. But there, too, I will oppose it most energetically'" (quoted in Zeylmans, *Who Was Ita Wegman?*, op cit, vol. 3, p. 435 [G]). In his Dornach address on 4.14.1935 (see below), Count Ludwig Polzer-Hoditz also spoke of these things: "There may be some among you here who heard Rudolf Steiner speak of a witchhunt against Frau Dr. Wegman and her work as a physician even back then, saying that this would destroy the Society" (quoted in Zeylmans, *Who*

Was Ita Wegman?, op cit, vol. 3, p. 334 [G]). At the end of the Curative Education Course and six months after the "esoteric executive council" and the Medical Section were founded, Rudolf Steiner— no doubt also with an eye to Ita Wegman's position—said, "There is no need for you to simply believe this but it can be deduced from all that occurs; back then, when the Christmas Foundation Meeting was to be set in motion, these positions of responsibility were carefully scrutinized with an exclusivity in regard to the quality of the human individuals who hold these positions that might strike some as ferocious. Given that the executive council at the Goetheanum arose from such foundations, it must inevitably be regarded as fully authoritative for what happens within the Anthroposophical Society. This executive council simply has to be seen as the executive that bears full authority for the diverse things that must be decided. Will this or will this not be understood in the future within the anthroposophic movement?" (Rudolf Steiner, *Heilpädagogischer Kurs* [in English: *Education for Special Needs: The Curative Education Course*, London: Rudolf Steiner Press, 1999], Dornach, 1990, pp. 186f). Eighteen years later, during a small meeting at the Sonnenhof, on Aug. 7, 1942, Julia Bort recalled comments about Ita Wegman that Steiner made shortly before his death. Werner Pache noted in his journal at the time: "He must also have told her that all, or a great many, would leave her in the lurch, but that he would not."

111   Letter from Ita Wegman to Mien Viehoff, 4.28.1933.

112   Ita Wegman wrote about this to Mien Viehoff on Apr. 28, 1933: "Honestly, I have to say that however pleased I am to hear Kolisko's lectures, I do not agree with his way of proceeding. Without further ado people [in Dornach] have become accustomed to me working in England; with Stein, too, there might have been some reconciliation. But now to include Kolisko as well is too much for them, and to see it printed in the program like that." Although Wegman always remained loyal to her companions and friends, covering up for much that she herself had certainly not initiated and therefore did not agree with, she did repeatedly express her concerns in her personal correspondence. In Feb. 1933 she wrote to Walter Johannes Stein in very direct terms: "I do not think that we can expect much collaboration from the Kolisko group. Kolisko has never wanted this, and will never want it; he will always do his own thing" (3.2.1933).

113   At the end of Sept. 1933, with Marie Steiner's agreement, Roman Boos published his book *Rudolf Steiner während des Krieges*

(Rudolf Steiner during the war), which tuned in to the mood of "national exaltation" in Germany. In his introduction, Boos wrote, among other things: "The incisive documents published in this volume on the theme of 'Rudolf Steiner during the world war' bring into sharp focus the figure of a man who, with heroic strength, battled lifelong through deeds and sufferings to make the German spirit a power of salvation within the history of humanity, so that it might exert a decisive and formative impact on contemporary events" [p. 1]; "The whole life of Rudolf Steiner is illumined by a great gesture whereby the German spirit is lifted from the creative powers at its very roots through courage, blood, suffering, and sacrifice to bear its spiritual fruits" [p. 11]; "As a portrait of the man, whose thinking and will never capitulate to powers of destruction, this book seeks to play a part in contemporary events. For this portrait can kindle our will to transform the general trend of events within our own actions from a will-o-the-wisp to a real task. Is the era of fatal resignation now close to its end? Are the powers that dare to take the reins of destiny now opening the gates to a renewal of history? Who in the world could not hope that this might be so?" [xxxixf]; "Self-reflection, manifestation of one's true nature, taking a grip upon one's own destiny is the 'made in Germany' hallmark tried and proven in the toughest trials. It is this yeast the world needs because it must burst asunder if not bound together by anything better than the soft putty of international pacifism" [xviii]. In 1934, in Munich and Berlin, Boos published his monograph on the "Rebirth of German Law" based on previous lectures he had given ("In lectures, addresses, and discussions with lawyers and laymen, the author has found a warm welcome in the new Germany for the fundamental ideas presented in this book, and likewise has received much stimulus for it" [p. 9]. See Uwe Werner, op cit, pp. 51ff, regarding the typical tenor of Boos's lectures on 1.23 and 24.1934, attended, at his request, by the National Socialist Party's chief justice). For many years, Boos had been one of Ita Wegman's harshest critics. At the Annual General Meeting in the spring of 1934, he was to hold the longest and most aggressive speech against her, speaking on that occasion of the "dark drive" of the "Declaration of Intent" and of an eradication of esotericism by Wegman and her circles; likewise of the "anal mysticism" and "anal esotericism" practised by them. He characterized Ita Wegman and the people connected with her as the "carcinoma of the Anthroposophical Society" (transcript, cf. note 167).

114 At the Michaelmas conference in 1933 (9.29–10.3), besides a performance of Steffen's "Fall of the Antichrist" and scenes from Faust, along with a reading by Albert Steffen from his own works, there were lectures by Roman Boos on "Tragedies of statesmanship in the works of Conrad Ferdinand Meyer," Willy Stokar on "Johannes von Müller (1752–1809) and his contemporaries," Friedrich Haeusler on "The origins of Switzerland in the context of medieval Italy," Guenther Schubert on "Jakob Burckhardt and our era," Friedrich Eymann on "Religion today," Max Leist on "The agricultural geology of Emmental" and Curt Englert on "Insights into problems of [Swiss] national education."

115 Letter from Ita Wegman to Albert Steffen, 7.29.1933.

116 Letter from Ita Wegman to Fried Geuter and Michael Wilson, 10.14.1933. Two days previously, Ita Wegman had written to Albert Steffen: "My dear Herr Steffen, During the medical conference, as I told you, I held a Class Lesson in the terrace room. From various quarters the wish has now arisen to hold a few more, and again I would like to give these in the terrace room. However, Dr. Wachsmuth is objecting to this, saying that your permission should first be obtained. Since my view is that no one has anything to say about whether or not I hold Class Lessons, and that the competency to do so is a matter for me alone to decide; and that this matter cannot be dependent on questions relating to rooms, I hereby inform you that I will give these Class Lessons in Medical Section premises at the Goetheanum if it is not possible to hold them in the other room. This Sunday and next, therefore, I will read a Class Lesson by Rudolf Steiner, after which I will be going away for a while. Yours sincerely, Dr. I. Wegman."

117 A letter, headed "Sanatorium Wiesneck, October 10, 1933, Buchenbach near Freiburg," and signed by Husemann and Schubert, runs: "Dear Colleague, You will no doubt have read the appeal by Dr. Wagner, Reich minister for medical umbrella associations, in issue 15 of the *German Medical Newsletter*, 10.7.1933. Excerpts from it were also published in the national press. The appeal is addressed to 'all physicians in Germany involved in biological medical procedures,' inviting them to amalgamate with their associations and affiliates in an overarching group that includes all biological physicians of every discipline. It is clear from this appeal that it does not involve a merely formal affiliation but instead intends to bring about closer contact between physicians of a 'biological' persuasion. It expressly states, 'Only after this federation has been formed will it become possible for all these medical procedures to obtain

the scrutiny or recognition which they deserve, and then be integrated into the training and further training of all physicians, for the benefit of all patients who need our help.' We have to welcome the fact that Dr. Wagner is not content with formal 'conformity measures' but instead aims to test medical disciplines that are outside the mainstream and ascertain what is 'valuable from all fields of medical practice.' Under these circumstances it is doubtless a matter of urgent importance that physicians in Germany working according to anthroposophic methods amalgamate in a federation so that their interests can be fully represented. As you know, Waldorf teachers and all enterprises connected with biodynamic agriculture have already formed similar associations. If we do not form such an association of physicians, any difficulties that arise at some juncture will find us without any protection or safeguard. For the inner consolidation of our group of physicians, likewise, such an amalgamation would be very welcome. Among other things this would enable us to exclude unqualified elements and others who illegally give themselves credentials as anthroposophic physicians, and deny them membership. Additionally, we must reckon on being required, at some point, to speak about 'anthroposophic medicine' to other physicians. Here it lies in all our interests for this to be done by colleagues who are best qualified to do so. The undersigned have long resolved upon these measures in discussions with our colleague Rascher in Munich who, as you may know, has close contacts with the core leadership of the NSDAP [National Socialist Party]. Dr. Rascher has declared his willingness to manage related negotiations with the authorities. We therefore ask that you tell us as soon as possible: 1) whether you are willing to join an 'association of anthroposophic physicians in Germany'; 2) whether you agree to name Dr. Rascher as the manager of this association; 3) We ask you to name the individuals who, in your view, are best-suited for representing anthroposophic methods effectively to other doctors, and who should therefore join the association executive; and 4) We ask you to inform us of any further points and perspectives you feel to be important.

Our proposal is not one we consider to be completely finalized; it is, rather, conceived in a broad enough way to allow inclusion of all justified interests. The thing of primary importance will be to form some kind of association, and the rest will then follow naturally. From these perspectives it does not seem necessary for anthroposophic physicians all to register separately in Munich. Please inform us if you have already done so. Since these matters are pressing, we ask you to reply immediately, with responses to points 1. and 2. at least, to the address above of Dr. Husemann. On the sixteenth of this month we will pass on to Dr. Rascher the communications we have received by that point. Yours sincerely, (signed) Dr. F. Husemann/Dr. R. Schubert." Cf. Uwe Werner, op cit, pp. 32ff, and Ernst Klee, *Auschwitz, die NS-Medizin und ihre Opfer,* Frankfurt, 1997, p. 219ff. and 350ff. in relation to Hanns Rascher, who also acted as NSDAP liaison officer within the Anthroposophical Society in Germany and whose son Sigmund, likewise a practicing physician, was later to undertake the cruellest experiments (including trials on death by hypothermia) on inmates of Dachau concentration camp. ("[Sigmund] Rascher, by education an anthroposophist (Free Waldorf School) has been described in the literature simply as a 'monster of medicine'" [Klee, p. 219]). In relation to "Reich medical president" Gerhard Wagner and the "conformity measures" applied to German physicians as the basis for realizing a Nazi health policy of eugenics, cf. Norbert Frei (ed.), *Medizin und Gesundheitspolitik in der NS-Zeit,* Munich, 1991; Fridolf Kudlien, *Ärzte im Nationalsozialismus,* Cologne, 1985; and Robert Jay Lifton, *The Nazi Doctors: Medical Killing and the Psychology of Genocide,* Basic Books, 2000.

118 Directly she received the newsletter and circular on Oct. 12; Ita Wegman enquired of, among others, Section members Eugen Kolisko, Heinrich Hardt, and Viktor Thylmann what stance they had toward the proposed federation. To Kolisko: "I would be glad to hear from you what answer you have given. If this comes about it seems to me that it will represent a most fateful alliance—primarily also because 'biological' methods cannot be construed as an anthroposophic approach. The Herr R.[ascher] referred to in the letter is also appointed to oversee other functions, of which you will no doubt have heard from Wolfgang W.[achsmuth]." To Hardt: "I would really like to know how you will reply to this enquiry. A great deal will depend in the near future on how physicians respond to it." To Thylmann: "Whether we can really go on working in accordance with R[udolf] St[einer] will depend very much on the answer to this circular by physicians working with the Section." Viktor Thylmann's reply arrived in Arlesheim only a few days later, and decisively rejected the circular ("I received the letter from Dr. H. a few days ago, and decided, after pondering briefly on it, not to reply at all. I haven't the slightest intention of getting involved with this, since I do not consider it the right course of action"). However, his letter already betrayed a

good deal of uncertainty in regard to the overall situation ("In the current situation it does not seem advisable to me to send a letter of rejection, since one does not know what sort of unpleasantness might arise for one in consequence," 10.14.1933). Hardt responded with no clear decision, while Kolisko wrote on 10.22.1933, "I did not receive the letter from Dr. H. But I have been informed of the planned federation that you mention and am in complete agreement with you. I reject this proposal as being quite wrong and misguided. Having discussed the issue with medical friends here, we have all reached the same outcome and will also pass on our views to members abroad at the next opportunity. We have to avoid exceeding our perfectly clear and simple spiritual tasks of medical work." Uwe Werner summed up the outcome of the activity undertaken by Husemann and Schubert (which acquired a legal form two years later at the end of April 1935): "Ultimately this...initiative came to nothing. Only around half of the physicians joined the association, and by the time it was to be integrated into 'conformity measures' only around 25 physicians were still engaged members. The fact that no such organization arose may well have helped ensure that anthroposophic physicians as such were not subjected to persecution" (Werner, op cit, pp. 166f).

119 "The Goetheanum leadership will increasingly identify itself with National Socialism. It seeks in every way to form a good relationship with those in power in Germany, and to organize things there in accordance with the wishes of this regime. Dr. Rascher, who has good connections with these powers, will now act as the one responsible for anthroposophic matters in Germany. There are also efforts underway, proceeding from Dr. Husemann and Dr. Schubert—no doubt at the advice of Dr. W[achsmuth]—to form an association of anthroposophic physicians and place this under the direction of Dr. Rascher. As you see, Germany is basically coming apart at the seams, and the Anthroposophical Society is being torn out of the structure Dr. Steiner gave it. The rulers in Germany and the Dornach leadership are in fact working parallel to each other in this respect. Things are very grave" (to Fried Geuter and Michael Wilson, 10.14.1933). In the spring of 1933 Guenther Wachsmuth was on a trip to Scandinavia, and gave an interview to Copenhagen newspaper in which he expressed very positive views of National Socialism: "It ought not to remain a secret that we [i.e., the Dornach executive council—author's note] regard with a sympathetic eye what is currently happening in Germany.... Stagnation means death for all spiritual and cultural life. Movement is necessary, and

the brave, courageous way in which the leaders of the new Germany are tackling current problems is, in my view, cause for nothing but admiration" (6.6.1933, quoted in Werner, op cit, p. 37). While in Scandinavia, Wachsmuth was informed by letter of the success of Hanns Rascher's discussions (cf. note 117) with leading Nazi circles, and had expressed his great pleasure at these developments ("For members, after all, it is also important to know, and will be welcomed by them, that we have met with such a positive response from this direction; and we also need to be clear that the former authorities previously did not show us such receptivity and interest. Today by contrast, we feel gratitude for the reception we meet with and for the fact that we are, at the same time, granted complete freedom to act and disseminate our ideas" [6.13.1933, quoted in Werner, ibid.]). Even after returning from his travels to Dornach, Wachsmuth continued—in accounts of his travels published in *Das Goetheanum* magazine—to accentuate and justify his unquestioning and positive assessment in a way that was close to absurd and which people like Ita Wegman found completely incomprehensible. He wrote, for instance, "It is good that the majority of our members are not given to weary and melancholic yearnings for a comfortable past nor meet today's complex events with merely doctrinal grumbling and dismay, but that instead such people are outnumbered in our membership by those who have the will to cooperate bravely and actively in solving current problems and tackling future tasks. At a time of general confusion around him, Goethe, alert to what was really happening, said, 'Here and now a new era in world history begins; and you can say that you were there when it commenced.' It is encouraging that those who wish to be 'there' predominate in our ranks as well" [quoted in Werner, op cit, p. 38]). Even before Wachsmuth's trip to Scandinavia, Rascher's superior at the SS news agency, SS Hauptsturmfuehrer ["captain"] Hauschild, had gone to Dornach at Rascher's suggestion and had been received there by Paul Eugen Schiller as "representative" of the executive council. Hauschild presented Schiller with a whole series of questions that were then answered in a great hurry, these responses later reaching Reinhard Heydrich (and possibly Heinrich Himmler). Uwe Werner comments on the origins of this statement by the executive council—which was officially signed by Albert Steffen and later repeatedly used as a reference document (by people such as Hermann Poppelbaum): "This unusual procedure later gave rise to the so-called Memorandum[!] issued by the executive council on May 20, 1933. It was a letter prepared in a hurry probably by Dr.

Otto Fraenkl with the support of Guenther Wachsmuth and Marie Steiner. Albert Steffen, president of the Society, was in Paris at this time. Fraenkl flew to see Steffen there on May 19" (ibid., p. 33). In fall 1933, in addition, at Rascher's suggestion and after a discussion with Guenther Wachsmuth, Marie Steiner sent a registered letter to Rudolf Hess regarding Rudolf Steiner's Aryan descent. Summarizing the responses of the Goetheanum in 1933, Uwe Werner wrote, "In Dornach, Albert Steffen, Ita Wegman and Elisabeth Vreede were opposed to National Socialism; but at that time Ita Wegman and Elisabeth Vreede were, for all practical purposes, already excluded from executive council work" (ibid., p. 40).

120 See here also Elisabeth Vreede's own, detailed account of the circumstances and the necessity for her actions in Elisabeth Vreede, *Zur Geschichte der Anthroposophischen Gesellschaft seit der Weihnachtstagung 1923* (in English: *On the History of the Anthroposophical Society since the 1923 Christmas Foundation Meeting*, in Zeylmans, *Who Was Ita Wegman?*, vol. 3, op cit), reprinted in Zeylmans, *Wer war Ita Wegman*, vol. 3, op cit, pp. 240ff, especially pp. 251ff.

121 It is clear that in this matter, also in relation to Karl König's involvement in Elisabeth Vreede's conference, Ita Wegman expressed extremely critical views. König, to whom Wegman's verbal comments were conveyed, even came to think that he would now be expelled from the Medical Section. Neither König's letter about this to Wegman nor her reply to him have survived. However, on Jan. 12, 1935, Wegman asked Margarethe Bockholt, who was staying in Berlin at the time (and giving lectures there), to speak again with König in person and to reassure him: "I'd like to ask you, please, to make contact with König in some way. I have heard he's giving a course with Bock, and I've received a letter here from him in which he seems to think I am expelling him from the Section following comments I made in response to the Dr. Vreede affair, of which you know. As always happens, these comments were circulated—Strohschein seems to have done this—and given the whole thing a different momentum, so that König gained the impression I no longer wished to have him in the Section at all. I have already written to him to say that I had no such intention, that I do not want him to leave the Section, but only that I found his actions problematic because he did not inform us what was happening, and in consequence we ended up with a silly situation on our hands, unnecessarily so. Well, you know how these things happen; misunderstandings arise, and so I'd be very grateful if you would speak to him in person."

122   Ita Wegman included in these activities a series of public lectures
that were extremely well attended, which she had initiated as a
weekly event in the Goetheanum's terrace room under the general
title of "Anthroposophic study of the human being as foundation
of healthcare appropriate in our time." The first speakers were Gerhard Suchantke, Margarethe Bockholt, Ernst Marti, and Werner
Pache.

123   Willem Zeylmans replied by return mail to Wegman's letter, writing on 12.16.1933: "At the beginning of October Miss Vreede
asked me whether I would be willing to participate now and then
in the general lecture evenings that she held on Tuesdays, which
she wished to establish on a broader basis than before. I naturally
had no objection to this. Further, she spoke of her plan to organize a series of lectures at Christmas, *alongside* the Christmas
conference, about the old and new Mysteries. She wished to invite
various speakers to give these lectures—not only physicians, but
including particular physicians who are used to speaking on general anthroposophic matters (apart from Dr. Hahn, Dr. Roeschl,
G. Kaufmann, as well as Dr. König, Kolisko, and me). I thought
this might be a good idea because we had just had the Michaelmas
conference from which Steffen had withdrawn, and no one was able
to tell how things would continue. The only condition I made was
that the lecture series should be offered as part of the Christmas
conference so that it could not be regarded as *oppositional.* That
is also how it was presented in Miss Vreede's letter [see note 120].
The whole uproar arose through the strange manner in which Steffen went about things. Although I knew the details of Miss Vreede's
plan, the way things came about now strikes me as very disagree-
able. Naturally, I don't wish to leave Miss Vreede in the lurch, but
I do doubt whether this way of proceeding makes sense any more.
I heard only much later that there were really serious differences
of opinion between the three executive council members up there.
In October the whole situation seemed to me like a kind of victory
by Boos over Steffen, and I saw no reason whatsoever therefore
to respect this state of affairs particularly. Only gradually did it
become apparent that, alongside this victory of Frau Dr. St. and
Boos over Steffen, a significant inner conflict was brewing. This is
always the unfortunate thing in our circles—that we never quite
know what is happening or what is not. Even now everything is circulating as rumor. Steffen is keeping quiet and allowing members
to make a mess of things. Thus we always face a choice between
waiting and just going on working in one's own field, or trying to

advance good, useful impulses and making something happen. In a deeper sense, Miss Vreede's impulse is a good one. If we'd had a proper picture of the situation in October, we might, though, have done better to hang on and wait a bit."

124 Letter from Ita Wegman to the English friends (members) in Clent and London, 12.18.1933.

125 Ibid.

126 Letter from Ita Wegman to Mien Viehoff, 12.18.1933.

127 Letter from Ita Wegman to the English friends in Clent and London, 12.18.1933.

128 Letter from Ita Wegman to Eugen Berthold, 121.19.1933.

129 Letter from Ita Wegman to Dorothy Osmond, 12.23.1933.

130 Directly after the Christmas conference (and the parallel event organized by Elisabeth Vreede), Ita Wegman made efforts to have a direct, personal discussion with Albert Steffen, writing to him already on New Year's Day: "Dear Herr Steffen, Now that the conference is over I would like to ask you warmly to meet me for a conversation. I am happy to meet you at any time, and can make myself available. Might I ask whether we could do this already on Jan. 2 or 3? You can phone and leave a message at the clinic about the best time for us to meet."

131 Letter from Ita Wegman to Joseph van Leer, 12.23.1933.

132 Ita Wegman sent another copy of this photograph to Nora Stein-Baditz on 1.5.1934, writing there in more detail about the origin and significance of the picture: "As a small greeting I'd like to send you a photograph of the Christ statue. This is a photograph that Miss Maryon once took, while the Doctor was still alive therefore. Miss Maryon herself gave me several copies of it. Now the same image is sold in larger format at the Goetheanum. Previously I kept these pictures for myself but now that you can buy them up there [at the Goetheanum] I'd like to make a gift of them to a few friends. These pictures I have here are connected with certain memories for me, since Miss Maryon took them, and because I'm sure they also passed through Dr. Steiner's hands."

133 Letter from Ita Wegman to Violetta Plincke, 12.23.1933.

134 Letter from Ita Wegman to Beeb Roelvink, 7.14.1933.

135 Letter from Ita Wegman to Maria Roeschl, 2.22.1935.

136 Letter from Ita Wegman to Rudolf and Gertrud Goyert, 1.3.1934.

137 Letter from Ita Wegman to the Wilson family, 1.5.1934.

138 Letter from Ita Wegman to Bernard Lievegoed, 1.17.1934.

139 "Everywhere one finds a widespread spirit of capitulation among members, against which one can make scarcely any headway.

Nor is it at all surprising if one knows that the anthroposophic members are simply unable to withstand bombardment by the National Socialist wave. It is very strange how each person comes to terms with this state, and no one any longer finds anything remarkable about being forced into line. The latest thing is that the Anthroposophical Society in Germany itself is to be integrated into these 'conformity measures' and will be led by Dr. Rascher, who will be in direct contact with the Nazis. One is obliged to sign a document stating one is in agreement with Hitler's worldview, which has been given the name *Ariosophia*. In the meantime, Rudolf Steiner is being further attacked by a party newspaper in Baden, and called the greatest swindler. On the one hand Rudolf Steiner is the subject of attacks, and on the other people form alliances with this pack. When one relates all these things it naturally sounds as if one were very sad about it; but it is different if you witness this fragmentation from close at hand and at the same time have the sense—as I do, for instance—that we know what the remedy is but are unable to use it because not enough people can get behind it in the fullest sense, in a way that would counter this capitulation. It would certainly involve a courageous and uncompromising stance to make headway, yet such headway cannot occur in isolation but requires many working together in community. That we make progress here and there can be seen everywhere, but that in itself will not accomplish very much. The really important thing is to form a new Michaelic community throughout the world. I also find it unspeakably sad that we have not yet achieved very much in England as counterweight that could work against what is happening in Germany" (letter from Ita Wegman to Maria Geuter, 1.18.1934).

140   In relation to Guenther Wachsmuth's markedly positive stance toward National Socialism and the diplomatic manoeuvring he expressly promoted in Germany, Uwe Werner writes, "He also had material grounds for his one-sided assessment. As treasurer he was concerned to preserve the Society not least in financial terms. The German members made a considerable contribution to funding the Goetheanum" (Werner, op cit, pp. 37f).

141   Letter from Ita Wegman to Karl Nunhoefer, 1.19.1934.

142   Letter from Ita Wegman to Erich Kirchner, 1.30.1934.

143   See note 57.

144   Letter from Ita Wegman to Bernard Lievegoed, 1.17.1933.

145   Letter from Ita Wegman to Eugen Kolisko, 1.24.1933.

146   Letter from Ita Wegman to Lothar Stettner, 1.23.1934.

147 Letter from Ita Wegman to Hilma Walter, 2.1.1934.

148 Letter from Ita Wegman to Sister Gertrud Pini, 3.6.1934.

149 Ibid.

150 Letter from Ita Wegman to Elise Wolfram, 2.1.1933.

151 Letter from Ita Wegman to Mien Viehoff, 2.2.1934.

152 Letter from Walter Johannes Stein to Ita Wegman, 2.27.1934.

153 Letter from Ita Wegman to Karl Schubert, 3.2.1934.

154 "I have been back since yesterday and would have liked to have had a discussion with Dr. Vreede today about the forthcoming general meeting, but heard that she went to Stuttgart yesterday. I just had time to speak with my English friends about the motion submitted by these 7 worthy gentlemen, which is to be presented at the general meeting, and also to have a brief conversation about it with Dr. Zeylmans in Holland. So it would be important also to continue these discussions with Dr. Vreede, and with you too. I want to submit a counter-motion which I have already formulated; but I don't want to send it off before speaking with Dr. Vreede" (letter from Ita Wegman to Eugen Kolisko, 3.1.1934).

155 Letter from Eugen Kolisko to Ita Wegman, 3.4.1935.

156 "Although she could have put her name to every single word of this document, she was deeply disconcerted and full of worries. She could see in advance that this statement would greatly intensify the battle in the Society, and that a split would become unavoidable. The inner obligation she had taken on when appointed as executive council member, and her love for the overall undertaking and work of Rudolf Steiner—including the form of the Society—led her to wish to avoid a split, or at least not to contribute to it" (Madeleine van Deventer, *Das Entscheidungsjahr 1934*, unpublished manuscript).

157 Cf. the reprint of the "Declaration of Intent" in Zeylmans, *Who Was Ita Wegman?*, op cit, vol. 3, pp. 387ff [G]. The text underwent further changes in Holland and England up to the annual general meeting. On another visit to Dornach and Arlesheim, Kolisko was no longer able to speak with Ita Wegman, who by now was ill, but he sent her the revised draft and wrote, "I am very sorry that you are ill and I send my heartfelt wishes to you for a speedy recovery. Attached is a copy from Grones containing the preliminary German wording of the Declaration of Intent. Today I received further revisions from Holland and England. Please keep this in a smaller circle until around 3:20, when all is ready. I believe all is progressing well and will be completed. Before the general meeting I will come here a little earlier to discuss everything, and will also write

to you beforehand so that you're kept informed of developments. Kaufmann sends many greetings to you. In England the Declaration has finally been accepted by the Executive Council. Zeylmans's reply brought a few more revisions and corrections which I will still need to incorporate. I'm traveling back to Stuttgart today" (undated, March 1934).

158   Letter from Ita Wegman to George Adams Kaufmann, 3.8.1934.

159   Ibid.

160   Letter from Ita Wegman to Heinrich Hardt, 3.8.1934.

161   Letter from Ita Wegman to Dorothy Osmond, 3.9.1934.

162   On the day after it, Ita Wegman wrote about this visit in a letter to Dorothy Osmond in England (3.9.1933): "Kolisko was here and brought with him a Declaration of Intent, which is very good. But strangely, the following occurred: as we ended the meeting we had with him, and I left the room, Kolisko—alone with a few physicians—started to castigate all the executive council members, including me. Then a fairly major confrontation began between him and the doctors, who naturally did not accept this. If things continue in this vein, naturally this initiative will be weakened as a result. Those who work together have to hold together, despite all the flaws one certainly has of course. Therefore, it increasingly strikes me that perhaps I should adopt a very different stance from the one I have taken thus far."

163   Letter from Ita Wegman to Jean Schoch, 3.13.1934.

164   Letter from Ita Wegman to Karin Ruths-Hoffmann, 3.17.1934.

165   Letter from Ita Wegman to Dorothy Osmond, 3.22.1934.

166   Regarding the writing of this statement Madeleine van Deventer wrote, "Now...the Declaration of Intent was a fact that existed, and as a member of the executive council Ita Wegman had to take a position on it. She discussed this with me for hours, and it resulted in her statement in the form of a letter to Herr Steffen, intended for reading out at the annual meeting. Once again—and for the last time—this letter testified to the full strength of her combative spirit! But those who pay subtle attention to it will not avoid hearing a certain distancing from the aims of the Declaration of Intent. Her statement that in the future she intended devoting herself entirely to her medical work also already show the germ of her future resolve" (Madeleine van Deventer, *Das Entscheidungsjahr 1934,* unpublished manuscript).

167   Quoted from the transcript of the annual general meeting of the General Anthroposophical Society on 3.27/28.1934, Archive at the Goetheanum.

168 Ibid., pp. 259f. Apparently Ita Wegman thanked George Adams Kaufmann later for his words, in a handwritten letter that has not survived, after which he wrote once more to her (in Arlesheim): "The words one wishes to speak to protect and defend may be almost as presumptuous toward spiritual reality as the words of those who launch an attack out of unconscious urges. One is not sure, then, if one has not in fact just done more damage. After speaking out like this, one has a sense of being jointly responsible for the negative things one hoped to avert. But especially if one has this feeling, your words of gratitude are so welcome—like a gift to the heart and a new bond, because, after all, you know that the will was good—that one *wished for* something better, and was also battling with oneself in a good sense."

169 "As soon as you can manage, you should leave Arlesheim for a little while. It strikes me that you will not so easily recover while you are still there. You need to 'breathe a different air'" (4.11.1934).

170 Letter from Hilma Walter to Viktor Thylmann, 4.11.1934.

171 Letter from Ernst Marti to Ita Wegman, 4.20.1934.

172 Later, after Ita Wegman recovered, one of her nurses looked back on this period in a letter and noted, "Her illness was inexpressibly painful for me, as for many others. Incomprehensible really" (Nurse Alma Ganz, Gnadenwald, 6.27.1934). A letter of support from Wilhelm Rudolf Goyert also described the mood among many people connected with Ita Wegman during the arduous illness that ran parallel to the events in Dornach: "My dear Frau Doctor, sending you my Easter greetings today, I do so with a timorous enquiry as to your health. I wonder how you will find the strength to recover after this gruelling Holy Week. My wife and I felt a profound hurt at the betrayal inflicted on the Dr—one that feels related to the hurt that the Lord's disciples must have felt and undergone in the week of Easter. To me it seems as if the love-radiant heart of the Goetheanum has stopped, and as if only the head now speaks dogmas and judgments it long since learned by rote. It is unspeakably painful— as if we must all once again pass through the suffering that Herr Dr. experienced during the [Goetheanum] fire, seeing in advance what further harm would still be done to us by 'human envy.' I know, dear Frau Dr., that words are simply inadequate to express something of the universal dimensions of this tragedy, which is only now beginning. Yet I need to write to you so that you know how closely connected we feel with you. I am very anxious indeed about your health, and hope that you, too, will soon recover again in the physical realm. We have such need of your guidance still. It always seems

to me that all the many hearts that beat for you in loyal friendship must also stimulate the powers of your own heart so that you soon recover, and that against this the adversaries can have no power. With warmest wishes and greetings, also from my wife, Your Wilh. Rud. Goyert" (4.21.1934).

173   For instance, on Apr. 17, 1934, Walter Johannes Stein wrote in a letter from London: "Dear Frau Doctor Wegman, Dr. Bockholt wrote to say that you are still ill, and this is why I am now writing to you at length. You know that much has not gone in this life as was really envisaged, and that this means therefore—for all of us as well as you—that some of our powers remain untapped, stored away as energies that we will not be able to draw upon until the end of this century. It is clear that for you in particular this rebuff will cause you to fall ill. Nevertheless, it must give you strength to know that you do not stand alone in this battle but that a very large number of people know themselves to be bound up with your destiny, and have perhaps been so for many millennia. These people experience what you suffer, and thereby can carry it with you. You know that I am bound to you with many feelings of gratitude and friendship, and that in thoughts I often attend your sickbed, most deeply and earnestly asking the powers that reign to stand by you and to ease your path. I don't wish to write anything about myself in this letter; only this one thing: that I, even if in a different way, must stand in the same battle as you. But I feel it as certain that everything that happens is only in order to give us strength, and again strength, for storms that will come over us in still greater and mightier form than current events. This is why I'm writing to you, because I feel that we must promise one another, whatever happens, to pass through these battles together in striving for a highest outcome. I say this, as you know, not for myself but for many. More clearly than before, the end of this century stands before my soul. Dr. Steiner accomplished the transition from the last third of the nineteenth century to the first third of the twentieth. Basically, it was this that still informed his life's work. We have now entered the second third of the century, and stand here alone and bereft, without his physical presence. And it is this pain, intensifying now, that has forcibly brought you to your sickbed. The last third will unite us with him again. In the first third he gave us his teachings. In the second we are alone with our feelings, and in the third we will have to prove whether we bear in our will what he gave us. The part of the Society that has now expelled you was not capable of accomplishing the transition into the second third of the century

that dawned at Easter 1934. These poor people thought that the impulse of the first third must be perpetuated. They believed that the purity of the teachings should be preserved. However, in truth, everything that Dr. Steiner gave us has entered the heart since Easter 1934, and must live there. While newly joining members may need to study his teachings in books, we who witnessed him at first hand are required to bear in our hearts the living inspiration that can arise from painful feeling. In the Mysteries, inspiration was only ever born from the passage through bitterest loneliness. That is where we stand. Where there is nothing but we ourselves. But I beg by the high powers that have stood behind you protectively through all times, that you feel the meaning and purpose of this aloneness. It is the power that binds us to Dr. Steiner at the end of the century. It is the most precious treasure of our life's path. When I try to hearken to what messengers of the spirit now tell us, I hear these words: *Born from loneliness / from grounds of worlds arise / sustaining feelings. / The world burden weighs / upon our being / yet sustaining powers / hold sway and ripen powers of will / in human hearts / when in the depths profound / we speak with lofty powers / about our destiny. / Within us lives / the guiding power of worlds of love / and wisdom's future meaning. / It cannot yet be seen / yet painfully felt; / and from the pain there ripens / feelings that will form us / into strong fighters / and faithful brothers / in distant times.* I send these words to you as a greeting. In devoted loyalty, Your Stein."

174   "From Friedl Schmidt, who was here for three days, I heard of plans to take Frau Dr. to Lake Thun; and I think this is a most happy solution so that she can at last escape the dire atmosphere in Dornach. I hope she will gradually overcome this illness, and I'd be most grateful if you would write again very soon to tell me how Frau Dr. is" (Karl König to Margarethe Bockholt, Pilgramshain, 4.30.1933).

175   Letter from Rudolf Meyer to Ita Wegman, 5.8.1934.

176   Letter from Georg Moritz von Sachsen-Altenburg to Ita Wegman, 5.11.1934.

177   After her recovery, Ita Wegman herself wrote an account of her illness (clearly as the basis for a verbal case history) which Hilma Walter subsequently edited slightly, anonymized ("A patient suddenly fell ill...") and to which she also added the treatments that had been used. The original transcript is as follows: "I suddenly fell ill without any forewarning. Apart from extreme tiredness, the only symptom was fever. The lack of any other symptoms suggested

it was the flu. But when the condition did not improve after a fortnight, and the fever did not fall below 38.5, the whole condition started to seem more serious. Dr. W[alter] examined me carefully but found nothing except a weak heart with weak cardiac sounds, but no noises and nothing on the lungs, nor any protein in the urine. My general state was not bad, but the fever did not abate. What was the illness? A sepsis was considered, an *Endocarditis lenta,* though I was not shivering, and the fever was not high enough. A blood test for staphylococcus proved negative. I grew ever weaker, and eliminations diminished. A Kaelin blood test was done—and produced a perfectly normal blood count. Treatment was primarily focused on the cardiac weakness and eliminations. For many weeks, the fever continued, rising each evening to between 38.3 and 38.5 despite all treatment. Before I give an explanation of the possible cause, I would like to describe how I experienced the fever. It arrived toward 8 p.m. and lasted until around 10 or 11 p.m., then gradually waned. It started with a coldness in the thigh, upon which hot compresses were well tolerated; then a general sense of warmth though the head remained cool; the heat accumulated in the feet and particularly the toes, as if it did not wish to leave the body. An unpleasant sense of awareness in the toes expressed itself in weariness but also stiffness and pain. Relief was only to be obtained by cold poultices repeatedly changed. As the fever grew, heart palpitations increased, for which Hyoscyamus proved a good remedy. I myself rubbed it into the heels and it immediately had a good effect on the heart. Cardiodoron, gold, antimony and stinging nettle were injected in alternation. Massage of the legs and arms with lemon and *Prunus,* and the back with equisetum. These massages had an excellent effect. The back massage with equisetum led immediately to diuresis, which, alongside the arm and leg massages, also had a good effect on circulation. Despite all these medicines, the fever was not ameliorated."

178   This seems likely based, among other things, on a letter from Eugen Kolisko of 5.18.1934, that mentions a marked improvement in Wegman's condition. (Kolisko was always kept well informed of her illness.) This improvement clearly made it possible for her to undertake the journey to Lake Thun. Kolisko writes, "I was very glad indeed to hear that you are feeling better, and will be able to go to the country. That is a great step forward." Wegman's later account of her illness on 7.14.1934 to Beeb Roelvink (see later in the text) seems to suggest that the improvement occurred *before* she went to Lake Thun; after outlining the spiritual turning point she

experienced, she wrote there, "And now my progress is such that my convalescence can safely and surely continue in the mountains and amidst nature." By contrast, Madeleine van Deventer—albeit in her very summary account of Wegman's illness (cf. Zeylmans, *Who Was Ita Wegman?*, op cit, vol. 2, p. 194 [G])—emphasized the initial change to Wegman's condition in Hondrich: "A marked improvement occurred already in the first week. Her temperature stabilized and she gradually learned to walk again." However, Ita Wegman herself, in her memorial address for Daniel Nicol Dunlop in 1935, showed (though after the passage of some time) that she had experienced the spiritual turning point in her illness while still in Arlesheim: "The patient knows very well if the physician's actions and thoughts are at odds with his situation. In my case I knew [after the spiritual experience] that my consultant—who had little hope I would get better—was wrong. The contrary view lived in my soul. I knew that I would recover after a while—and no one can deprive one of this inner certainty."

179 Errors of punctuation and grammar have been corrected in this and following quotes from Ita Wegman's notebook entries and manuscripts.

180 Letter from Ita Wegman to Maria Roeschl, 2.22.1934.

181 Even at the annual general meeting, on 12.29.1925, Albert Steffen had given a positive summary of Ita Wegman and her work since Rudolf Steiner's death, saying, "Frau Wegman continued to direct and develop the clinic in an outstanding way, so that it now has no less than seven physicians working there. She founded and developed the children's home, and has achieved the finest successes with children in need of special care. Then there is her connection with Lauenstein, which also promises to develop in an excellent way. She has accomplished these deeds in the medical realm, which, specifically, could not have been expected anywhere other than here. Then Frau Dr. Wegman took over the Class Lessons, and in this connection also undertook trips with Herr Dr. Wachsmuth and Fraeulein Dr. Vreede to England, Prague, Paris and Vienna, with related conferences. Frau Dr. Steiner was unable to take part in these trips since she was so busy with her work here—something also that can be said of me. I am somewhat tied down here by the journal we have been publishing weekly. It must also be mentioned that Frau Dr. Wegman initiated a quite new form of nursing training in Arlesheim, in two courses; and that, through her close collaboration with excellent physicians in our movement, we can look ahead with much confidence and hope that what Herr Dr. Steiner

intended with this new form of medicine will be realized and come to fine fruition" (quoted in Zeylmans, *Who Was Ita Wegman?*, op cit, vol. 3, pp. 152f [G]).

182   In Ita Wegman's literary estate was found a long, undated, six-page, typewritten account—or a draft lecture or the transcript of a lecture—relating to this prehistory and the problematic issues surrounding continuation of executive council work with only three individuals. The manuscript includes the following: "Since the Christmas Foundation Meeting is of such importance, specifically now again, I would like to say a little about it, describe how it came about. Every person has a different view of the Christmas Foundation Meeting and its impulses. But what I now present are conversations that took place between Dr. Steiner and myself. Often others were present too, but many of these conversations also occurred only between the two of us. After the Goetheanum burned down, Rudolf Steiner was continually concerned to 'organize' the Society anew, or as he often also put it, to 'galvanize' it. He said that the Society was half-dead. One group of members had become very intellectual, while the other kept lamenting the good old days— before ideas about threefolding had arisen—when the old esotericism still flourished. Many of the latter did not have the least glimmer of understanding of the threefolding idea, or any sympathy for it, whereas the former were precisely the ones drawn to Anthroposophy through it. Much was undertaken for the purposes of clarification. Speaking to me, Dr. Steiner said the following: the older members had had too much esotericism without digesting it, while the young members had had too little. The old Society nurtured by Dr. Unger and his group, but also by Frau Dr. Steiner, had failed completely. And Rudolf Steiner was still seeking solutions and ways to inaugurate change. He was deeply downcast. In 1923, the courses at Penmaenmawr and Ilkley took place. And to me it seemed as if, from this moment on, a solution had suggested itself to Rudolf Steiner. He spoke of how the consuming fire that had destroyed the old Goetheanum had revealed mighty secrets that were slowly coming into focus for him in their greater contexts. Mystery knowledge, he said, has now become free, and this Mystery knowledge, which was safeguarded in the diverse earlier Mysteries, was now to become part of the teachings of Anthroposophy. But the Society, he said, must be reorganized. Here he no longer mentioned a need to galvanize the Society or give it a new impulse, but organize it anew. He spoke these words after his trip to England, and great activity then arose within his being. It was as if the

necessary changes could not be introduced quickly or thoroughly enough. A series of lectures were held in Vienna, where he spoke about the workings of Michael. A gathering of physicians was also held at the house of van Leer who, with Dr. Glas, invited some of the Viennese doctors and other individuals. The evening was a great success. Dr. Steiner was bursting with originality, and engaging in a rapid crossfire of conversation with the physicians. He sat in the middle of them, alternating between seriousness and humor; a Viennese joke would be fired off—only comprehensible to the Viennese—triggering salvoes of laughter. The evening was unique; and it was astonishing to realize that Rudolf Steiner was not only a great researcher and outstanding esotericist but also the most charming conversationalist. It seemed as if the Viennese coffee that we drank later animated him still more. But here I'd like to note in passing another thing it is important to know, which can also perhaps help us to understand certain individuals who are currently playing a strange role. Dr. Husemann had also come from Stuttgart, with a few books. He thought he should also be present at a gathering of physicians, and should have his say too. In a much-concealed way, his intellectual appraisal was that Dr. Steiner really ought not to be giving medical lectures, but that he, Dr. Husemann, should be doing this. Now it sometimes happened that Rudolf Steiner could read other people's thoughts. And so, when Husemann came up to him, Dr. Steiner greeted him in an ice-cold way and asked what he was doing there, saying that he didn't need his scholarly approach one bit. Pointing to the books Husemann had brought, he said he could just pack them up again, all except for Frau Dr. Kolisko's study of the pancreas. Husemann was greatly put out. It was after this evening that a decision was made to write the book on medicine. 'I cannot do this with the other physicians,' said Dr. Steiner, 'they are all so self-opinionated in their lack of knowledge; I can only do it with you—and it will have a good outcome.' This decision was then communicated to van Leer who, as president of Weleda, was always on the keen lookout for books on anthroposophic medicine. After staying in Vienna we drove to Holland, with the aim of reinvigorating the national Society there, which was in the doldrums, with a visit from Dr. Steiner and a lecture cycle by him. A new general secretary also needed to be appointed, and it was thought that Herr de Haan should take this on. Now Dr. Steiner did not say much when he heard this. But in the evenings, after the lectures, when we were sitting together at the Hotel Doelen, Dr. Steiner very subtly drew attention to the qualities possessed by Dr. Zeylmans, saying that the Dutch Society should consider itself fortunate to have as a member a physician with such wide-ranging knowledge. And then, through questions and replies it eventually became apparent to de Haan that he was not the best candidate to lead the Dutch Society; and that Dr. Zeylmans should relinquish his private practice and dedicate himself entirely to leading the Society. This was all done so naturally that one felt regretful such self-evident solutions cannot be the norm. What Dr. Steiner proposed came to be in Holland; Dr. Zeylmans was appointed by him as general secretary. In Dornach the work continued in a systematic manner. Dr. Steiner gave the magnificent lectures on the Mysteries that you no doubt know, and which really re-fertilized the whole of anthroposophic knowledge. Then one day Dr. Steiner told me what he was planning. Through a new form of organization, which he himself wished to bring about, he wanted to try to give the Society an entirely new and different form with a executive council that would stand by him, with which he could work, and which he himself would appoint. I also want to note here that for a while Dr. Steiner said that if things could not be shaped as he wished, he would try to start again from small beginnings, with a small group of people, and structure things esoterically like a kind of order that would work out into the world without the burden and ballast of a Society. So this initially was the new organization he had in mind. Then he also talked to me about the Sections he wished to establish; various Sections, one for painting, one for music; but that he had not yet found the people he considered suitable for this. At this gathering, of which Albert Steffen also spoke, Rudolf Steiner said that if things followed traditional lines, Frau Dr. Steiner ought really to be deputy chair [of the executive council] but that he no longer wished to follow traditional ways, but new ways instead. He had therefore chosen Albert Steffen as the deputy chairman, and had other, also very important tasks in mind for Frau Dr. Steiner. Then, a few days later he asked me what I thought of having Fraulein Dr. Vreede in the executive council as well. He said this would be good for the continuity of the Anthroposophical Society to include her since she had been involved so much throughout. Frau Dr. Steiner and Fraulein Dr. Vreede, he said, would join the executive council as associates. From the very outset Dr. Steiner told me that I, as his secretary, should always organize things with him. This is the true account of preparations for the Christmas Foundation Meeting. The way in which the Doctor presented it was a surprise for everyone—no one knew of it. But it contained cosmic will of so pronounced a kind that all who were involved in its origins were very aware that other laws held sway here than had previously been at work in how things were done in the Anthroposophical Society. The Christmas Foundation Meeting itself was a mighty event. It was so mighty that Rudolf Steiner himself told me that, after invoking all the elements, all spirituality, a dire backlash would occur if henceforth people did not develop spirituality. 'In former times,' he told me, 'a person who had initiated an esoteric act of this kind might have had to pay for it with his own sudden death. But now, by the power of Christ, such things are possible; and because humanity in its current state needs this, one has to have the trust and also the courage to undertake such mighty things.' This is the history of the Christmas Foundation Meeting. What happened afterward should perhaps be kept for another occasion. I have spoken of all this because it strikes me as so impoverished an undertaking for three people on the executive council to say, in ordinary human terms, that they wish to lead the Society with just the three of them in accordance with the Christmas Foundation Meeting. This is just a small-minded and all too human way of playing with great phrases."

183   In a letter dated May 19, 1934, which Wegman had received at the beginning of the second week of her stay in Hondrich, Kolisko first outlined developments that had occurred since the last general meeting. This included the following: "We are making headway despite the great difficulties. But it now seems necessary to me for something new to happen so that activities currently only undertaken by those who have been 'expelled' can unite and gain more coherent form. The enclosed letter is founded on this idea, and is addressed by us to diverse friends and members. This is intended as preparation for a gathering where the bases of such an affiliated group can be elaborated. We have taken the initiative to do this and would like to inform you of this straight away so that you are kept in the picture from the outset. On June 3, we'd like to hold the preparatory meeting in A[rlesheim] so that friends there can discuss these matters with us. If you yourself have any suggestions relating to this or any comment, we would all be very grateful, especially since we cannot count at present on you attending in person.

"It is very clear now that a joint effort by all those involved will be necessary since otherwise a general fragmentation would occur. And this joint effort must develop in a way that nurtures the trust for developing a new Society with specific aims. This is intended to be the first step in that direction." The circular enclosed with this letter by Kolisko was composed by him and Juergen von Grone, and countersigned by Elisabeth Vreede, Willem Zeylmans van Emmichoven, Pieter de Haan, Daniel Nicol Dunlop, and George Adams Kaufmann, and had been dispatched one day previously to Madeleine van Deventer, Gerhard Suchantke, Karl König, Herbert Hahn, Maria Roeschl, Ernst Lehrs and Ernst Marti. It contained an announcement about a large gathering in Stuttgart to clarify further steps, the reason for which was given in the following introductory words: "Events since the general meeting have led to such grave decisions that we believe a joint mustering of all our powers to be essential. We have to gain clarity about both the inner and outer conditions under which we can continue our work on behalf of the General Anthroposophical Society in the present circumstances. Our groups, above all the important fields of work for which our members bear responsibility in various locations arose, after all, on the common ground that Rudolf Steiner laid down for us at the Christmas Foundation Meeting. They mostly cannot survive in a healthy, living way without this common ground. Today, therefore, destiny poses this very significant question for our inner initiative: How will we seek to continue nurturing this common, sustaining life of our movement to the best of our ability in the situation we currently find ourselves in? Especially for the leading members of our circles, and those who hold positions of responsibility, there is a need therefore to hold a larger meeting where, after discussing this situation, we may also resolve in what form, as affiliation of independent groups of the Anthroposophical Society, we will continue to bear our common responsibility—which has grown to be of still more central importance in the light of recent events." In the next few weeks, Wegman received further reports from Kolisko, or information circulars about these proposed meetings and resolutions in England, Holland and Germany. On June 30 and July 1, 1934, these activities eventually led to establishing the "United Free Anthroposophical Groups" (cf., for instance, Lili Kolisko, *Eugen Kolisko. Ein Lebensbild,* Gerabronn-Crailsheim 1961, pp. 359ff).

184   In a letter dated 4.27.1934, a week after he returned from the general meeting, Löffler wrote to Wegman about this as follows: "If you don't find a more suitable place to go to recuperate in real, relaxing tranquility, please do come to us in Gerwalde. I assure you that you would have a very pleasant time here with us, and would be surrounded with nothing but love."

185   Letter from Ita Wegman to Fried Geuter and Michael Wilson, 6.14.1934.

186 Draft letter from Ita Wegman to Frl. Von Hohnert, undated (around 7.14.1934).

187 Letter from Ita Wegman to Beeb Roelvink, 7.14.1934.

188 Letter from Ita Wegman to Madeleine van Deventer, 6.20.1934.

189 Letter from Ita Wegman to Hilma Walter, 6.28.1934.

190 Letter from Ita Wegman to Madeleine van Deventer, 6.25.1934. After returning from her long journey to Palestine and Italy, Ita Wegman acknowledged in a letter to Jules Sauerwein that she had more or less kept her—very clearly formulated—travel plans to herself before she set sail. She wrote very frankly: "I was also a little anxious that my friends would fail to understand why one would undertake such a long journey after such a severe illness as I had suffered, and that they would consider this too tiring for me. So I kept fairly quiet about it, and it became known only after the trip had gotten well underway."

191 Letter from Ita Wegman to Carl Alexander and Gertrud Mirbt, 7.26.1934.

192 "The idea is increasingly developing in me to travel to Arlesheim and deal with everything there that needs dealing with, and primarily to discuss with you how the future should be shaped. This does not mean I feel strong enough yet to start work; that is not the case, but I can talk to people and discuss things with all of you" (letter from Ita Wegman to Madeleine van Deventer, 8.12.1934).

193 Ibid.

194 "Glorious trips into the mountains were undertaken. She was also very preoccupied with the fate of the Theban Legion in St. Maurice. Then we discovered a botanical rock garden above Bourg St. Pière. Frau Doctor would sit there often in the mornings on rocky outcrops and study the plants. She categorized the alpine plants very determinedly and looked lovingly upon every single blossom" (Madeleine van Deventer, quoted in Zeylmans, *Who Was Ita Wegman?*, op cit, vol. 3, p. 194 [G]).

195 Emil Bock, *Reisetagebücher. Italien, Griechenland, Heiliges Land,* Stuttgart, 1986, p. 83.

196 Forty-two years later, Siegfried Pickert in Dornach gave the following account of this visit: "Destiny once allowed me...the good fortune—I was in need of a little recuperation and therefore this task fell to me—to accomplish certain personal services for Ita Wegman. This was in 1934 when, after her serious illness, she was convalescing in the Valais canton in Switzerland. In my own somewhat fragile state I could act as her chauffeur when needed, and did so very gladly indeed—for this was of course a very appealing

thing! I can remember one thing in particular; naturally I tried to drive carefully and sensibly. But I often found that she did not care to travel at such a tempo: 'Please drive faster, why does one sit in a car like this!' ... On one occasion we made an excursion to Milan, from Ticino. I remember that we visited many art galleries there, and that Ita Wegman was accompanied by various people. Finally we entered a church whose every surface from top to bottom was painted with images from the Old and New Testament. We had a full guided tour with an older lady (who was really very inwardly connected with these fine pictures). We, Ita Wegman's companions, had more or less had enough of the tour although a good number of the Old Testament images remained to be studied, and so we sat down quietly on the pews. But Wegman—also, as I believe, out of kindness to this person, who had taken it upon herself to describe it all—completed the whole guided tour, tirelessly interested in everything" (quoted in Peter Selg, *Der Engel über den Lauenstein,* pp. 126f). In Siegfried Pickert's view, Ita Wegman completed the full tour "also" out of kindness to the guide—but no less due to her own interest in all depictions of the events in Palestine, which she studied intensively not just for their artistic quality but more so in relation to the events they portrayed. (We can get a vivid sense of this, too, from Wegman's extensive collections of paintings of Gospel scenes, whose motifs are arranged in a thematically ordered series; Ita Wegman Archive.) Liane Collot d'Herbois also recorded the following in her memoirs: "Ita Wegman loved visiting art galleries and was so enthusiastic in looking at pictures that no one could keep up with her. She could spend hour after hour walking around and delighting in what she saw. She liked paintings best, especially from the Italian Renaissance: of Christ, John the Baptist, Paul. To view such paintings filled her with new strength; she felt sustained by them" (Liane Collot d'Herbois, *Erinnerungen an Ita Wegman. 50 Jahre Ita Wegman-Fonds für soziale und therapeutische Hilfstätigkeiten,* Easter 1993, p. 40).

197 In her pocket guide book to the region (G. Olaf Matson, *The American Colony Palestine Guide, Jerusalem 1930*), Ita Wegman underscored passages that related to Alexander in Jaffa and Jerusalem ("In 332 BC, Jaffa, along with the rest of Palestine, experienced a radical change of masters, that is from Eastern to Western, under Alexander the Great, King of Macedonia" [p. 223]. "In 334 BC, Alexander, King of Macedon, on his rapid march through Syria after his victory over Darius, sent Jaddua, the High Priest, a message ordering him to transfer his allegiance from Darius to himself,

and to pay him tribute. Jaddua answered that he could not so easily renounce his legitimate master, so Alexander continued his march upon Jerusalem. When the conqueror arrived at Mt. Scopus, just north of the city, instead of meeting with preparations for armed resistance, Alexander was surprised to see the gate thrown open, and a procession of priests in all their sacerdotal robes, and a crowd of people in snow-white clothes, headed by Jaddua robed in purple and scarlet, with a mitre on his head and the name Jehovah on his breastplate, come forth and slowly proceed up the hill toward him. No sooner had Alexander seen the Priest than, to the surprise of his army, he advanced to meet him, and saluted him reverenetly" [p. 31]). Twenty-one months earlier, in December 1932, Walter Johannes Stein had sent her from Constantinople a copy of the bust of Alexander by Lysimachos, and told her of his plans—which he did not in the end realize—to travel on via Ankara and Issus to Jerusalem: "This is the route Alexander took with his army. We may be in Bethlehem for Christmas" (12.12.1932; for more on Stein's studies in Constantinople and his political efforts in Turkey, see the account by Johannes Tautz, *Walter Johannes Stein. Eine Biographie* [in English: *Walter Johannes Stein: A Biography,* London: Temple Lodge, 1990], Dornach, 1989, pp. 199ff). In another letter to Wegman on 1.1.1933, about his experiences in Ankara, Stein wrote, "I am leaving today, very pleased by what has been achieved. Yesterday, on the dot of midnight (New Year) I was received by Kemal Pascha Atatürk [who considered himself a successor to Alexander the Great, and emphasized his descent from Gilgamesh and Sumerian civilization, cf. Tautz, pp. 200f], who held a long conversation with me. He urged me to write to him when I have discovered anything further in my research. I have spoken a good deal about Dr. Steiner here, and gave a lecture at the Gazi Institute, which was disussed in the newspaper. Above all I publicized the Gilgamesh epic, which was unknown here previously. I narrated it first at the Philological Institute, highlighting the importance of Dr. Steiner's intepretation of it. This made such a strong impression that it was eventually printed in the newspaper. I held many hours of discussions with all the government's ministers: with the foreign minister on politics and the economy, with the minister of education on Turkish history and pedagogy, with the director of the Society for Turkish Historical Research, the director of the Turkish Central Bank (on finance) and the director of the ministry of statistics (on trade and commerce). I am getting to know the minister of health, and spoke to the minister of agriculture about rearing chickens etc. Briefly, I gained a comprehensive picture and was hosted by important poets. I met writers and journalists, and spoke everywhere of Dr. Steiner. Hurrah!!! Many warm greetings, your Dr. Stein. [P.S.:] I will be in Stuttgart on 1.8."

198 Margarethe Bockholt, *Palästinareise 1934*. a 17-page typescript. This very detailed account by Bockholt was found among Ita Wegman's papers and had clearly been forgotten for decades ("Unfortunately, no report of this trip [to Palestine] is extant, and in the meantime all Wegman's companions on the journey have died." Madeleine van Deventer, quoted in Zeylmans, *Who Was Ita Wegman?*, op cit, vol. 2, pp. 194f [G]). This was despite the existence of a handwritten note by Kalmia Bittleston, preserved in Arlesheim, which stated, "Dr. Bockholt kept a diary of the time when they were there, and when she came back she had it typed out and gave copies as presents."

199 Cf. the relevant accounts in Emil Bock: *Reisetagebücher. Italien, Griechenland, Heiliges Land*. Stuttgart, 1986. In the course of his translations of the Gospels—which he completed in December 1933(!)—Emil Bock (1895–1959) had first undertaken a trip to Egypt and Palestine in the spring of 1932. At the suggestion of Eduard Lenz he then led a larger group of priests and members on a second trip in the spring of 1934 (4.11–5.9) to explore the polarity he had discovered there between the lands of Judaea and Galilee, at the same time further deepening this experience for himself. Bock's account of Palestine, written following these two trips, is a wonderful document by a brilliant, highly spiritual, and historically learned traveler who was capable of looking beyond the obstacles to such a journey in the early twentieth century ("Travel in the truest sense of the word—so that the traveler becomes a pilgrim who encompasses temporal and human, spiritual dimensions rather than just covering geographical miles—is to a large extent now a thing of the past. The enrichment of soul, the inner transformations that could, until our contemporary crises, be found by visiting sacred sites—since one could still sense something of the lives that had unfolded there—must in the future be sought and found in purely inner ways" [Emil Bock, 1948 in *Reisetagebücher*, p. 10]). At the same time, Bock's account is highly significant for our understanding of Wegman's journey to Palestine. We can, it is true, be fairly sure that Wegman was aware (having ordered a copy of his "Thoughts on Translating the New Testament" [1930–1933]) of Bock's discoveries of 1932—to which Bock first made reference in the text accompanying his translation of the Gospel

of St. Matthew in August 1932; and that she had quite clearly spoken with him (or someone who had been on the group trip with him) before she embarked on her own trip, taking the same route, staying in the same accommodation and making use of the same person—Merezian, see below—who had helped Bock on his own travels. Nevertheless it is also true that the parallel nature of these two trips is specifically characteristic of anthroposophic and Christological experiences around the year 1933, and as such their spiritual dimension should not be underestimated. While National Socialism rampaged in Germany and established its deathly rule (observed attentively by both Bock and Wegman), and in Dornach the gravest incursions took place, of clearly "demonic" character, so that the true spiritual dimension of these years started to be completely covered over (or destroyed), the future powers of an esoteric Christ impulse could still manifest here.

200 In 1931, Georg Moritz von Sachsen-Altenburg had given Wegman the two books by Emmerik—transcribed by Clemens von Brentano—entitled "The Life of the Holy Virgin Mary" and "The Bitter Passion of Jesus Christ" (Regensburg, 1926 and 1931). Wegman was however already familiar with their content since Madeleine van Deventer owned these two volumes. In her memoirs, Liane Collot d'Herboid wrote, "On one occasion Ita Wegman disappeared into her room with these two big volumes, and was so immersed in them that she saw no one for three days. She read them from A to Z, scarcely sleeping while she did so" (*Persönliche Erinnerungen an Ita Wegman*, p. 10).

201 Merezian operated a "Levant Travel Service" in Jerusalem, which had started back in 1920. After her return from Palestine, to thank him for guiding them and for the many conversations they had, Ita Wegman sent him the book she had published in 1929, *Aus Michaels Wirken* [From the work of Michael] (which Merezian thanked her for in turn in a letter, saying that it brought him "many new and valuable insights"; 12.19.1935). Emil Bock, for his part, gave Merezian a hectographed copy of his diaries, which the Armenian guide likewise studied with great interest.

202 After returning from her trip, Ita Wegman recorded in writing many details of the locality around the Church of the Sepulchre and the stations of the Via Dolorosa. These descriptions began with the words: "The Via Dolorosa lies close to your heart. Where is it? This is the burning question that lives in you. And: Where did the Mystery of Golgotha take place?" Wegman's accounts show how she was much irritated by the various buildings constructed over

the holy sites, and the (often rivalrous) religious communities they belonged to, along with the tourism, commercialization, and trivialization; but that despite this she was also deeply moved by the Church of the Sepulchre and its surroundings ("When one walks from one place to another in the church, despite all the things that create confusion there, one does gain a sense of the sanctity of the place").

203 Cf. Anna Katharina Emmerick, *Das bittere Leiden Jesu Christi*, pp. 7ff. Emil Bock visited the place in 1932 and 1934, noting in retrospect after the trip of 1932: "On Mount Zion we came upon the 'House of Caiphas' that lies in a beautiful, peaceful garden. A piece of mosaic on the ground is said to show the place where Peter denied Christ. Very near to this we found the room of the Last Supper: a surprisingly ceremonial, Gothic hall. Crusader mood. Did the Knights Templar decorate it in this way? Today it belongs to the Mohameddans who use it only as a vestibule to the mosque of David's grave. In an adjoining chamber there is a copy of David's grave, the original of which stands in a room lower down in the house, to which only the "faithful" are allowed access. Although the tradition of the grave of David contains only a kernel of truth, this means that the Last Supper location is already divested of its private nature. The house was a site of worship and ritual; the Coenaculum belonged to a fraternity, perhaps a group of the order of Essenes who in a special sense felt themselves to be "sons of David." The longer we stayed in the Coenaculum, the more fully it was pervaded with the substance of that self-sacrificing departure of Christ from himself, which took its source there, hovering around the Last Supper path and passing through Golgotha and beyond it to the events of Easter and Ascension" (Emil Bock, *Reisetagebücher*, p. 334). In 1934, by contrast, he wrote, "Then we visited the Coenaculum which hitherto had been one of the most striking places in Jerusalem. I had it in mind to see if we might visit the other rooms in the house but we came up against a whole series of disappointments. The Arabs have turned the Coenaculum into a mosque, inserting a tasteless prayer alcove into the grandiose Gothic. Tawdry colored patterns have been painted on the windows and the ground is now carpeted so you can only walk there barefoot. In addition, the wardens of the house are so eager to be paid for everything that I gave up the attempt to see anything more than the room of the Last Supper" (ibid., p. 385).

204 "The place where Jesus was baptized. The loamy waters of the Jordan flow sluggishly on their way. We are already visibly in the

world of the Dead Sea. All primary events in Christianity reveal a harmony of image with the cosmos. The Jordan baptism occurred at the lowest place on the surface of the earth: the Christ being descending from heaven to earth follows the trajectory of fallen earth and humanity into the depths of death. The place of the baptism is a quiet, unremarkable place. Again it becomes clear to us how much the Christ events occurred on a quiet, small scale" (Emil Bock, op cit, pp. 338f).

205 Writing about his second trip to Palestine, Emil Bock also described his impressions of the Dead Sea: "We really have arrived on the moon. A landscape surrounds us that reveals how the earth could have become moon.... The sublunary sphere of postmortem life is tangibly around us here: as if we had died. We gaze through the transparency of an earthly landscape as if seeing death from the other side. I'm expressing what our souls feel, and trying to portray the fact that the level of the Mediterranean lies 400 meters above us. The impressions surrounding us here are among the strangest in our lives. The sunset has the feel of glassy colors, as if the sun in the sky were becoming moon-like in character" (Emil Bock, op cit, pp. 402f). Describing his return to Jerusalem, Bock writes further, "Only now, breathing more easily, do we sense the heavy, ahrimanic spell this world laid upon us, despite our cheerfulness and joy. It was certainly instructive to spend such a long while in the salty depths. But then it appeared to us to be enough, and many had the sense that they could not have borne it any longer. We have undertaken the strangest journey, close to the bounds of our capacities" (ibid., p. 407).

206 In 1932, Emil Bock wrote as follows about his first encounter with Jerusalem's temple mount: "Suddenly we are standing on the ancient temple square. A mystery hovers in the air. The loftiest, strictest silence can really be felt to live in these stone surfaces void of people. Only afterward do we learn that the square has been open to Muslims only since midday. Piercing sun glows bright above the fantastic architectural forms of the cliff cathedral and the circling walls, whose high arched openings present the strangest glimpses. Here we are at the place of the Old Testament rites of worship, which subordinated all the sacred sites of nature—sacred mountains, groves, grottoes. As every day of our trip was subsequently to show us, these exist in Palestine in a unique wealth and fullness. A monotheistic spirit holds sway in strict grandeur here, where abstraction entered into religion. You can get a feeling of the forces of age that governed humankind in the Old Covenant. Here

there lived something that made humankind old. Islam, which today possesses the Temple of Solomon, is, owing to its potentized intellectualism, the true inheritor of the unaltered and preserved Old Covenant. Shivers of sanctity in enmity with nature waft into our soul here from ancient times" (Emil Bock, op cit, p. 330).

207 Emil Bock likewise wrote, "In Emmaus we were encompassed by a friendly and fruitful world. The gaze looks down upon broad plains and toward the Mediterranean. The lovely garden of the talkative priest, Müller from Barmen, did us good after the sterner impressions in Jerusalem and the desert" (Emil Bock, op cit, p. 390).

208 Letter from Ita Wegman to Madeleine van Deventer, 10.5.1934. Cf. Rudolf Steiner, *Christ and the Spiritual World: And the Search for the Holy Grail,* Rudolf Steiner Press, 2008, CW 149, lecture, 12.31.1913 (see also later in the text).

209 Emil Bock, op cit, p. 354.

210 After his trip in the spring of 1932, Emil Bock wrote of this: "The whole super-earthly impression of withdrawing to the mountain…does not depend [here] on what one actually sees but is due to the ether world which we sense in intensified fashion through the contrast with the landscape around the Dead Sea—as if one has not just climbed a few hundred meters but has ascended beyond the Earth and Moon sphere into the true sphere of the sun. Here the Earth seems like an island preserved from the times of ancient Sun. Jerusalem is a residue of Saturn, the desert a portion of Moon, and Galilee a vestige of ancient Sun. We can experience this vividly on this summit in particular. In the desert we saw that the Earth might have rigidified entirely into Moon. Here we see how a natural potential to become Sun has been preserved" (Emil Bock, op cit, p. 414).

211 "Whereas in Judaea we can experience death, in which there nestles a completely chaotic, teeming activity that has only the appearance of life, here we can sense too much life, drawn away from the earth. One is so wrapped in this warm, watery atmosphere that it is difficult to form earthly, sharply contoured thoughts. And the life of spirit that unfolds here can really only culminate in a kind of comfortable satisfaction and mugginess. At least, there is always the danger of this. Of Judaea and Galilee—as it has now become—one might almost say that the one has too many death forces, the other too much life. Here at the Sea of Galilee, also, all the miracles took place, and are more related to the elements. Healing, and driving out of the devil took place here on many occasions, as well as both occasions of feeding. In Capernaum the healing of

Peter's mother-in-law also occurred. She was described as falling ill because of her sibyl nature. It is surely understandable that here, at the Sea of Galilee, ancient clairvoyance and sibyl oracles could long be preserved" (Margarethe Bockholt). In his 1932 diary, Emil Bock wrote, "The atmosphere of the lake is very powerful. The heavy sultry quality of the atmosphere gives an even greater sense of mystery. There is something unreal about the landscape. One can understand how the Gospels hover between imaginative and physical reality. Here nature brings you slightly out of yourself. Here we can start to understand the disciples' awareness, which must still have had something of a balance between day and night.... The Jordan between the sea of life and the ocean of death is an image of human incarnation unfolding between pre-birth reality and the salt-bearing element of death. The etheric revelations of Christ all occur in Galilee. Just as the mountain of temptation lies near to Jericho and the Dead Sea, so the mountain of transfiguration is close to Nazareth and the Sea of Galilee. The Mount of Olives near Jerusalem balances between them" (Emil Bock, op cit, pp. 350f).

212   Letter from Ita Wegman to Madeleine van Deventer, 10.21.1934.

213   Only a few weeks before, Emil Bock for his part (directly following his own second trip to Palestine) had begun to work over the diary notes of his two trips with a view to publishing them privately, at the same time embarking on a written account of his major studies of Jewish history and the Old Testament, which he had been working on intensively for years. These were published the moment Wegman returned to Arlesheim in Nov. 1934 as "Ancient History: Thoughts on the Spiritual History of Humanity."

214   Letter from Ita Wegman to Madeleine van Deventer, 10.24.1934.

215   Emil Bock, *Reisetagebücher*, p. 364.

216   Rudolf Steiner, *Bausteine zu einer Erkenntnis des Mysteriums von Golgotha* (in English: *Building Stones for an Understanding of the Mystery of Golgotha*, Rudolf Steiner Press, 1972), CW 175, Dornach, 1996, p. 284 (author's emphasis).

217   Of Wegman's handwritten correspondence during her travels, only the—few—letters she wrote to her colleagues in Arlesheim (in particular to Madeleine van Deventer) have been preserved. An extant reply from Emil Leinhas, dated 11.25.1934, shows us that as soon as she arrived on Capri, Wegman clearly embarked on a renewed correspondence with larger groups of people, discussing future projects and also already formulating ideas for ways to handle processes in Dornach. Wegman had written to Leinhas from Capri to discuss the second edition of the book she and Steiner had written

together, *Extending Practical Medicine* (London: Rudolf Steiner Press, 1997; also translated as *Fundamentals of Therapy*, Chestnut Ridge, NY: Mercury Press, 1999), at the same time, evidently, also expressing something of her stance toward the internal conflicts in the Anthroposophical Society. In his reply, Leinhas detailed various issues relating to the new edition, writing as follows at the beginning of his letter: "I thank you for your friendly lines from Capri, and would first like to convey my warmest wishes for the new beginning of your work. I hope that your health will have improved to the point where you can take up your tasks again afresh with full vigor. Your long absence will no doubt allow you to see some things in a different light from previously. I can already see this from your kind letter, and was very pleased; I, too, in recent months have come to the view that the so-called issues in the Society are of no significance, and that it will take only a little time before the reserves still remaining in the Society from Dr. Steiner's work are fully exhausted. Then the collapse will become outwardly apparent, too. Anthroposophy itself will not be affected. It will find other means to work, as is clearly being prepared already. The outer impulse still lacking for this will no doubt be provided by world events in the near future."

218   Letter from Ita Wegman to Madeleine van Deventer, 10.24.1934.

219   Letter from Ita Wegman to Sister Hedwig Walter, 12.12.1934.

220   Werner Pache, *Tagebuch.* There Pache noted on the current situation in curative education: "The economic situation is becoming ever more difficult. Grave decisions must be made throughout the curative movement. Gerswalde is struggling. Muehlhausen is at risk of collapsing. Erlacher has gone. We will have to give up with Sweden." Seven days later Werner Pache left for an exploratory trip, held discussions with leading colleagues in Altefeld, Berlin, Gerswalde and Schloss Hamborn, and summed up his conclusions as follows: "In most places things are still possible, in contrast to the schools. Grave news: Kolisko is leaving the [Stuttgart] school. It could be a good thing if something strong emerges from this. All the more important that the institutes survive."

221   Ita Wegman wrote in a later letter to Elisabeth Dank (1.31.1935): "I myself actually experienced more of the Old Testament in Palestine—the generations and all that is connected with this—than the Christ; and so I am longing already to return and be present there at the beginning of spring, since I am sure that everything would be completely different there then. *And it is surely true that it is still possible to experience the Christ there in early spring; you see, an*

old member told me that the Doctor had told her that one could have a small glimmer of it every spring in Palestine" (author's emphasis).

222 As Ita Wegman wrote six months later to her Jewish colleague Emil Weiss, who was practicing in Pardes Hanna-Karkur (and evidently had recently emigrated there), she wanted to realize this spring trip to Palestine in the not too distant future. At the end of this letter she wrote of this: "I have heard that you like it better in Palestine now, and that things are going well for you. As for me, I would gladly return to Palestine again; I would like to experience this land again in the spring, in particular" (5.28.1935).

223 In his Christmas card, Herbert Hahn referred to a conversation he had with Wegman at her mother's birthday, in which she had evidently summed up her own development hitherto and hinted at her future intentions. Recalling this conversation and affirming it, Hahn wrote, "It made a great impression on me to hear you say that some people seek to become a pure mirror of what Dr. wished for and still wishes" (Zeist, 12.22.1934).

224 Letter from Ita Wegman to Franz Löffler, 12.12.1934.

225 Letter from Ita Wegman to Fried Geuter, 12.14.1934.

226 Letter from Ita Wegman to Fried Geuter, 11.23.1934.

227 Letter from Ita Wegman to Eleanor Merry, 12.17.1934. According to Werner Pache's diaries, Ita Wegman also spoke of this spiritual experience in Arlesheim two weeks later on the last day of that year, at a New Year gathering: "Frau Dr. Wegman speaks gently of the presence of Christ. She thought at the beginning [of her illness] that her earthly task was over. But Dr. Steiner and Christ came to her in a vision; they nodded to her, affirming that she should start to work again. From this moment, I hope, we may all gain benefit."

228 Letter from Ita Wegman to Eleanor Merry, 12.17.1934.

229 Walter Johannes Stein's reply, which he wrote already on 12.21 in London, included the words: "I am inexpressibly pleased that the experiences you had [while away] were so profound and so uniquely and intrinsically your own. This has great significance both for this life now and in the future."

230 "Weihezeit" instead of "Weihnachtszeit": in a letter from Wegman to Eleanor Merry on 12.17.1934.

231 Letter from Ita Wegman to Hilma Walter, 11.22.1934.

232 For instance, in a letter that Gerhard Suchantke wrote to Ita Wegman recalling a Christmas festival, he said, "I thought of the beautiful, tall tree with the red roses, all the festive faces of the staff, and not least of you, dear Frau Doctor—of what you yourself put

into such days. Most especially I think of a Christmas festival—I believe it was 8 years ago.... Based on notes of conversations with Herr Dr. Steiner, you spoke about the festival period from Advent to Pentacost as stages of the Christian path of suffering and initiation" (12.27.1934).

233   Cf. also Madeleine van Deventer's report of Wegman's illness and travels, quoted by Zeylmans, which ends by commenting as follows on Wegman's return to Arlesheim in November 1934: "In conversations she told us that from now on the new Christianity would be the focus of her efforts. Likewise the Christianizing of medicine had become a burning issue for her" (Zeylmans, *Who Was Ita Wegman?*, op cit, vol. 2, p. 195 [G]).

234   Letter from Ita Wegman to Jules Sauerwein, 12.18.1934.

235   That Wegman regarded her return from illness and convalescence as a radical "new beginning" (and as biographical precursor, likewise, to the new beginning of Christological work in Arlesheim) is something she stressed immediately after her recovery (see above: "My life has been *given back* to me anew; I feel the inner obligation to shape it in a deeper way than hitherto. For all of us a new period must begin and is announcing itself like the glowing light of dawn! Let us remain free in allowing to work upon us what the higher worlds intend, and what we yearn and petition for from below" [author's emphasis]). Ten days before the Holy Nights began, on 12.14.1934, she had written in this vein to Fried Geuter: "For my part, I am fortunate to be well again, and there was no doubt significance in my enforced withdrawal from everything for a period. I experienced this as benevolent grace, as I did, likewise, the chance to fill my soul with impressions of distant lands, which soothed my recent bitter experiences in the Society. *And so I am now able to begin afresh*" (author's emphasis). Werner Pache noted Wegman's address of 12.24 in his diary in these words: "Frau Dr. Wegman spoke: 1934/35 from Easter onward refers back to 1902, from Christmas. It was after this that Dr. Steiner began to promulgate Christianity in *Christianity as Mystical Fact* (SteinerBooks, 2006). Now this starts to bear fruit. Every year more fruit will grow from the seed that Dr. Steiner planted at the beginning of the century. This starts with 1935, which Dr. Steiner described as being of such importance. This is a mighty context. How will things look in 33 years from now if no further fruits can ripen from seeds that Dr. Steiner planted (to be precise, this will begin in 1925 plus 33 years, or 1958), thus in 1967? In other words as we embark on the last third of the twentieth century. This must give us the impulse to

gather all our strength to prepare seeds, within modest bounds. What can this consist of? *Reinvigorating* the spiritual treasures of Anthroposophy. It is this she wishes to attempt to begin with us during the 13 Holy Nights. She wishes this attempt, in all modesty, to be seen as *a new beginning*" (Werner Pache's emphasis).

236 Letter from Ita Wegman to A.M. Gibaud, 1.30.1933.

237 Letter from Ita Wegman to Mathilde Enschedé, 4.10.1935.

238 Werner Pache recorded the following in his diary: "Jan. 5, 1935: After a short presentation of no great importance, Stein initiated a free group discussion. Wonderful sight: Stein, Zeylmans, de Haan, Kaufmann, Grone, Kolisko, Bockholt, Hauschka, Marti, Rudolf, Maddy and others. The past 33 years are discussed in terms of actual details. Stein recounts his work on the oil war, Japan, mongolism, the forthcoming rise of Islam. Reflections on the Mystery of Golgotha in the ether (1934) and the appearance of the Resurrected Christ in the ether light. Free. Hopeful (1.6.1935): Evening in the clinic: Fr. Dr. Wegman, Vreede, Stein, Dunlop and others. Recollections of the last days of Dr. Steiner and the period following his death. The start of the difficulties."

239 Letter from Ita Wegman to Hilma Walter, 1.15.1935.

240 In various situations—as already immediately after her recovery from illness in the spring of 1934 (cf. page 86); Wegman emphasized not only the need for a calm, composed and understanding stance but once again stressed the importance of patient endurance without seeking to found new organizational forms. On 2.14.1935, she wrote in this vein to Bernard Lievegoed: "What I always want to impress on you all is not to seek new forms already. It is good to work for a while without as yet having a form but instead connecting with each other through insight and trying to develop an associative way of working through mutual esteem. I am quite certain that a form will emerge from this, will be given to one at some point as a spiritual gift. We must just keep ourselves inwardly open and prepared."

241 At the end, to the question from Dunlop and Kaufmann, "Will you join with us in England? Frau Dr. Wegman stresses that...she feels herself entirely *free* of all responsibility" (diary entry by Werner Pache, Pache's emphasis).

242 Letter from Ita Wegman to Hilma Walter, 1.15.1935.

243 Letter from Ita Wegman to Wilhelm Goyert, 4.2.1933.

244 Draft letter from Ita Wegman to Walter Johannes Stein, 1.9.1935.

245 Undated (January 1935). Wegman also wrote to Hilma Walter on 1.15.1935: "The feeling I used to have that a part of the Christmas

Foundation Meeting is still alive in England is one I don't really have any more. A new situation exists there. I have given it my full attention and find, naturally, that it requires a new stance of me."

246   Cf. Emanuel Zeylmans van Emmichoven, *Who Was Ita Wegman?*, op cit, vol. 2, p. 262 [G].

247   Letter from Ita Wegman to Alice Wengraf, 7.24.1935.

248   Letter from Ita Wegman to Walter Johannes Stein, 1.9.1935.

249   Letter from Ita Wegman to Herbert Hahn, 3.28.1935.

250   Directly after her return from Palestine, at the end of November 1934, Ita Wegman had told Willem Zeylmans van Emmichoven that holding the Class Lessons was one of her most urgent spiritual tasks, and that she would further intensify her efforts in this regard. Zeylmans reported this as follows in a letter to George Adams Kaufmann on 12.13.1934: "She started to speak about the Class of her own volition [in contrast to the theme of the 'United Free Groups' which was a subject broached by Zeylmans, and in relation to which Wegman signalled her support 'but at the same time wished to keep herself somewhat free of it']. This work is for her the most important of all. But since in general she wishes to lead an (outwardly) tranquil life, she says that if we wish it she will try to stay for something like 3 weeks in succession at each center, and then give 7 to 9 Class Lessons during this time. Three weeks in London, three weeks in The Hague (no doubt Stuttgart will not be possible for the time being), a longer time in Arlesheim, and then with us again."

251   Letter from Ita Wegman to Walter Johannes Stein, 1.9.1935. Wegman evidently telegraphed Dunlop immediately after January 6. On January 8 Stein wrote back to her from London: "Dunlop just showed me your telegram. He was somewhat disconcerted by it. He said, 'The style of it is as friendly as could be, but it is an absolute refusal.' I tried to tell him that you are very pleased with the work in England, and that this was more to do with your inner reflections on what your real task is now, but he was still very sad. He said, 'I cannot tell the members this without upsetting them; and I will just say that the date of Dr. Wegman's arrival has not yet been fixed. Perhaps it is important for you to know this.'" Three weeks later, Stein wrote again to Wegman an extensive and ultimately insistent letter in a style very characteristic of him: "Dear Frau Doktor Wegman, I'd like to tell you how people here see the situation of the English Anthroposophical Society. It has long been sleeping, but awoke due to the fact that you came here, and Nunhoefer came, that the New School gained much stimulus through

the visits of diverse people (Kolisko, Schubert, etc.). This awakening led to more vitality. I won't mention Clent in this context since, though excellent work is done there, this has less impact on the work in London. But along with my lectures, which also reached many non-anthroposophists, all this has kindled much life. The connection with the provinces is more lively, many lecturers are traveling around, and everywhere people are starting independent initiatives. The physicians likewise are participating more in our general anthroposophic life. Yesterday, for instance, almost all of them came to the lecture—Stounton, Wood, Broman, etc. Weleda made a profit this month for the first time. You can say that the movement is outwardly blooming. That's the objective picture. The disputes in the Society no longer play any role. The members who found this problematic have left the Society. Those who remain want to work, no more than that. It was in these circumstances that the members, via Dunlop, asked whether you would be able to nurture the esoteric life here on a regular basis. However, this request occurred in a form that did not allow you the possibility of giving a positive answer. I don't wish to go over the details—the fact arose and determined the situation. I would now ask you to consider the following. You know very well that at the moment the movement outwardly flourishes it inevitably needs the esoteric aspect. You know this, and I know that you know it. All I can say is this: Please give this. You do not need to be invited nor anything else. You know that the right things will be done simply because you come— that the right arrangements will arise. Kaufmann reported on his conversations with you, and his report will not lead to anything positive. He received the message that you are dissatisfied with the English movement. What are people to make of this when they are full of good will, are waiting for you with longing, and wish to deepen their work esoterically alongside their outer work? They cannot even understand it, for they have never before had a Society that functions so well. I know that certain things have irritated you; but it is just that the English always think in terms of organization. Please don't ascribe too much importance to it—please consider what is positive. As things stand at present, damage will be done whatever you may say in writing or via a messenger. I tell you that you have no choice; it is absolutely essential that you come. You could not answer to Dr. Steiner for it if you failed to come now. We all love you, and all want to work with you. If anything has come between us it must certainly be due to a misunderstanding, some kind of clumsiness. The members only wish for one thing:

to work. And they know that they work well, but they want to deepen this work. I therefore beg you, the moment you receive this letter, to pack and travel here. Please come at least for the period of the general meeting. Though the program has long been fixed and sent out, there are two lectures by me included in it, one of them at a time when the Class Lesson should be held. Please put this right—give the Class Lesson on that Sunday. Give a report of your travels instead of my other lecture. Open your inner being to the people here and give what you have to give. Then go back to your other necessary work elsewhere. Frau Doktor, please do listen to me. There's nothing more to add. I know that what I am proposing is the right thing. I beg you warmly to do it. My greetings to you in honour of our good, old connection, very warmly, your Stein. [P.S.] A lecture by me on Salome has been arranged for Friday, February 8 at 8.15 a.m. I know that Dr. Steiner does not wish this lecture to be given. I am very clear about this. He told me this more insistently than ever. He wants you to report on your travels, your experiences instead. And if you do not do so and save me, I will be in a desperate situation. And on Sunday at 10.45, the time when the Class Lesson should be given, I am supposed to speak about the [supplementary] exercises and the soul's development. And I know that if I do this that Dr. Steiner will dash me to pieces. Frau Dr. Wegman, if I died suddenly, you might well come to my funeral. And now I beg you: come to the living" (1.31.1935).

252   "The situation of the Anthroposophical Society within which the Class was really given is now so different from what it was after the Christmas Foundation Meeting that I have a feeling that the Class connected with this Society has a quite different position now from before. And as I told you previously, I want to return to the founding impulse of the Michael School, which is inherent in the Michael School itself, rather than being tied to the Anthroposophical Society. I have an inward obligation toward this Michael School, and I want to orient my actions in accordance with this obligation, and bear responsibility for it. I wish to re-awaken awareness in people for this spiritual union. And for this reason the School must be led differently from before" (letter from Ita Wegman to George Adams Kaufmann, 6.19.1935).

253   With this in mind, too, Wegman refused to hold a Class Lesson at the general meeting of the English Society since it had (from her perspective) distanced itself from the Christmas Foundation Meeting (cf. page 150f). Retrospectively she wrote to Dunlop, "In such a situation I could neither properly envisage nor undertake the

work of the First Class, *which was after all given as an important impulse within and as part of the Christmas Foundation Meeting"* (1.6.1935; author's emphasis).

254 See Peter Selg, ch. 3–6, in *Rudolf Steiner and the School for Spiritual Science: The Foundation of the "First Class,"* (Great Barrington, MA: SteinerBooks, 2012): ch. 3, "The Contribution of Ita Wegman"; ch. 4, "The Ritual Act and the Rose Cross"; ch. 5, "Ita Wegman Holds the Class Lessons"; and ch. 6, "Ita Wegman's Introductory Words to the Class Lessons."

255 Letter from Ita Wegman to Gertrud Goyert, 1.29.1935. Shortly after this Wegman wrote as follows on this theme in a letter to Elisabeth Dank: "Everything after all is so different from how it was. One has to stay much more with one thing and protect it like a treasure, for otherwise everything will be robbed and stolen from you. That's why I will have to stay here for a while now in order, as I feel it, to build a strong castle" (1.31.1935).

256 Letter from Ita Wegman to Gertrud Goyert, 1.29.1935.

257 Gertrud Goyert's extensive reply to Wegman's letter, written on February 5 in Cologne and sent to Arlesheim, is particularly illuminating about the situation of those who had hoped (and continued to hope) that Wegman would collaborate in the "united free anthroposophic groups," but at the same time respected her spiritually founded views. Goyert's remarkable text ran as follows: "I send you my warm thanks for your kind letter. I was very pleased to receive such full and loving words from you, and I was well able to understand why Dr. Steiner saw you as the Society's secretary and wanted you to be in written communication with the members. The reason I want to reply to you in detail today is that we have long wished to advance the things that seem necessary to us through a conversation, but without anyone binding themselves to new decisions. If we must decide at a later stage, this can happen at another time; first, though, let us speak freely.

"Your inner involvement in the processes at work, dear Frau Doctor, is one for which I have full understanding, even though it has to be said that our other friends experienced deep disappointment. The enthusiasm and courage to create something new may have been founded on the hope that you would, one day, unite your efforts with those of our friends in working in a future-oriented way. Consolation for this disappointment may lie in these friends' experience of the tangible proximity of Dr. Steiner himself, which does not allow them to fall into despondency but will instead continue to give their work wings. He is, I know, also with you, and at some point I'd like to tell you how I experienced this connection on one occasion. But he is also with the others who still live on the hill [Dornach] and battle so bitterly with those outside in the valleys. It is not easy for me to say this, but I believe that we are distinguished from the others because they are unable to do this, cannot see the positive powers within us. As far as we two are concerned, Herr Goyert and myself, we regard ourselves as 'Society-weary.' We do not wish to create a new form for the Society the moment an old one collapses. Nevertheless, it seems clear that further work is only possible by joining with others in the future. There is danger of grave isolation since the members who are not part of the free Societies in England, Holland and Germany will remain alone and thus not find their way to you. I have often had to hear this and do also think that things will take this shape in the future. The slander spread from the other side is too powerful not to have effect. Why do we therefore stay with the form of the Society? Not to serve a partisan cause but because we wish to nurture a life of spirit in the future, and because our love for Dr. Steiner continually rekindles in the spirit and can multiply in the love for people who work with us, and who take this work to heart. Soon, no doubt, we will be prohibited from speaking the word Anthroposophy in public. Will a broad stream of spiritual life nevertheless pour through all lands? In the countries where the free groups exist, the separate institutes stand as islands. The living practice of Anthroposophy is to manifest in them. But the other aspect is needed, too: Anthroposophy as worldview. Can this be cultivated more effectively than by means of a loose Society form, a federation? All the people who act within this form are free and independent after all. The difficulty you see in this might perhaps be resolved by recalling Dr. Steiner's emphasis at the Christmas Foundation Meeting that the members of the executive council are not members of the Society. That already clarifies their special position. I have to wonder at the precision with which Dr. Steiner governed the spiritual relationships between people in the physical realm. I can only envisage a healthy and wholesome work of the united groups in the future if you, too, dear Frau Doctor, add your name to the friends as a gift. This in no way constricts your free work or the hearkening to your inner being, for I can well understand that your will and work goes further than that of our friends. Dr. Steiner established the Class, after all, in connection with the School of Spiritual Science at the Goetheanum. What will happen if, at the next gathering, a decision is to be made to expel the "disruptive" members? This expulsion is also to include the two executive council members who were only provisionally excluded last year. The reading of the Class is intimately connected with the life of the members who participated in it. One would not want to fail to cultivate this. In fact, there is not all that much to say about this in writing. The Sections were based on the individuals present. Now those individuals are being sent away while their work is retained, and something quite different is made of it than was first initiated. If all this is taken away, what happens to the esoteric stream that flowed through it? We have to be very concerned about the future of the agricultural work. As far as I know, none of our friends is a member of the 'Ring' [agricultural research group]. What possibility will there be to obtain the soil preparations? The medicines produced by Weleda in Stuttgart have been felt in many cases to be completely ineffective, and it is possible that our friends may have to take a hand in this in some way. The archive [of the Goetheanum] also ought to be preserved appropriately. All these are questions which one could discuss very well in community with the friends. The text which Dr. Poppelbaum sent to the members of the Society contains such spiteful distortions that one does not wish to engage with it; and yet since you are subject in it to such cruel attacks—shouldn't something happen in response? Dornach and Hamburg are named as the source of this script; and I have to assume that the lady in Haus Hansi must have had a hand in its composition. Herr Dr. Zeylmans in Holland will also have told you about the latest experiences. Herr Goyert who is preoccupied with quite other issues than those I am expressing here will also write to you at some point since at present it does not seem possible for us to come to visit you in Arlesheim. For today, dear Frau Doctor, please take this letter as a sign of my inner commitment. Herr Goyert sends his warmest greetings, as do I. Your Gertrud Goyert. [P.S.] It is Inge's birthday today—she is 22 and therefore has come of age! The operation proved successful and she is well." Ingeborg Goyert had suffered from polio since the age of 7. At the recommendation of Rudolf Steiner, who often stayed with the Goyerts when he was in Cologne, she was eventually admitted to Wegman's clinic in Arlesheim and was treated there by her and Steiner (cf. Ingeborg Goyert, *May I help you?* Paderborn, 1999).

Especially after the general meeting on 4.14.1935, further letters arrived in Arlesheim asking Wegman for clarification of her "neutral" stance or seeking her clearer and more active alignment with the "united free anthroposophic groups," which however she never ultimately agreed to. On 5.13.1935, for instance, Luise von Zastrow (also on behalf of Johanna von Keyserlingk) wrote, "When we last saw each other in Sasterhausen, you said that it wasn't in fact necessary for members to belong to one faction or another. Now, given the collapse of the Society at the last general meeting, a new situation has arisen that requires new decisions. The leaders of the working group with its legion of supporters fought hard and suffered badly in this battle for justice. And were fighting, too, for Frau Dr. Wegman. If, as member, I no longer wished to side with the working group, it would seem to me as if I were just leaving other friends to fight and suffer while nevertheless wishing to benefit from the fruits of this battle. Surely it is more Michaelic to take a clear stance in which one acknowledges oneself as one of the heretics, even sharing in their errors. Or at least to enter into a certain narrower partisanship than to remain aloof from all parties? For us at a distance, dear Frau Wegman, it is hard to see what stance you have adopted toward recent events and toward the members of the working group!" Ita Wegman replied only a few days later, in a letter dated 5.20.1935, writing as follows to Luise von Zastrow (with a request to share the letter with Johanna von Keyserlingk): "As to the working groups. Their stance is of course right for they allow members to participate who can no longer be connected with the Goetheanum. No doubt people do still need some such connection. For me the idea of a spiritual union is more telling, where interpersonal relations are nurtured more, which will ultimately mean that the split into two groups will fall away. However, earthly circumstances do not allow these feelings of mine to be realized. Therefore, when you ask me whether new membership cards [issued by the 'working group' or the 'united free groups'] would be necessary to clarify the situation, then I have to say that I believe one cannot do without these cards in the near future. Yet I know that a large number of people who cannot go along with the Goetheanum cannot, either, decide to join the working groups. Really this includes all the people who currently work in the clinic and the diverse institutes, and also many young people. In the future, therefore, I will probably take the stance of standing quite independently, without joining any affiliation, yet working in full sympathy with those who also value having something of our work, and offering a place for those who do not wish to ally themselves with any party. In line with this, when things are running more smoothly, I will again hold the School [Class]. That is roughly my position at present, and my inner voice is telling me that this is probably also in harmony with what Rudolf Steiner wishes." In a reply to Ludwig Polzer-Hoditz, in which she thanked him once again for his speech at the general meeting ("What you did at the general meeting was fine and good!" [see the further text and note 280]), Wegman wrote ten weeks later in a concluding note (and after acknowledging a correspondence between Polzer-Hoditz and Lili Kolisko): "For me, things have now come to a final conclusion. There are so many misunderstandings that I think it better to let things rest. We all thought we were doing the right thing. It is more important to look forward now than to look back" (7.9.1935).

258   Letter from Ita Wegman to Alice Wengraf, 1.31.1935.
259   Letter from Ita Wegman to Klara Zupic-Dajceva, 2.1.1935. We do not know when and by what means Wegman heard of this meeting, but she was aware of it by no later than the third week in January, via a letter from Walter Johannes Stein dated 1.17 in which he wrote, "Very late yesterday evening Dunlop had me called. He had a report in front of him, a transcript in Italian of a meeting of members, a small enclave at the Goetheanum as it seems. There consideration was given to dismissing you and Dr. Vreede from the executive council and expelling Dunlop, Zeylmans, De Haan, Kolisko and Grone from the Society." The three motions that were eventually submitted to the general meeting of 4.14 were worded thus: "(Motion I) The two executive council members Frau Dr. Ita Wegman and Frl. Dr. Elisabeth Vreede, who have shown their disregard for the will of the Society by actions that bear the character of self-expulsion, will no longer be acknowledged as members of the executive council. Frau Dr. Ita Wegman and Frl. Dr. Vreede are relieved of their positions as executive council members of the General Anthroposophical Society. The General Meeting views as impossible any further activity by the two named persons on behalf of the General Anthroposophical Society. (Motion II) The General Meeting proposes that the founders and representatives of the so-called Association of Free Anthroposophical Groups, messrs. D. N. Dunlop, George Kaufmann, Dr. F. W. Zeylmans, P. J. de Haan, Juergen von Grone, Dr. E. Kolisko, have ceased to be members of the General Anthroposophical Society. (Motion III) The General Meeting asks that the executive council no longer recognize as part of the General Anthroposophical Society those national Societies and groups that have amalgamated in the Association of Free Anthroposophical Groups, without however withdrawing membership from the individuals belonging to such a group" (quoted

in Zeylmans, *Who Was Ita Wegman?*, op cit, vol. 3, pp. 28f [G]). Werner Pache's diary entry on January 20 also suggests that Wegman first heard about the procedures underway in Dornach from the letter from Walter Johannes Stein that arrived on January 19: "On 12.20 a meeting was apparently held between the 'executive council' (consisting of only Wachsmuth and Steffen, since Frau Dr. Steiner is bedridden because of her knee) and the General Secretaries (insofar as these were appointed by the Easter resolution), in which discussion concerned the forthcoming 1935 general meeting: The six (Dunlop, Kaufmann, Zeylmans, Haan, Kolisko, Grone) are to be expelled; Vreede and Frau Dr. Wegman are to be dismissed as executive council members, and thus also effectively expelled." Pache recorded the immediate reaction to this news from Elisabeth Vreede and Ita Wegman: *"Vreede thinks that everything possible should be done to prevent this happening, issuing of documents. Frau Dr. Wegman thinks: 'We must suffer everything that is to come, so that the truth comes to light'"* (author's emphasis).

260   In another letter sent to France 12 days later, Wegman wrote, "It is most remarkable that people who work with the Goetheanum can invoke such huge feelings of hatred. One would have thought that if they have really united with Dr. Steiner they would also find love within themselves. We will just have to accept these things with real composure and try repeatedly to be connected with each other, and, by behaving in a non-aggressive way, adopt a different stance" (to Mme. Boussel, 2.13.1935).

261   Klara Zupic-Dajceva in Zagreb had written as follows to Ita Wegman on 1.12.1935 in relation to the events in Dornach and the general meeting resolutions in 1934: "It is our profound conviction that certain powers were at work in this split which were seeking to do all they could to harm the Society. If people had been thinking clearly, things ought not to have come to this. One cannot expel someone if all have an equal right and were appointed by Dr. Steiner. Dear Frau Dr. Wegman, you have been deeply insulted. Please forgive this for the sake of the great cause involved. Christ was more insulted than anyone else has ever been on earth. This very grave guilt *of all of us, really of all the members,* can be compensated for only by great forgiveness. I believe that it is somehow interwoven with the karma of every single member that things happened like this. In each of us a cleft existed somewhere through which the devious nature of these things could enter. It may seem ridiculous to you but I believe in the power of solemn promises and vows. If many of us who witness what has happened but do not see

the reasons for it could now forget all the supposed or 'exaggerated' causes, and focus only on the fact of the split in the Anthroposophical Society; and if we all sought continually to engage our inner will in meditation as in a prayer, then a reconciliation would come about."

262 Letter from Ita Wegman to Hermann Poppelbaum, 2.12.1935.

263 In the letter of 2.12.1935, Wegman replied to Poppelbaum's assertion that Rudolf Steiner only appointed Elisabeth Vreede to the executive council at Wegman's request ("The first four of these people appointed to the executive council were chosen by Dr. Rudolf Steiner himself. He then included Miss Vreede, too, at Frau Dr. Wegman's express request"). She wrote, "The purpose of my letter is not to write about myself, but I must strongly reject the impertinence of your statement that Dr. Steiner was persuaded by me to include Miss Vreede in the executive council. Do you really think that Dr. Steiner would have been governed in his actions by personal sympathies when he appointed the executive council? Quite other motives were at work. The executive council was appointed in accordance with quite different and more dignified laws than those you so thoughtlessly assume when you write, 'He then included Miss Vreede, too, at Frau Dr. Wegman's express request.' This is an enormous error and I do not wish to let it pass since it involves a slur on Dr. Steiner that I will never permit."

264 Letter from Hermann Poppelbaum to Ita Wegman, 4.24.1935. For her part, in March 1935 Elisabeth Vreede wrote a (relatively) detailed refutation of Poppelbaum's account (*On the history of the Anthroposophical Society since the 1923 Christmas Foundation Meeting*, reprinted in Zeylmans, *Who Was Ita Wegman?*, op cit, vol. 3, pp. 240ff [G]), which she also submitted to Ita Wegman before its publication. Ita Wegman largely concurred with Vreede's record of events, but in a letter of 3.22.1925 asked her to make an important addition—which Vreede did not in the end do. In her letter, Wegman wrote, "Yesterday I forgot to say something I had also discussed with George Kaufmann; we wondered whether you could add a last sentence to your history document stating that it has not yet been possible to correct a few things in the text such as some details of the events at executive council meetings. I am thinking here of the Alexander question, the esoteric nature of the Class. Your document would gain weight by this. *I do not think that I should start to engage with this issue, since the whole thing relates too closely to me; and yet these two things contain the core of the whole drama*"

(author's emphasis). Cf. also Peter Selg, *Elisabeth Vreede. 1879–1943,* Arlesheim, 2009, p. 186ff.

265 Letter from Ita Wegman to Franz Löffler, 4.3.1935. The same day, and in almost the same words, Wegman also wrote to Gustav Ritter in Sweden: "Here in the Society we are experiencing hugely difficult times, and it is not yet clear what the consequences of the next general meeting will be. No doubt we can expect the final act of the Christmas Foundation Meeting. I experience these events as destined and inevitable, and hold out no hope. I am also writing this letter with this sense, so that no old things stay hanging over me such as letters I haven't yet replied to." One day later (4.4.1935) she wrote to Walter Johannes Stein: "It is my karma to stand at the very center of these things, and also to be the focus of all attacks."

266 On 1.17.1935, already, Wegman wrote to Maria Rascza in Stuttgart: "Since the beginning of December I have been back in Arlesheim, and am trying to settle back into work. *But it is much harder than I thought,* since the situation here in the Society is very difficult indeed. Whether one wishes it or no, one is drawn into a situation that I personally find completely alien and nonsensical" (author's emphasis). Four weeks later, again, Wegman wrote to Beeb Roelvink to say that the situation "is actually much, much harder to cope with than I myself imagined" (2.14.1935).

267 Letter from Ita Wegman to Gerhard Suchantke, 1.25.1935.

268 Peter Selg, *Ita Wegman und Arlesheim,* Arlesheim, 2006, pp. 15ff. The last text which Ita Wegman published in her lifetime was a brief foreword to a legend recounted by Nora Baditz (cf. Peter Selg, *Die letzten drei Jahre. Ita Wegman in Ascona 1940-1943* [in English: *The Last Three Years: Ita Wegman in Ascona, 1940–1943,* SteinerBooks, 2014], pp. 175f). On 10.21.1942 she wrote to Werner Pache about the importance of this legend: "It is really essential to look at this story again, for all this took place in Arlesheim after all and—as Rudolf Steiner says—was even given to certain people as a kind of glimpse of insight enabling them to later found the anthroposophic movement in Arlesheim and Dornach."

269 Letter from Ita Wegman to Fried Geuter, 2.21.1935.

270 See note 259 for the exact wording of these motions.

271 In relation to Ita Wegman, it was stated that through her support for the "Statement of Intent" and the subsequent "United Free Anthroposophic Groups" she, like Elisabeth Vreede, had departed from "the founding principles and a unified Anthroposophical Society" and that she had engaged "in open conflict with the due and proper governance of the Society." It was further stated that

the "existence" of the letter from Ita Wegman that had been read
out at the previous year's annual general meeting offered "final
proof" that "the author had relinquished all objective and human
entitlement to act as a member of the executive council" (*Was in
der Anthroposophischen Gesellschaft vorgeht. Nachrichten für
deren Mitglieder [Newsletter]*, year 12, nos. 11/12, Mar. 17, 1935,
p. 43; author's emphasis).

272   With reference to the forthcoming general meeting, and as introduction to the motions printed immediately after this article, it stated
the following among other things: "Each of us must ask whether
our duty lies in comfortable toleration which merely allows things
to run their course in order to avoid conflict, and preserves the
appearance of solidarity before the world—thus abandoning the
ideal of an alert and pure spirituality, and sabotaging in advance
all new efforts by the Society to devote itself to spiritual knowledge on a rigorously ethical foundation. Or is it our duty, rather,
to employ our full moral powers to help fulfil Dr. Steiner's greatest wish for the movement he initiated: that it might be said of
this movement that a Society once existed which dedicated itself to
spiritual study and research, and did not tolerate any idle esoteric
dilletantism when this sought to raise it head and plant charlatan-
ism in its midst?" (*Was in der Anthroposophischen Gesellschaft
vorgeht. Nachrichten für deren Mitglieder [Newsletter]*. Year 12,
nos. 11/12, March 17 1935, p. 43). For the further thrust of Marie
Steiner's argument, cf. Emanuel Zeylmans, *Who Was Ita Wegman?*,
op cit, vol. 3, pp. 42ff [G].

273   Letter from Ita Wegman to Elisabeth Vreede, 3.28.1935.

274   Ita Wegman wrote to Hilma Walter on May 3, thus over two
weeks after the annual general meeting: "It is in fact necessary to
set a few things straight, and I will need your help to do so. How
great is the hatred of Frau Dr. Steiner against me, and to satisfy
this hatred, the work of Rudolf Steiner is to be destroyed." In her
notebooks at this time, Wegman recorded two initial accounts in
which she precisely documented the events of March 29 and 30,
1925 (cf. these accounts in Zeylmans, op cit, *Who Was Ita Wegman?*, vol. 3, pp. 119ff [G]). After receiving Wegman's letter, Walter also recorded her recollections in writing on 5.8.1935, noting
her growing unease and anxiety at the time about Rudolf Steiner's
state of health, and her memory of Ludwig Noll communicat-
ing with Marie Steiner. Wegman's account included the following
words: "It is incomprehensible to me, and painful, that anyone
can speak of guilt or blame in this context, of blame for informing

someone too late. When Dr. Noll heard this news he informed Frau Dr. Steiner in very clear terms how things stood. I was very downcast after publication of my account of the sickbed of Dr. Steiner in the Goetheanum newsletter ['The sickbed and the last days and hours of Dr. Steiner's life,' in *Was in der Anthroposophischen Gesellschaft vorgeht. Nachrichten für deren Mitglieder.* 4.19.1925] when I heard that Frau Dr. Steiner had been very upset about this article, and thought that I ought to have telephoned her sooner. At the time Dr. Noll said he would ensure that Frau Dr. Steiner knew of and understood the situation we were in. I know that he did this in a true and honest way. And I am therefore all the more astonished that now, after ten years, these things have surfaced once more with the aim of casting blame again. Frau Dr. Steiner herself is very well aware of the true course of events." At the end of the account in her letter, Hilma Walter summed up her own stance on all this: "It has never before been so apparent to me how little one can do to counter the Memorandum and its effects if there is no will for reconciliation behind the judgments made there. Likewise, people are now simply unable to do anything other than see everything in one particular light. To look on and have to suffer from the consequences of this is already very hard, but also a great lesson which can help us to make all the more headway inwardly" (5.8.1934).

275   See note 254.

276   As Ita Wegman explained in various letters, in Hamborn she wanted to continue the work on the Gospel of St. Mark that she had started in 1934, and make this the basis of all future activities: "My proposal for the work in Hamborn is to focus on the working of Christ both before and after the Mystery of Golgotha. We will then be uniting past and future within the work of Christ. This is an ambitious undertaking, and certainly cannot be accomplished in just one gathering, but we first need to form a large circle and then connect it to its center with radial lines" (2.14.1935). A week later, in a letter to England (to Fried Geuter in Clent), Wegman spoke again of her intended gathering, connecting it now with her trip to Palestine, her experience in Constantinople in September 1934, and the focus on Germany and Switzerland of work she had since undertaken. Starting from a reference to her continuing reticence about plans she had formerly pursued in England, she wrote, "The fact that many anthroposophists are now going to England seems to me to recall the way, in olden times, the Greeks were drawn to Rome and the rest of Italy to work culturally there; and no doubt

this is something karmic. For my part, by contrast, I received an important impulse—this happened in Constantinople—not to leave Germany in the lurch, but to devote my energy more to this country. You will recall that I thought that one couldn't do very much there, and that German culture should be rekindled somewhere else. But strangely, an experience in Constantinople showed me that various things are still possible in Germany if one can only take the right measures. This thought continues to trouble me, and this is also why I will slowly and surely reconnect with Germany; and why I have decided to organize a conference at Easter in Hamborn.... Arlesheim and also Germany—in this case Hamborn—need to receive a hugely powerful spiritual impulse at Easter" (2.21.1935).

277 Letter from Ita Wegman to Mathilde Enschedé, 4.10.1935.
278 Letter from Ita Wegman to Gottfried Bahr, 3.19.1935.
279 Letter from Ita Wegman to Gerhard Suchantke, 3.19.1935.
280 As Ita Wegman reported in a letter to Wilhelm Goyert, Polzer's initiative was based on a spiritual experience: "He told me that he felt spiritually called upon by Dr. Steiner—and recounted a dream to me—to do something for the Society to prevent it being broken apart by the machinations of spirits who were seeking to destroy Rudolf Steiner's work" (4.2.1935). A day after Wegman dictated this letter, Polzer had a further such experience in Mariensee (Austria), which led him to compose his Dornach speech the next morning and the words of his official motion ("A voice told me, 'Lodge a request to speak in Dornach, otherwise you will be unable to have a voice.' And so I did this immediately on waking" [quoted in Thomas Meyer, *Ludwig Polzer-Hoditz. Ein Europäer*, Basel 1994, p. 344]). For an overall spiritual understanding of Polzer's aims and efforts, we should also note that he was connected with the First Class and Ita Wegman's task in relation to it: "I had to...support Frau Dr. Wegman...at the general meeting. Since Dr. Steiner entitled me to hold the Class in the Michael School, and since he specified that this Michael School was in the closest connection with Frau Dr. Wegman, I regarded it as my duty to defend Frau Dr. Wegman, and to stand by her side" (Polzer-Hoditz, quoted in Meyer, *Ludwig Polzer-Hoditz,* op cit, p. 343). In his long speech, of great integrity, Polzer described the "Memorandum" as "destructive, fanatical incitement" that continued the moral slanders previously perpetrated against Ita Wegman. He then placed key emphasis on wholesale misjudgment of and intentional blindness to Wegman's task with the Class (cf. note 254), and said, "Now I must speak of my understanding of the role of Frau Dr. Wegman as colleague of

Rudolf Steiner in the Class. Rudolf Steiner, you see, very clearly designated her as his colleague in this respect. I find it mistaken simply to conflate his Class colleague and collaborator with the role of Secretary in the executive council, which in this case strikes me as an insult—and there have been no lack of insults. It is clear to me what Rudolf Steiner meant by his 'colleague' in this regard. Appointment of this colleague, thus of his helper and assistant in founding and sustaining a Mystery school, could only be based on a profound destiny connection which Rudolf Steiner perceived in full consciousness and to which he wished to do justice. I have absolutely no doubt that this was the case. Thus Rudolf Steiner was in fact telling Frau Dr. Wegman that she bore a great destiny.... The initiative to found the esoteric Michael School came, as Rudolf Steiner said, from Frau Dr. Wegman. In taking up this initiative, the esoteric union of destiny was created which is necessary for the modern Mysteries.... When Rudolf Steiner returned from England in 1924, he indicated on various occasions that he gradually wished to give the Class a ritual framework. In the context of this developing ritual element within the Michael mystery, he spoke at admissions in September of the handshake and the promise that was also to be made to Frau Dr. Wegman. This was an indication that this union of destiny also had significance for the Michael mystery" (quoted in Zeylmans, *Who Was Ita Wegman?*, op cit, vol. 3, pp. 334f [G]). In his memorial text for Ita Wegman written eight years later, immediately after her death (*In memoriam Frau Dr. Ita Wegman 1943*), Polzer noted, in addition, that he had decided to support Ita Wegman many years before the 1935 general meeting, during a Class lesson that had been hugely disrupted by Roman Boos: "The battle against Frau Dr. Wegman took forms that bordered on the demonic. Dr. Roman Boos became the instrument of this, and brought it to a culmination. I was present; Frau Dr. Wegman was holding a Class lesson. Seemingly by chance, I was sitting right at the front that day, and was able to observe everything that occurred. Frau Wegman had just begun, when Dr. Boos came rushing on to the podium from behind, pale and agitated in appearance, and started to hurl insulting words at Frau Dr. Wegman. It was an assault in the worst sense, the disruption of a ritual act. Other executive council members responded only weakly to this incident, and from then on I knew where my place was. Despite what happened on this occasion the persecution intensified, and Dr. Roman Boos was further employed as battering ram" (ibid., p. 409).

281 Letter from Ita Wegman to Gerhard Suchantke, 4.3.1935.

282 Ibid.

283 Ibid.

284 Letter from Ita Wegman to Franz Löffler, 4.3.1935.

285 Herbert Hahn wrote to Wegman to offer his express support for Polzer-Hoditz's initiative. On Apr. 8, 1935, six days before the general meeting, he formulated his stance as follows: "The shape that things have now assumed, which appears irreparable for a long time to come, seems to me to be the conclusion of tragic developments. The chorus of oppositional voices has grown so loud that there seems only one course of action: to take this tragedy upon oneself, at the same time maintaining a clear, spiritual protest, and through quiet, fruitful work in smaller groups prepare for the new situations that must eventually emerge. It is my conviction that this is the way to do battle with such strong adversary powers." As far as we can tell from the available documents, Herbert Hahn was one of those who most deeply understood Wegman's stance (cf. his important recollection of 12.22.1934 in note 223). At the catastrophic general meeting in 1934 he himself had given an address which, alongside that by George Adams Kaufmann, was far and away the most spiritually important speech. There he recalled Rudolf Steiner among other things, and said of Eugen Kolisko— whom the previous speakers had massively attacked to the point sometimes of mockery: "We often heard Dr. Steiner speak in a smaller gathering in Stuttgart, and he frequently addressed specific things to the very people who least understood whom his words were addressed to. These same people listened, laughed, and later used such words as weapons. All sorts of things can be said about Dr. Kolisko and his flaws. I have not heard anyone say yet that in 1922, at the Goetheanum where Dr. Kolisko gave lectures, the view existed that individuals such as Dr. Eugen Kolisko were worthy of the very greatest esteem, and that this was based on their inner truthfulness ('Individuals such as Eugen Kolisko, MD, cannot be esteemed highly enough by the anthroposophic movement.... When I hear him speak, as on this occasion, about the 'free life of the spirit,' I have the sense that he is speaking truth to our hearts, and that his whole life is dedicated to this truth [in Rudolf Steiner, *Damit der Mensch ganz Mensch werde*, CW 82, Dornach, 1994, pp. 246f]. Times change! Such things were once said. And now it is said that such people have gone rapidly downhill. A little while ago only. I saw Dr. Kolisko working with children in The Hague, and his work was still productive. I have to say that I can see no difference between then and now" (transcript, page 175; cf. note 167).

286 See the text of Polzer's important speech that, despite the outcome of the vote, strongly affected the general meeting, in Zeylmans, *Who Was Ita Wegman?*, op cit, vol. 3, pp. 333ff [G]; and Meyer, *Ludwig Polzer-Hoditz*, op cit, pp. 596ff. In relation to the background to Polzer's address to the general meeting and his experience in Arlesheim during the night between April 14 and 15, cf. the account by Thomas Meyer, op cit, pp. 345ff. Six days later Ita Wegman wrote to Walter Johannes Stein in London: "Old Count Polzer has completely transformed himself. Whereas he used to feel connected with the old brigade, he has changed his views over many years—and stands up for these views courageously. He spoke at the general meeting, warning that one should not go too far with these things and should not forget Rudolf Steiner's esoteric intentions; and he articulated this view very beautifully. I am sending you a transcript of his speech, which I find important since an old esotericist and friend of Steiner here expresses things that he himself surely did not so fully accept to begin with" (4.22.1935).

287 On 4.10.1935, Wilhelm Rudolf Goyert wrote to Albert Steffen: "I hereby raise an objection with the whole fibre of my being to the motions at the general meeting on April 14; specifically, 1) against the dismissal of Frau Dr. Wegman and Frl. De Vreede, 2) against exclusion from membership of messrs. Dr. Kolisko, v. Grone, Dr. Zeylmans, de Haan, Dunlop, Dr. Kaufmann, 3) against alteration of the statutes, which does not accord with what Dr. Steiner intended at the 1923 Christmas Foundation Meeting. I would like to remind you of your own solemn promise whereby you have often stated that you yourself would not remain in the executive council if one of the other executive council members were to leave it. If you recall these words of yours, you cannot concur with such a resolution. I have submitted a motion and then withdrawn it since in this same motion I myself spoke of a trust that I can no longer have in the light of recent events. Nevertheless I here repeat the motion since I am convinced that the persons concerned—in this case yourself, Frau Dr. Steiner and Dr. Guenther Wachsmuth—ought not to shift the responsibility for such monstrous action to the members, but should bear responsibility for all times to come for the consequences of this action." The wording of Goyert's motion ran simply: "I propose that no vote is held relating to the dismissal of Frau Dr. Wegman and Fraeulein Dr. Vreede from the executive council, nor about expulsion from the Society of messrs. Dr. Kolisko/von Grone/Dr. Zeylmans/de Haan/Dunlop/Kaufmann.

This decision should be transferred to the chair Albert Steffen and to Frau Dr. Steiner and Dr. Guenther Wachsmuth."

288 Letter from Ita Wegman to Wilhelm Goyert, 4.2.1935. Walter Johannes Stein likewise regarded these events in the Society from a similar perspective, that of inevitable destiny, though he saw them in a far more optimistic light. Six days before the general meeting he wrote to Ita Wegman from England: "You can imagine that my thoughts are turning to you at this time. But in everything occurring now I can see only positive aspects. It was necessary to sunder you from this Anthroposophical Society—not only for you but for Rudolf Steiner himself. This has been done now by excluding such key anthroposophists from the Society. Here processes come to the fore whose meaning will only become apparent in configurations at the end of the century. Nothing more remains for you to do, therefore, than to walk through these events—which are the final ones—with true inner tranquility in your heart. Thus you will be free and able to do what should long since have been done" (4.8.1935).

289 "At the general meeting of April 16, 1935, this Society has made clear its will, by majority decision, that it no longer desires my work. It no longer wishes me to act in the function R. Steiner gave me as executive council member. There is naturally no more dispute required in relation to this demonstration of majority will. If a majority decision, engineered by propaganda through slanderous texts against me—through a one-sided Memorandum that does not correspond to the truth—is to determine the wrongness or, rather, rightness of my actions, then the Society is acting only in accordance with association principles, since it is after all impossible that those who cast their votes in this way can form any judgment about such complex circumstances as existed. Since they could not do this, they have felt and acted as members of an association. They have said to themselves that there are very grave problems in the executive council which are impacting on members, and this is endangering the Society. They read and hear of these difficulties in the Memorandum. What other choice do they have then, than to join with all the rest and call for these trouble-makers to be removed? This standpoint is comprehensible, and each person must decide for himself whether it accords with the moral and Christian principles that should hold sway in our Society. I always regard a mass decision as dubious, and therefore there is no point in being indignant or defending myself" [Notebook].

290 Letter from Ita Wegman to Carlos Santos, 5.23.1935.
291 Letter from Ita Wegman to Gerhard Suchantke, 4.24.1935.

292 Letter from Ita Wegman to Hilma Walter, 5.3.1935.

293 On May 19 1935, Ita Wegman wrote to a former patient who had little connection with Anthroposophy the following relaxed yet incisive words: "The Anthroposophical Society is clearly not entirely satisfied with my work because it wishes this work to be smaller-minded in nature than I understand it. I also wish to adhere far more to Rudolf Steiner's intentions than the Society finds good. I am therefore no longer on the Society's executive council, and am freer to work in the way I see fit."

294 Letter from Ita Wegman to Hilma Walter, 5.3.1935. Five months later, Wegman wrote again to Gertrud Spoerri, saying, "The work is progressing and the fact that I am no longer in the executive council means I feel liberated from a great deal of pressure, and can continue working positively, unhampered by feelings of enmity" (9.23.1935). A few other people in Wegman's proximity likewise regarded the developments set in motion by the general meeting in this light, including Walter Johannes Stein who, on receiving news from Wegman that she had been dismissed and, as she certainly saw it, expelled from the Society ("Now the remarkable thing has occurred, dear Dr. Stein, that you are still a member of the Society, while I am not! Have you considered this situation?"), and having perused the text of Polzer's speech at the general meeting, he wrote, "It really is astonishing that I remain in the Anthroposophical Society while you do not. But it makes no difference. The Society Dr. Steiner founded was based on reincarnation; he stated expressly that it will depend on souls themselves whether they form the selfless resolve to descend to the earth. Isn't it possible to be excluded from this Society. All the rest is temporal misapprehension. As far as the work is concerned, you are free and may devote yourself to your true task.... We can be grateful for Polzer's speech, but these things are not decided by speeches. What has gone astray here will be redeemed by karma. The 1,600 [members] who voted in favor of the expulsions will have to do the opposite at the end of the century. There are some who will do this with insight, while others needed this stance of opposition to prepare for it" (4.24.1935).

295 Just ten days before the general meeting, and with an eye to forthcoming events, Wegman had written to Walter Johannes Stein in England: "If it were just to do with me it would not be so bad, but there are many institutions connected with me, many people in turn involved in these, who invest their energy in this work. These events are upsetting everything, and human powers are not adequate to stand firm against the storm. And so one has to gather

all one's forces to prevent catastrophes sweeping through the institutes. It may also be that these catastrophes are inevitable and that we should take the point of view that a completely new beginning is necessary" (4.4.1935). If we consider the consequences of the general meeting, and the previous and ongoing slander campaign against Ita Wegman, and study the relevant documents, the extent to which such activities aimed to paralyze and destroy the intentions associated with Wegman (far beyond questions of her office and role) soon becomes apparent ("as certain dark powers certainly intend"). Even in an apparently unimportant letter which Ita Wegman wrote to Adele von Heydebrand on May 6, 1935, the level at which the conflicts continued after 4.14 becomes very clear: how people's emotions were stirred up and how they were prevented from pursuing their individual paths. Wegman wrote, "Dear Frau von Heydebrand, when you were at the general meeting with me and Frau Moll, you told me that you would be glad to do something for us, such as drawing people's attention to our clinic and our training courses. I enclose a few brochures with the training program. I am very keen to ensure that these courses continue in the right way, and so I'd like to ask you to do what you can to publicize them, and perhaps see if you can interest this or that person. Frau Moll knows so many people, doesn't she, and may be able to help. I am also asking because something very strange happened recently. A young girl who came here from one of our institutes to attend the training courses went to see the secretariat at the Goetheanum in regard to membership [of the AS] and there encountered the most unbelievable attempts to turn her against us. She was reproached for not taking courses at the Goetheanum, in eurythmy and so forth, and when she said that she did not wish to train in eurythmy, but in nursing, and that she had no gift for eurythmy either, she received this reply: 'Yes, people always think that to begin with, but later they find they do have a great gift for it.' Then she was asked whether she had read the Memorandum, and when she replied that she was not yet a member, they were somewhat embarrassed but continued nevertheless with accusations and slander against the clinic. That is how they are behaving up there, and if we do not gather all our forces to defend ourselves against these attacks, they will succeed in undermining and destroying our work. And so I'd like to ask all of you who do sense that Rudolf Steiner remains connected with this work, to help us by recommending the clinic and setting the record straight, so that this work is not destroyed. I would be really very grateful to you, dear Frau von Heydebrand,

and also Frau Moll, for such help. I hope you are well. With warm greetings from your Dr. I. Wegman. P.S. Some people may only wish to attend part of the course, and this is certainly possible from our point of view."

296 Letter from Ita Wegman to Sister Hetha Ross, 5.14.1935.

297 Letter from Ita Wegman to Beeb Roelvink, 5.28.1935.

298 Letter from Ita Wegman to Gustav Ritter, 7.29.1935.

299 Cf. Peter Selg, *"Ich bin für Fortschreiten"* [in English: *I Am For Going Ahead,* SteinerBooks, 2012], pp. 146ff. It is interesting to note here that as soon as she returned from Palestine Ita Wegman had begun to ask individuals whether they really wished to commit themselves to working with her; and that she undertook such collaboration in awareness of the spiritual importance of the Arlesheim clinic, initially also as the basis for future dissemination of medicine indications and therapy recommendations. While it is true that after 1934/1935 Wegman gladly continued to advise many physicians, including non-anthroposophic ones, she also urged her anthroposophic colleagues to be increasingly mindful of the wellsprings of their healing work, and restricted the scope of those to whom such knowledge was circulated. On 2.18.1935, for instance, she replied to queries from the anthroposophic physician Hans Mothes, who had a practice in Essen: "You mention...that you already wrote to me several months ago saying you would like to come here to gain further insight into the indications Dr. Steiner gave for treatment. When you wrote to me I myself was very ill, and unable to correspond. But now I'd like to reply that these indications were personally given to me by Dr. Steiner during work at the Clinical-Therapeutic Institute. Many of these indications found their way into the medical courses, *Natura* magazine and the supplementary sheets. The basis of the therapeutic measures that have now become practice for many physicians must be traced back to the collaborative work undertaken between Dr. Steiner and me. It is now my view that I have no further obligation to publicize these indications, except in the narrower confines of work here at the clinic. The events in the Society and the way various physicians have acted against the Medical Section has led me to take the position that I will only speak about therapeutic issues in smaller gatherings with those who clearly undertake to collaborate honestly with me."

300 Back in January 1935, five months before his death, Wegman had written to Dunlop: "I am connected to you not only personally, but also through Rudolf Steiner" (undated, Jan. 1935). For more

on Dunlop's connection with Rudolf Steiner, cf. the monograph by Thomas Meyer, *D.N. Dunlop: A Man of Our Time*, Temple Lodge 1996.

301 "I received the sudden news from England that Mr. Dunlop is gravely ill; I am therefore traveling to England to offer him medical assistance." Wegman wrote this in a letter to Beeb Roelvink shortly before her departure, and left for England around midnight on 5.28.1935. According to Thomas Meyer, Wegman visited Dunlop with Hilma Walter, who also arrived speedily from Clent: "Yet the two physicians were denied any influence on the course of treatment offered to Dunlop" (Meyer, *D. N. Dunlop,* op cit, p. 321 [in German edition, *D.N. Dunlop. Ein Zeit- und Lebensbild,* Dornach, 1987]).

302 At several places the text below deviates stylistically from the translation by Thomas Meyer in his Dunlop biography (pp. 323ff, German edition) and is a little more faithful to Wegman's German style.

303 Joseph Emmanuel van Leer (1880–1934). Ita Wegman worked very closely with him for many years on the Weleda board of management. He put his private means and his financial and political skills at the service of the anthroposophic movement. He died completely unexpectedly seven months before Dunlop (and directly before Wegman's return to Arlesheim) while on a business trip to Baku (Soviet Union).

304 Letter from Ita Wegman to Eleanor Merry, 7.1.1935.

305 Letter from Walter Johannes Stein to Ita Wegman, 6.23.1935. Eugen Kolisko's weighty decision to emigrate to London—which marked the end of his collaboration with Helene von Grunelius, who died soon after this, and led to an exile condemned to failure that culminated in his own death three years later (but did, however, give decisive aid to Karl König's Camphill initiative in Scotland)—was directly connected with Dunlop's death. Cf. Thomas Meyer: "'Dann werde ich sterben...' Eugen Koliskos letzte Jahre in England," in *Mitteilungen aus der anthroposophischen Arbeit in Deutschland,* no. 183/199; Peter Selg, *Helene von Grunelius und Rudolf Steiner's Kurse für junge Mediziner. Eine biographische Studie,* Dornach, 2003; Hans Müller-Wiedemann, *Karl König. Eine mitteleuropäische Biographie im 20. Jahrhundert,* Stuttgart, 1992.

306 C. Bessenich / Paul Buehler / O. Eckstein / C. Englert-Faye / Otto Fraenkl / Emil Grossheintz / Ehrenfried Pfeiffer / H. Poppelbaum / Paul Eugen Schiller / Guenther Schubert / Richard Schubert /

Jan Stuten, *Denkschrift über Angelegenheiten der Anthroposo-phischen Gesellschaft in den Jahren 1925 bis 1935*, Dornach, 1935, p. 113.

307 Letter from Ita Wegman to Frl. Duve.

308 Letter from Ita Wegman to Eleanor Merry, 11.22.1935.

309 Letter from Ita Wegman to Willem Zeylmans, 11.16.1935.

310 Letter from Ita Wegman to Fried Geuter, 11.25.1935.

311 One and a half years later, Ita Wegman was to urge Eugen Kolisko, too, to realize his "School of Spiritual Science" in collaboration with the Anthroposophical Society in London, despite the fact that the latter had been making life difficult for him in various ways. She wrote, "Dear Herr Kolisko, you may laugh at this and say, "I want nothing more to do with the Anthroposophical Society in London"; you may wish to create something quite different which has no connection with the Society. Yet it seems to me that, through Dr. Steiner, we are after all still part of this Society, and that this needs gradually to undergo a metamorphosis. Such transformation must head in the direction of a loose coherence of activities with people in the Society. The Anthroposophical Society as such ought to be a greater community—that of the new Christians, who seek to inte-grate the reality of the risen Christ into themselves. Of course, this does not have to be said in so many words, but we must hold it in our hearts. Only by this means will we successfully accomplish real spiritual deeds" (6.10.1937).

312 Cf. Peter Selg, *The Last Three Years: Ita Wegman in Ascona, 1940–1943*, Great Barrington, MA: SteinerBooks, 2014 (cf. espe-cially notes 24 and 25 in that volume regarding the early history of Casa Andrea Cristoforo and the Motta Farm. Wegman was first offered partial acquisition of the land at Motta on 8.28.1935).

313 Ita Wegman's mother, Henriette Charlotte Maria Offers-Wegman (born 11.27.1851) died in Ita Wegman's presence on 1.18.1935 at the age of 83 in Ryswyk, Holland. Three weeks after her mother's death, Wegman wrote to her colleague H. C. Rudersdorff, the GP who had previously cared for her: "My mother's departure into the world of spirit is in fact not a farewell for us, but has become a far more intense sense of belonging together" (2.12.1935). Cf. the letter to Henriette Offers-Wegman, Ita Wegman's mother, and the personal meditation for her 73rd birthday, given by Rudolf Steiner in November 1924 (while in his sickbed), in Peter Selg, *"Die beseelte Menschensonne." Ein Herz-Meditation Rudolf Steiners*, Arlesheim, 2011 (photograph of Henriette Offers-Weg-man on page 16).

Books in English Translation
by Peter Selg

ON RUDOLF STEINER:

The Destiny of the Michael Community: Foundation Stone for the Future (2014)

Rudolf Steiner and Christian Rosenkreutz (2012)

Rudolf Steiner as a Spiritual Teacher: From Recollections of Those Who Knew Him (2010)

ON CHRISTOLOGY:

The Lord's Prayer and Rudolf Steiner: A Study of His Insights into the Archetypal Prayer of Christianity (2014)

The Creative Power of Anthroposophical Christology: An Outline of Occult Science · The First Goetheanum · The Fifth Gospel · The Christmas Conference (2012); with Sergei O. Prokofieff

Christ and the Disciples: The Destiny of an Inner Community (2012)

The Figure of Christ: Rudolf Steiner and the Spiritual Intention behind the Goetheanum's Central Work of Art (2009)

Rudolf Steiner and the Fifth Gospel: Insights into a New Understanding of the Christ Mystery (2009)

Seeing Christ in Sickness and Healing (2005)

ON GENERAL ANTHROPOSOPHY:

Spiritual Resistance and Overcoming: Ita Wegman 1933–1935 (2014)

The Last Three Years: Ita Wegman in Ascona, 1940–1943 (2014)

From Gurs to Auschwitz: The Inner Journey of Maria Krehbiel-Darmstädter (2013)

Crisis in the Anthroposophical Society: And Pathways to the Future (2013); with Sergei O. Prokofieff

Rudolf Steiner's Foundation Stone Meditation: And the Destruction of the Twentieth Century (2013)

The Culture of Selflessness: Rudolf Steiner, the Fifth Gospel, and the Time of Extremes (2012)

The Mystery of the Heart: The Sacramental Physiology of the Heart in Aristotle, Thomas Aquinas, and Rudolf Steiner (2012)

Rudolf Steiner and the School for Spiritual Science: The Foundation of the "First Class" (2012)

Rudolf Steiner's Intentions for the Anthroposophical Society: The Executive Council, the School for Spiritual Science, and the Sections (2011)

The Fundamental Social Law: Rudolf Steiner on the Work of the Individual and the Spirit of Community (2011)

The Path of the Soul after Death: The Community of the Living and the Dead as Witnessed by Rudolf Steiner in his Eulogies and Farewell Addresses (2011)

The Agriculture Course, Koberwitz, Whitsun 1924: Rudolf Steiner and the Beginnings of Biodynamics (2010)

Karl König's Path to Anthroposophy (2008)

ON ANTHROPOSOPHICAL MEDICINE AND CURATIVE EDUCATION:

Honoring Life: Medical Ethics and Physician-Assisted Suicide. A Consideration from an Anthroposophical Point of View (2014); with Sergei O. Prokofieff

I Am for Going Ahead: Ita Wegman's Work for the Social Ideals of Anthroposophy (2012)

The Child with Special Needs: Letters and Essays on Curative Education (Ed.) (2009)

Ita Wegman and Karl König: Letters and Documents (2008)

Karl König: My Task: Autobiography and Biographies (Ed.) (2008)

ON CHILD DEVELOPMENT AND WALDORF EDUCATION:

I Am Different from You: How Children Experience Themselves and the World in the Middle of Childhood (2011)

Unbornness: Human Pre-existence and the Journey toward Birth (2010)

The Essence of Waldorf Education (2010)

The Therapeutic Eye: How Rudolf Steiner Observed Children (2008)

A Grand Metamorphosis: Contributions to the Spiritual-Scientific Anthropology and Education of Adolescents (2008)

An independent newsletter by and for members of the Anthroposophical Society, published in association with the ITA WEGMAN INSTITUTE FOR BASIC RESEARCH INTO ANTHROPOSOPHY, Arlesheim, Switzerland

deepening@wegmaninstitut.ch   Issue 3.1 | January 5, 2014

CONTENTS:

*

I have essentially characterized the task of the fifth post-Atlantean epoch, as I have described that in this epoch it becomes the task of humanity consciously to confront evil as an impulse in world evolution.

~ Rudolf Steiner, 18 Nov. 1917, GA 178

*

A NOTE TO SUBSCRIBERS

This issue of *Deepening Anthroposophy* is produced as a special edition in both English and German. Beginning with this issue, it will be possible to order paper copies of *Deepening Anthroposophy*. The cost per issue mailed to the US will be $9. The international rate is $12 / £7.5 / CHF 11 /

Deepening Anthroposophy began in April 2012 as an independent newsletter by and for English-speaking members of the Anthroposophical Society worldwide. Since March 2013, it has been produced in association with the Ita Wegman Institute for Basic Research into Anthroposophy, in Arlesheim, Switzerland.

The purpose of this newsletter is to provide a space for cultivating Anthroposophy and deepening our awareness of the tasks of the Anthroposophical Society, in accord with the impulse of the Christmas Conference of 1923. The Christmas Conference was Rudolf Steiner's final attempt to encourage our work with Anthroposophy to take on an enduring "esoteric direction" for the sake of its healthy continuance: "The prosperity and fruitful development of the anthroposophical cause will depend upon a true understanding of the esoteric direction that, from now onward, will be implicit in the anthroposophical movement" (July 18, 1924, CW 240; see also CW 260). It is hoped that a newsletter devoted to basic research into Anthroposophy will contribute to this goal.

—*Thomas O'Keefe, deepening@wegmaninstitut.ch*

Ita Wegman Institute
for Basic Research into Anthroposophy

Pfeffinger Weg 1a, ch 4144 Arlesheim, Switzerland
www.wegmaninstitut.ch
e-mail: sekretariat@wegmaninstitut.ch

The Ita Wegman Institute for Basic Research into Anthroposophy is a non-profit research and teaching organization. It undertakes basic research into the lifework of Dr. Rudolf Steiner (1861–1925) and the application of Anthroposophy in specific areas of life, especially medicine, education, and curative education. Work carried out by the Institute is supported by a number of foundations and organizations and an international group of friends and supporters. The Director of the Institute is Prof. Dr. Peter Selg.